CHARLES G. FINNEY

TRUE CHRISTIANITY

Compiled and edited by F. G. Kuruvilla

Anchor-Cross Media
Cambridge, Massachusetts
www.anchorcross.org

Anchor-Cross Media
P.O. Box 381682
Cambridge, MA 02238
World Wide Web: www.anchorcross.org

Anchor-Cross Media is a division of Anchor-Cross Ministries, Inc.

The front cover painting of Jesus praying in Gethsemane is by Matthew Philleo. Used with permission. The back cover painting of Charles Finney is by Waldo and Jewett, 1834. Used with permission of the Oberlin College Archives.

ISBN 0-9742727-0-1

Preface

In December 1833, Charles Finney denied communion to those who were slaveholders in his church. This bold stance, taken over thirty years before slavery was made illegal in the United States, typifies the character of this courageous preacher. On a national day of fasting in 1841, the first sin he preached on was the manner in which Native Americans had been treated by the government. Finney's significance in shaping the conscience and very history of America is unquestioned. As Allen Guelzo writes, "It would be hard to tell the story of the American Republic before the Civil War without giving Charles Grandison Finney one of the starring roles."

However, Finney's message was far from exclusively focused on social or political causes. In fact, to the frustration of many social activists, he believed that the best way to solve society's problems was to preach the gospel. Finney sought to transform people with a gospel message that changed their hearts, and he insisted that it be *all* of their hearts. His powerful and convicting messages challenged people to submit their entire lives to the Lordship of Jesus Christ — this included renouncing materialism, worldly fashion, secular entertainment, and of course, slavery. Few people today have the courage to speak against the culture of the world as Finney did, but God surely blessed his ministry. Over half a million people became Christians under Finney's preaching.

This book is a collection of lectures drawn from *Lectures to Professing Christians*, the *Way of Salvation*, and *Lectures on Revivals of Religion*. They are grouped into four topics: repentance, prayer, witnessing, and spiritual growth. The chapters were originally sermons or lectures delivered by Finney that he later revised to be more suitable for print form. Because most of the book is drawn from *Lectures on Revivals of Religion*, one will notice a continuity and cumulative progression from chapter to chapter. (There is an appendix detailing the origin of each chapter in this book.) When reading the book, it is easy to feel the passion that Charles Finney preached with. One is convicted by his direct style that he obviously hopes will be clearly heard, understood, and applied. Some of the chapters in this book are among the most convicting pages written in the last two hundred years. Chapter 4 on repentance is an unforgettable experience, feeling more like a hammer than a lecture. The chapters on prayer and witnessing (5-12) have more insight into the subject that any modern book I have read. Fortunately, he loved to tell real illustrations of the truths he taught — these are of a great help in understanding practical applications.

Finney greatly believed that his works should be simple and easily understood by any audience. Thus he took much effort to make his preaching easily comprehensible by using plain language and many stories. In that spirit, I have edited each chapter to make it more readable for the twenty-first century reader. Some words like damask, groat, or weal are simply not used much anymore, while other words like careless have changed their meaning somewhat. For example, when Finney describes the careless sinner, he means the apathetic sinner, someone who has no interest in the things of God. I have changed such words to their modern equivalents. I have modernized the punctuation usage, and sometimes also his sentence structure to improve readability. In the interest of brevity, as well as not wanting to stray into topics unfamiliar or confusing to today's reader, many of the chapters have also been shortened. However, I have intentionally retained the parts in each chapter where he asks the hearer to respond in application. These are obviously derived from the fact that these were originally sermons to a live audience. Hearing his pleas to the audience is very moving, and is part of the power of each chapter. My goal with this book is to produce an easily readable text that faithfully reproduces the substance *and* style of Finney's original lectures.

I would especially like to thank Tyler VanderWeele for his proofreading the manuscript and for his numerous suggestions to improve clarity. I am very grateful to Raymond Yim, Peter Park, and Nicole Rim for their help in the cover design and typesetting. Finally, I would like to thank Raymond for his being a constant source of encouragement to me in the completion of this work.

May God continue to use this work for his glory.

Finny Kuruvilla
Cambridge, Massachusetts
September 2003

Table of Contents

Part I

REPENTANCE

Chapter 1

DISCERNING YOUR CHARACTER

"They feared the LORD, *but also served their own gods." (2 Kings 17:33)*

When the ten tribes of Israel were carried away captive by the king of Assyria,[1] the land was filled with strangers from different idolatrous nations who knew nothing about the religion of the Jews. Very soon wild beasts increased in the land and lions killed many people, and they thought it was because they did not know the god of the country, had offended him, and he had sent the lions among them as a punishment. So they asked the king, who told them to get one of the priests of the Israelites to teach them the manner of the god of the land. They took this advice, and obtained one of the priests to come to Bethel and teach them the religious ceremonies and forms of worship that had been practiced there. And he taught them to fear Yahweh as the God of that country. But still they did not receive him as the only God. They feared him, that is, they feared his anger and his judgments, and to avoid these, they performed the prescribed rites. But they "served" their own gods. They kept up their idolatrous worship, as this was what they loved and preferred, though they felt obliged to pay some reverence to Yahweh as the God of that country. There are still many people, professing to fear God, and perhaps possessing a certain kind of the fear of the Lord, who nevertheless serve their own gods — they have other things to which their hearts are supremely devoted, and other objects in which they mainly put their trust.   WOW

---

[1] In 722 BC, Israel was invaded by the armies of Shalmaneser, king of Assyria, and the people were deported from their homeland. This is recorded in 2 Kings 17:3-6.

There are, as you know, two kinds of fear. There is that fear of the Lord that is the beginning of wisdom, which is founded in love. There is also a slavish fear, which is a mere dread of evil, and is purely selfish. This is the kind of fear that is possessed by those people spoken of in the text. They were afraid Yahweh would send his judgments if they did not perform certain rites. This was the motive they had for paying him worship. Those who have this fear are supremely selfish, and while they claim to revere Yahweh, they have other gods whom they love and serve.

There are several classes of people to whom this applies, and my goal is to describe some of them in such a way that you may know your character. To serve a person is to be obedient to the will and devoted to the interests of that individual. It is not properly called serving where only certain deeds are performed, without entering into the service of the person. To serve someone is to make it one's business to do the will and promote the interest of that person. To serve God is to make religion[2] the main business of life. It is to devote one's self, heart, life, powers, time, influence, and all, to promote the interests of God, to build up the kingdom of God, and to advance the glory of God. Who are they who, while they profess to fear the Lord, serve their own gods?

1. Those of you who have not enthusiastically renounced the ownership of your possessions, and given them up to God. It is self-evident that if you have not done this, you are not serving God. Suppose a gentleman were to employ a clerk to take care of his store. Suppose the clerk were to continue to attend to his own business, and when asked to do what is necessary for his employer who pays him his wages, he says, "I really have so much business of my own to attend to, that I have no time to do these things." Would not everybody cry out against such a servant, and say he was not serving his employer at all? His time is not his own, it is paid for, and he has only served himself. So where a person has not renounced the ownership of himself, not only in thought, but practically, he has not learned the first lesson in religion. He is not serving the Lord, but serving his own gods.

2. That person who does not make his occupation a part of his religion does not serve God. You hear a person sometimes say, "I am so busy all day at work that I do not have time to serve God." He thinks he serves God for a little while in the morning, and then attends to his

---

[2] Finney uses the word "religion" to mean devotion or obedience to God. He uses it often throughout the book. It is unfortunate that this word has negative connotations in Christian circles today, since the Bible (see James 1:27) and many historic Christian writings use it in a positive sense.

worldly business. That person has left his religion where he said his prayers. He is willing perhaps to give God the time before breakfast, before he gets ready to go to his own business. As soon as that is over, he goes to his own work. He perhaps fears the Lord enough to say his prayers night and morning, but he serves his own gods. That person's religion is the laughing stock of hell! He prays very devoutly, and then, instead of engaging in his business for God, he is serving himself. No doubt the idols are very satisfied with the arrangement, but God is completely displeased.

3. Those of you who devote to the Lord only that which costs you little or nothing are serving your own gods. There are many who make religion consist in certain acts of piety that do not interfere with their selfishness. You pray in the morning with your family, because you can do it then very conveniently, but do not allow the service of Yahweh to interfere with the service of your gods, or to stand in the way of your getting rich, or enjoying the world. The gods you serve make no complaint of being offended or neglected for the service of Yahweh.

4. Those who suppose that the six days of the week belong to them, and that only the Sabbath is God's day, serve their own gods. There are many who suppose that the week is their time, and the Sabbath God's, and that they have a right to do their own work during the week, to serve themselves and promote their own interests, if they will only serve God on the Sabbath. You that do this do not serve God at all. If you are selfish during the week, you are selfish altogether. To suppose you had any real piety would imply that you were converted every Sunday and unconverted every Monday. But is this the idea of the Sabbath, that it is a day to serve God instead of other days? Is God in need of your services on the Sabbath to keep his work going?

God requires all your services as much on the six days as on the Sabbath. He has designated the Sabbath for unique duties, and required its observance as a day of rest from physical toil and from those fatiguing cares and labors that concern the present world. Because the gospel is to be spread and sustained by the things of this world, God therefore requires you to work all the six days at your secular employments. But it is all for his service, as much as worship is for the Sabbath. The Sabbath is no more for the service of God than Monday. You have no more right to serve yourselves on Monday than you have on the Sabbath. If any of you have regarded the matter this way, and imagined that the six days of the week were your own time, it shows that you are supremely selfish. I beg of you not to consider that in prayer and on the Sabbath you are serving God at all, if the rest of the time you are serving yourself. You have never known the radical principle of serving the Lord.

5. Those people who will not make any sacrifices of personal comfort are serving themselves, or their own gods. Suppose your servant were to say, "I cannot do this," or "I cannot do that," because it interferes with his personal comfort. He cannot do something because he likes to sit on a cushion and work. Or he cannot do something else because it would separate him from his family for an hour and a half. What! Is that doing service? When a person enters into service he gives up his ease and comfort for the interest of his employer. Can any person be supremely devoted to the service of God, when he shows that his own ease and comfort are dearer than the kingdom of Jesus Christ, and that he would sooner sacrifice the salvation of sinners than sit on a hard seat, or be separated from his family an hour or two?

6. Those who grudgingly give their time and money, by constraint, and not with a cheerful heart, are serving their own gods. What would you think of your servant, if you had to force him all the time to do anything for your interest? How many people are there who when they do anything for Christianity, do it grudgingly? If they do anything, it is difficult. If you go to one of these people and want his time or money for any religious goal, it is difficult to get him interested. It seems to go across the grain and is not easy or natural. It is clear he does not consider the interests of Christ's kingdom the same as his own. He may make a show of fearing the Lord, but he "serves" some other gods of his own.

7. Those who always ask how little they may do for religion, rather than how much they may do, are serving their own gods. There are many people who seem always to ask how little they can get by with in what they do for God. If this is you, it is a simple matter of fact that you have never set your hearts on the goal of promoting Christianity in the world. If you had, you would ask, "How much can I do for this goal and for that goal?"

8. They who are saving up wealth for their families, to elevate and promote them, are serving gods of their own and not the Lord. Those who are thus aiming to elevate their own families to a different sphere, by saving up wealth for them, show that they have some other goal to live for than bringing this world under the authority of Jesus Christ. They have other gods to serve. They may pretend to fear the Lord, but they "serve" their own gods.

9. Those who are making it their goal to accumulate so much prop-

erty that they can retire from business and live comfortably, are serving their own gods. There are many people who profess to be the servants of God, but are eagerly engaged in gathering property, intending to eventually retire to the country and live in comfort. What do you mean? Has God given you a right to a perpetual rest, as soon as you have made so much money? Did God tell you, when you professed to enter his service, to work hard so many years, and then you might have a perpetual holiday? Did he promise to excuse you after that from making the most of your time and talents, and let you live in comfort the rest of your days? If your thoughts are set upon this notion, I tell you, you are not serving God but your own selfishness and sloth.

10. Those people who would sooner gratify their appetites than deny themselves things that are unnecessary, or even hurtful, for the sake of doing good are serving their own gods. You find people that greatly love things that do them no good, and others even form an artificial appetite for what is positively loathsome, and they will chase after it. No arguments will make them abandon it for the sake of doing good. Are such people absorbed in the service of God? Certainly not. Will they sacrifice their lives for the kingdom of God? Why, you cannot make them even give up a cut of tobacco! A weed that is harmful to health and loathsome to society — they cannot give it up, even to save a soul from death!

Who does not see that selfishness predominates in such people? It shows the astonishing strength of selfishness. You often see the strength of selfishness showing itself in some such little thing more than in things that are greater. The real state of a person's mind strongly stands out, showing that self-gratification is his rule, when it will not give place, even in a little way, to those great interests for which he should be willing to lay down his life.

11. Those people who are most readily moved to action by appeals to their own selfish interests show that they are serving their own gods. You see what motivates such a person. Suppose I wish to get him to pledge for building a church, what must I say? Why, I must show how it will improve the value of his property, or advance his party, or gratify his selfishness in some other way. If he is more excited by these motives, than he is by a desire to save perishing souls and advance the kingdom of Christ, you see that he has never given himself up to serve the Lord. He is still serving himself. He is more influenced by his selfish interests than by all those benevolent principles on which Christianity is based. The character of a true servant of God is the opposite of this.

12. Those who are more interested in subjects other than religion are serving other gods. If you find them more ready to talk about other subjects, more easily excited by them, more awake to learn the news, they are serving their own gods. Many are more excited by the economy, or the question about war, or about the fire, or anything of a worldly nature, than about revivals, missions, or anything connected with the interests of religion. You find them completely engaged about politics, but if you bring up the subject of religion, ah, they are afraid of excitement! This shows that religion is not the subject that is nearest their hearts. A person is always most easily excited on that subject that lies nearest his heart. Bring that up, and he is interested. When you can talk all day about the news and other worldly topics, and when you cannot possibly be interested in the subject of religion, you know that your heart is not in it. If you pretend to be a servant of God, you are a hypocrite.

[handwritten margin note: Politics]

13. When people are more interested in their own fame than God's glory, it shows that they live for themselves, and serve their own gods. You see a person more annoyed or grieved by what is said against him than against God. Whom does he serve — who is his God, himself or Yahweh? A minister may be thrown into frenzy because somebody has said a word derogatory to his scholarship, his dignity, or his infallibility, while he is as cool as ice at all the abuses thrown upon the blessed God. Is that person willing to be considered a fool for the cause of Christ? Did that person ever learn the first lesson in religion? If he had, he would rejoice to have his name slandered for the cause of Christianity. No, he is not serving God — he is serving his own gods.

14. Those who do not make the salvation of souls the great and leading goal of their lives are serving their own gods. The aim of all Christian institutions, that which gives value to them all, is the salvation of sinners. The end for which Christ lives, and for which he has left his church in the world, is the salvation of sinners. This is the business that God puts his servants about. If anyone is not making this business the main goal of his life, he is not serving the Lord, but instead his own gods.

[handwritten margin note: Soul Winning is very important]

15. Those who seek happiness in religion, rather than usefulness, are serving their own gods. Their religion is entirely selfish. They want to enjoy religion, and all the while are asking how they can get happy states of mind. And they will go only to such meetings, and sit only under such preaching, which will make them happy. They will never ask whether that is the way to do the most good or not. Now, suppose your servant should be like this, and were constantly planning how

to enjoy himself. If he thought he could be most happy in the parlor, stretched on the sofa, with a pillow under his head and another servant to fan him, he would refuse to do the work that you had for him and urgently required. Instead of showing a desire to work for you, a care for your interest, and a willingness to pour himself out with all his powers in your service, he wants only to be happy! It is just so with those professed servants of Yahweh, who want to do nothing but sit on their handsome cushion, and have their minister feed them. Instead of seeking how to do good, they are only seeking to be happy. Their daily prayer is not, like that of the converted Saul of Tarsus, "Lord what will you have me do?" but instead, "Lord, tell me how I can be happy." Is that the spirit of Jesus Christ? No, he said, "I delight to do your will, O God."[3]

16. Those who make their own salvation their supreme object in religion, are serving their own gods. There are many in the church who show by their conduct and even acknowledge in their language that their main goal is to secure their own salvation — their grand determination is to get their own souls to the firm towers of the heavenly Jerusalem. If the Bible is correct, all such characters will go to hell. Their religion is pure selfishness. "For whoever would save his life will lose it, but whoever loses his life for my sake will save it" (Luke 9:24).

REMARKS

1. See why so little is accomplished in the world for Jesus Christ. It is because there are so few that do anything for him. It is because Jesus Christ has so few real servants in the world. How many professing Christians do you suppose there are in this church, or in your whole acquaintance, that are really at work for God, and making a business of religion, and pouring themselves out to advance the kingdom of Christ? The reason why religion advances no faster is that there are so few to advance it and so many to hinder it. You see a group of people trying to get the merchandise out of a store on fire. Some are determined to get the merchandise out, but the rest are not engaged with it, and they divert their attention by talking about other things, or hinder those at work by finding fault with their way of doing it, or by holding them back. So it is in the church. Those who desire to do the work are greatly hindered by the objections and resistance of the rest.

2. Understand why so few Christians have the spirit of prayer. What should God give them the spirit of prayer for? Suppose someone were

---

[3] Psalm 40:7-8, quoted in Hebrews 10:7

engaged in his worldly schemes and God gave him the spirit of prayer. Of course he would pray for that which lies nearest his heart, that is, for success in his worldly schemes, in order to serve his own gods. Will God give him the spirit of prayer for such purpose? Never. Let him go to his own gods for a spirit of prayer, but let him not expect Yahweh to grant the spirit of prayer while he is serving his own gods.

3. You see that there are many professing Christians that have not begun to be religious yet. A man said to one of them, "Do you feel that your property and your business are all God's, and do you hold and manage them for God?" He said, "Oh, no. I have not gotten as far as that yet." Not gotten as far as that! That man had been a professing Christian for years, and yet had not got so far as to consider his property, business, and all that he had as belonging to God! No doubt he was serving his own gods. For I insist that renouncing one's possessions is the very beginning of Christianity. What is conversion, but turning from the service of the world to the service of God?

4. It is great dishonesty for people to profess to serve the Lord, and yet in reality serve themselves. You who are performing religious duties from selfish motives are in reality trying to make God your servant. If your own interest is the supreme goal, all your religious services are only desires to make God promote your interests. Why do you pray, keep the Sabbath, or give your property for religious goals? You answer, "For the sake of promoting my own salvation." Indeed! Not to glorify God, but to get to heaven! Do you not think the devil would do all that, if he thought he could benefit by it and be a devil still? The highest form of selfishness must be to get God with all his attributes enlisted in the service of your mighty self.

And now, my hearers, where are you all? Are you serving the Lord, or are you serving your own gods? Have you done anything for God? Have you been living as servants of God? Is Satan's kingdom weakened by what you have done? Could you say now, "Come with me, and I will show you this sinner and that sinner converted, or this backslider and that backslider reclaimed, or this weak saint and that weak saint strengthened and helped?" Could you bring living witnesses of what you have done in the service of God? Or would your answer be, "I have been to meetings regularly on the Sabbath, heard a great deal of good preaching, and I have generally attended the prayer meetings, and we had some precious meetings, and I have prayed in my family, and two or three times a day in my closet, and I read the Bible." And in all that you have been merely passive, as to anything done for God. You have feared the Lord, and served your own gods.

Chapter 2

THE SALVATION OF THE WICKED IMPOSSIBLE

"If it is hard for the righteous to be saved, what will become of the ungodly and the sinner?" (1 Peter 4:18, NIV)

The teaching of the text is that the salvation of the righteous is difficult and that of the sinner impossible. I am now to show why the salvation of the wicked is impossible.

Here let me first state that by "the righteous" it is not meant those who have never sinned. It could not be difficult to save those who have never sinned against God. They are in fact already saved. But these righteous ones are those who having been sinners, come to have faith in Christ, and become "heirs of the righteousness that comes by faith."[1] It is vitally important to consider here that the governmental difficulty in salvation, because of your having sinned, is completely removed by Christ's atonement. This is true no matter how great your guilt, if you will only have faith in Jesus and accept his atonement as the ground of pardon for your sins.

Hence the difficulty in saving sinners is not simply that they have sinned in the past, but that they now continue sinning and not believing on the Lord Jesus Christ. The salvation of sinners is therefore impossible.

1. The sinner cannot be saved, because salvation from sin is a necessary

---

[1] Hebrews 11:7

condition of salvation from hell.[2] Being saved from sin must come first. Every sinner knows, and on reflection and self-inspection, he must see that his state of mind is such that he cannot respect himself. Until he meets the demands of his own moral nature, the elements of blessedness cannot therefore be in him.

He also knows that he does not want to have anything to do with God — he is afraid of God. He both dreads and hates his presence, being afraid to die and go near to God where death carries all people. He knows that all his relations to God are extremely unpleasant. How certainly then may he know that he is utterly unprepared for heaven.

Now the sinner must be saved from this guilty and detestable state of mind. No change is needed in God, his character, government, or position toward sin. But the greatest possible change is needed on the part of the sinner. If salvation implies fitness for heaven, and if this implies ceasing from sin, then of course it is naturally and forever impossible that any sinner can be saved without holiness.[3]

2. The peace of heaven forbids that you should go there in your sins. I know you expect to go there in the end. Your parents are there, as you hope and believe, and for this reason you even more want to go there, that you may see them in their glory. You say, "Oh, I would like to be where my father and mother are." And do you think you can follow them, in your sins? What could you do in heaven if you were there? What could you say? What kind of songs could you sing there? What sort of happiness, fitted to your heart, could you hope to find there?

Your pious mother in heaven — oh how changed! You heard her last words on earth — for they were words of prayer for your poor guilty soul. But now she shines and sings above, all holy and pure. What sympathy could there be between you and her in heaven? Remember what Christ said when someone told him that his mother and his brothers stood outside, wanting to see him. He said, "Who is my mother and who are my brothers? Whoever does the will of my Father in heaven is my brother and sister and mother" (Matthew 12:48,50). Therefore the law of sympathy in heaven is not based on earthly relationship, but on oneness of heart — on the common spirit of love and obedience toward their great common Father.

---

[2] Supporting this, Jesus is often referred to in the Bible as Savior from sin, not from hell. For example, "You shall call his name Jesus, for he will save his people from their sins" (Matthew 1:21).

[3] A reference to the verse, "Strive for... the holiness without which no one will see the Lord" (Hebrews 12:14).

Do you then expect that your mother would be glad to see you — that she would spread her garment over you and take you up to heaven? Oh, if she were told that you were at the gate, she would rush down to say, "Oh my sinning child, you cannot enter heaven. Into this holy place nothing can by any means enter that 'does what is detestable or false.'[4] You cannot — no, you cannot enter!"

If it were left to your own mother to decide the question of your admission, you could not come in. She would not open heaven's gate for you. She knows you would disturb the bliss of heaven. She knows you would damage its purity and be an element of discord in its shared feelings and in its songs.

You know that it did not have to be this way. You might have given your heart to God before, and then he would have shed his love abroad in your soul, given you the Holy Spirit, and made you ripe for heaven. But you would not give your heart. Everything was done for you that God could wisely do, all that Christ could do, all that the Spirit of God could consistently do. But all was in vain. All came to nothing because you would not give up your sins, even for everlasting life. And now will heaven let you in? No. Nothing that does what is detestable can by any means go inside.

3. Besides, it would not be comfortable for you there. You were never quite comfortable in spiritual company on earth. In the prayer meeting you were unhappy. As one individual said, "Oh, what a place this is! I cannot go across the street without being spoken to about my soul. How can I live here?" Let me tell you, it will be just as bad — no, much worse for you in heaven. That can be no place for you, sinner, since you hate most of all those places and scenes on earth that are most like heaven.

4. The justice of God will not allow you to participate in the joys of the saints. His relations to the universe make it necessary that he should protect his saints from company like you. They have had their discipline of trial in such company long enough. Their eternal reward will bring everlasting relief from this torture of their holy emotions. Oh how will God, their infinite Father, put around them the shield of his protection upon the mountains of paradise, which lift their heads eternally under the sunlight of his glory!

His sense of propriety forbids that he should give you a place among his pure and trusting children. It would be so unfitting — so unsuitable! It would throw such discord into the sweet songs and shared

---

[4] Revelation 21:27

feelings of the holy! Besides, as already said, it would not be kind to you. It could not soothe, but only grate and annoy your spirit. Oh if you were forced to be there, how it would torment and irritate your soul!

What then will become of the ungodly and the sinner? They will certainly not be in a desirable place or position. Not with the righteous in the judgment, for this God's word has often and most solemnly affirmed. Christ himself affirms that, when all nations are gathered before him for judgment, he will separate them one from another, as a shepherd divides the sheep from the goats. This separation, as the description shows, brings the righteous on the right hand and the wicked on the left. He says he will separate them one from another not according to their nationality or their family connections, but according to their character as friends or enemies of God.

Oh, what a separation must this be in families and among dear earthly friends! On this side will be a husband — on that a wife. Here a brother and there a sister, here one of two friends and there the other, parted forever — forever! If this great division were to be struck between you today according to present character, how fearful the line of separation it would draw! Ask yourselves where it would pass through your own families and among the friends you love. How would it divide college classes — and oh, how would it strike many hearts with terror and dismay!

It is asked, where shall the ungodly appear? I answer, certainly not in heaven. But they must be in the judgment, for God has said that he would bring the whole human race into judgment, and every secret thing, whether it is good or evil. All are to be there, but some are on the right hand and some on the left.

The ungodly and the sinner will appear in that day among the damned — among lost angels, doomed to the place prepared for their eternal home. Jesus has himself told us so. The very words of their judgment are on record, "Then he will say to those on his left, 'Depart from me, you cursed, into the eternal fire prepared for the devil and his angels' " (Matthew 25:41). This is indeed the only place for which they are prepared. This is the only company to which their hearts are friendly. They have chosen to belong to Satan's government on earth, at least in the sense of doing precisely what he would have them do. Now therefore, after such training in selfishness and sin, they are clearly fit for no other company than that of Satan and his angels.

Let it not surprise any of you to be told that the friendly sinners of earth, remaining enemies to God and radically selfish, are preparing themselves for the company of the arch spirit of evil. Just observe what restraints are put around sinners here. Observe how obviously they feel restrained, and show that they are impatient and uncomfortable. It may be read out of their very hearts that they would be glad to be vastly more wicked and selfish in their outward life if they could. It is wonderful to see how many ways God's providence has walled in the sinner's path and hedged him in from explosive sin.

But let these walls be torn away. Let all care for his reputation among good people perish forever from his soul. Let despair of ever gaining God's favor take full possession of his heart, and fasten its iron grasp upon him. Then what will he become? Take away all the restraints of civil society, of laws and customs, of Christian example, and of Christian society. Let there be no more prayer made for him by pitying Christian friends, no more counsel given, or request made to persuade him towards the good. Then tell me, where is the sinner? How terribly will sin work out its dreadful power to corrupt and madden the soul! Bring together many desperate wretches, in the madness of their despair and rage and wrath against God and all the good, and oh what a fearful world would they make! What can be conceived more awful! Yet this is the very world for which sinners are now preparing, and the only one for which they will be found to be prepared for in the judgment.

As this is the only world for which the sinner is prepared, so it is the only one that is appropriate given his influence for mischief. Here only, here in this prison-house of woe and despair, can sinners be effectively prevented from doing any further mischief in God's kingdom. Here they are cut off from all possibility of doing any more harm in God's universe.

In this earthly state one sinner destroys much good. Each and every sinner does much evil. God looks on, not unconcerned, but with amazing patience. He tolerates a great deal of evil to be done for the sake of securing an opportunity to attempt the power of patience and love upon the sinner's heart. You are abusing his love and defeating all his kind intentions, but still God waits, until the point is reached where patience ceases to be virtue. Beyond this point, how can God wait longer?

Here you find ample room for doing mischief. Many are around you whom you influence to evil and urge on towards hell. Some of them would be converted if not for your influence to hold them back and ensnare their souls. If this were the place, I could name and call out some of you who are exerting a deadly influence upon your associates.

Ah to think of the souls you may ruin forever! God sees them and sees how you are playing into the devil's hands to drag them down with you to an eternal hell. But before long he will take you away from this sphere of doing evil. He will forever cut off your connection with those who can be influenced to evil, and leave around you only those associates who are ruined, despairing, and maddened in sin like yourself. There he will lock you up, discard the key, and let you rave on, swear on, curse on, and madden your guilty soul more and more forever! Oh what inmates are those in this prison-house of the guilty and the lost! Why should not God make such a place for such beings, so lost to all good, and so given up to all the madness and guilt of rebellion?

There alone can sinners be made useful. They refused to make themselves useful by their voluntary agency on earth. Now God will make use of them in hell for some good. Do you ask me if I talk about sin being made useful? Yes, to be sure I do. God never permits anything to occur in his universe unless he extracts some good from it, overruling its influence, or making the correction and punishment of it a means of good. This is a great consolation to the holy that no sinner can exist from whom God will not bring out some good. This principle is partially developed in society here, in civil government. Government can make great use of those people who will not obey the law. It can make them examples and lift them up as beacons of warning to show the evil of disobeying wholesome laws. A great many people have had strong impressions made on their minds when riding through Auburn on the railroad.[5] They have observed those lofty frowning walls and towers that enclose and guard the culprits confined within. Many a hard heart has trembled before those walls and the terrors of those cells behind. If the outside view does not help to awe the spirit of transgression, give them the inside view and some of its heart-desolating experience. These things do good. They tame the passion for doing evil and impress a healthy fear on the hardened and reckless. If so under all the imperfections of human government, how much more under the perfect administration of the divine!

God cannot afford to lose your influence in his universe. He will rejoice to use you for the glory of his mercy, if you choose. Oh yes, he will put away your sins as far as the East is from the West, and will put a robe of beauty and glory upon you, a sweet harp in your hands, a song of praise on your lips, and the melody of heaven's love in your heart. All these are yours if you choose. But if you will not, then he has other

---

[5] A reference to the Auburn State Prison in New York.

attributes besides mercy that need to be illustrated. Justice will come in for its claim, and to illustrate this he will make you an example of the bitter misery of sinning. He will put you deep in hell. The holy, seeing you there, will see that God's kingdom is safe and pure, and in their everlasting song they will shout, "Great and amazing are your deeds, O Lord God the Almighty! Just and true are your ways, O King of the nations! Who will not fear, O Lord, and glorify your name? For you alone are holy. All nations will come and worship you, for your righteous acts have been revealed" (Revelation 15:3-4).

If you will not repent, this is the only way that God can make you useful in his kingdom. He has tried every means of bringing you to repentance, but all in vain. He cannot get you to agree. Of course there is no alternative but to make you an example to deter all other moral agents from sinning.

There is no other way for God to meet the demands of the public welfare, but to make you an example to show his abhorrence of sin. God is most thoroughly economical of his resources. He manages everything to the very best account. Everything must, under his hand, be made conducive in some way to the general good. Even of your misery he will be as economical as he can, and will carefully turn it all to the very best account. Every groan and every throb and pang of your agonized soul will be turned to use. Yes, count on it, all this agony, which does you no good, but is to you only pure and unalleviated misery, will be a warning beacon, under God's hand, crying out in tones of thunder, "Stand away! Stand away, lest you come into this place of torment. Stand far away from sin — fear this awful sin. Watch against it, for it is an awful thing to sin against Yahweh. I have tried it, and here I am in unspeakable pain!" Oh what a testimony, when all hell shall produce one mighty accumulated groan — a groan, whose awful voice shall be, "Stand in awe and do not sin, for God is severe in his judgments upon the guilty."

Oh sinner, think of it. God wants you now to cry out to every fellow-sinner, and warn him away from the brink of hell. Will you do it? What are you in fact doing? Are you preparing yourself to go out as a missionary of light and love and mercy to those in darkness? Are you preparing your wings as an angel of mercy to bear the messages of salvation? No, you refuse to do this, or anything of the sort. You hate to preach such a gospel and to preach it so! But God will make you preach it in another way. As I said, he is thoroughly economical of the resources of his kingdom, and all must do something in some way for his glory. He will have everything preach — saints preach and sinners preach. Yes, sinners in hell must preach for God and for his truth. He will make your very groans and tears preach, and they will tell over and over the dreadful story of mercy abused and sin persisted in, and growing worse and worse, until the bolts of vengeance broke at last upon your guilty head! Over and over will those groans and tears repeat the fearful story, so that when the angels shall come from the farthest regions of the universe, they shall cry out, "What is here? What do those groans mean? What do those flames mean, twisting around their miserable victims?" Ah, the story then told will make them cry aloud, "Why will God's creatures sin against his throne? Can there be such madness in beings gifted with reason's light?"

These angels know that the only thing that can secure public confidence in a ruler is fidelity in the execution of his law. Hence it is to them no wonder that God should punish sin with the most exemplary severity. They expect this, and seeing its awful demonstrations before their eyes, serves only to more deeply impress on their souls the holiness and justice of the great and blessed God.

REMARKS

Come then, repent and believe the gospel if you would be saved.

But what are you doing? Do you flatter yourselves that the work of salvation is so easy that it may be safely and surely done during a few of life's last moments? Will you presume, as the man did who said he should need only five minutes to prepare to die? Hear his story. What was the result of his system? Disease came on. It struck him with its strong hand. Delirium set in. Reason tottered and fell from its throne, and so he died! Consider what news we hear of others who once sat as you now sit, and once heard the gospel as you hear it now. There, one is dead, and now another — and now another. In rapid succession they drop from the stage of mortal life — and what next? Soon we shall meet them in the fearful judgment!

Are you aware that the smooth sea of temptation carries you on to the rapids of death? Were you ever at Niagara Falls? How smooth and deceitful those waters, as they move along up above the current of the suction from below. But lower down, see how those same waters roar, and dash, and foam, and send up their thick mists to the heavens above you. Yet in the upper stream you glide gently and noiselessly along, dreaming of no danger, and making no effort to escape. In a moment you are in the awful current, plunging headfirst down. Where are you now?

And what should you do? Like Bunyan's Christian pilgrim[6], put your fingers in both ears and run, shouting, "Life! Life! Eternal Life!" How many of you are sliding along on the smooth, deceitful stream, yet only just above the awful rapids and the dreadful waterfall of death! What if, this night, delirium should strike you? Or what if the Spirit should leave you forever, saying, "He is attached to his idols, leave him alone"?

Surely, oh sinners, it is time that you should set down your foot in most fixed determination, and say, "I must and I will have heaven! How can I ever bear the doom of the damned?"

---

[6] A reference to the main character in John Bunyan's book *The Pilgrim's Progress*, written in 1675.

Chapter 3

TRUE AND FALSE REPENTANCE

"For godly grief produces a repentance that leads to salvation without regret, whereas worldly grief produces death." (2 Corinthians 7:10)

In this text, the apostle refers to another letter that he had formerly written to the church at Corinth on a certain subject for which they were greatly to blame. He speaks here of the effect that it had in bringing them to true repentance. They had a godly grief. Here was the evidence that their repentance was genuine. "For see what earnestness this godly grief has produced in you, but also what eagerness to clear yourselves, what indignation, what fear, what longing, what zeal, what punishment! At every point you have proved yourselves innocent in the matter" (2 Corinthians 7:11).

In the verse that I have taken for my text, he speaks of two kinds of grief for sin: one producing repentance that leads to salvation, the other producing death. He refers to what is generally understood as two kinds of repentance. I will now show:

I. What true repentance is.

II. How it may be known.

III. What false repentance is.

IV. How it may be known.

It is urgent that professing Christians were taught to better discriminate the nature and character of various religious exercises. If it were so, the church would not be so overrun with false professors.[1] I have recently been often led to examine, over and over again, the reason why there is so much false Christianity, and I have tried to discover what the root of the problem is. It is notorious that many suppose themselves to be religious who are not so according to the Bible. Why is it that so many are deceived? Why do so many, who are still impenitent sinners, get the idea that they have repented? The cause is certainly a lack of discerning instruction about the foundation of religion, and especially a lack of discrimination between true and false repentance.

I. WHAT TRUE REPENTANCE IS

1. Repentance is a change of mind about the nature of sin. To one who truly repents sin looks very different than it does to someone who has not repented. Instead of looking desirable or fascinating, it looks the very opposite, completely detestable, and he is surprised at himself, that he ever could have desired such a thing. Impenitent sinners may look at sin and see that it will ruin them, because God will punish them for it. But it still appears inherently desirable. They love it. They roll it under their tongue. If it could end in happiness, they would never think of abandoning it. But to the other it is different. He looks at his own conduct as perfectly hateful. He looks back on it and exclaims, "How hateful, how detestable, how worthy of hell, such a thing was in me."

2. Repentance is a change of mind about the nature of sin in relationship to God. Sinners do not see why God threatens sin with such severe punishment. They love it so much themselves that they cannot see why God should look at it in such a way as to consider it worthy of everlasting punishment. When they are strongly convicted, they see sin differently. In their mind, they see sin in the same light that a Christian does, and then they only lack a corresponding change of heart to become Christians. Often a sinner sees its relationship to God to be such that it deserves eternal death, but his heart does not go with his mind. This is the case with the devils and wicked spirits in hell. Note that a change of mind is necessary to true repentance, and always precedes it. The heart never goes out to God in true repentance without a previous change of mind. There may be a change of mind without repentance, but no genuine repentance without a change of mind.

---

[1] The term "professors" is what Finney often uses for professing Christians. A professor claims to be a Christian, though may not be so in God's eyes. The term has nothing to do with an academic professor.

3. Repentance is a change of mind regarding the tendencies of sin. Before the sinner thinks it utterly unbelievable that sin should have such tendencies as to deserve everlasting death. However, his mind may be fully changed on this point without repentance, but it is impossible that a person should truly repent without a change of mind. He sees sin, in its tendency, as ruinous to himself and everybody else, soul and body, for time and eternity, and against all that is lovely and happy in the universe. He sees that sin tends to harm himself and everybody else, and that there is no remedy but universal abstinence. The devil knows it to be true. And possibly there are some sinners now in this congregation who know it.

4. Repentance is a change of mind regarding the guilt of sin. The word "repentance" implies a change in the state of the mind including all this. The apathetic sinner is almost devoid of right ideas about the guilt of sin. Suppose he admits in theory that sin deserves eternal death, he does not believe it. If he believed it, it would be impossible for him to remain an apathetic sinner. He is deceived if he supposes that he honestly holds an opinion that sin deserves the wrath of God forever. But the truly awakened and convicted sinner has no more doubt of this than he has of the existence of God. He sees clearly that sin must deserve everlasting punishment from God. He knows that this is a simple matter of fact.

In true repentance there must be a corresponding change of heart. The change of heart involves sin in these four areas: its nature, its relations, its tendencies, and its guilt. The individual who truly repents, not only sees sin to be detestable and vile, and worthy of abhorrence, but he sincerely abhors it and hates it in his heart. A person may see sin to be hurtful and detestable, while yet his heart loves it, and desires it, and clings to it. But when he truly repents, he most heartily abhors and renounces it.

In its relation to God, he feels towards sin as it really is. And here is the source of those outpourings of sorrow in which Christians sometimes break out, when contemplating sin. The Christian sees its nature, and simply feels disgust. But when he views it in relation to God, then he weeps. The fountains of his sorrow pour out, and he wants to get right down on his face and pour out a flood of tears over his sins.

Then as to the tendencies of sin, the individual who truly repents feels it as it really is. When he views sin in its tendencies, it awakens a vehement desire to stop it, and to save people from their sins, and roll back the tide of death. It sets his heart on fire, and he goes to praying, laboring, and pulling sinners out of the fire with all his might, to save them from the awful tendencies of sin. When the Christian sets his mind on this, he will stir himself to make people give up their sins. Just as if he saw all the people taking poison which he knew would destroy them, and he lifts up his voice to warn them to beware.

He feels correctly, as to the guilt of sin. He has not only an intellectual conviction that sin deserves everlasting punishment, but he feels that it would be so right, so reasonable, and so just, for God to condemn him to eternal death, that instead of finding fault with the sentence of the law that condemns him, he thinks it the wonder of heaven, a wonder of wonders, if God can forgive him. Instead of thinking it hard, severe, or unkind of God that stubborn sinners are sent to hell, he is full of adoring wonder that he is not sent to hell himself, and that this whole guilty world has not already been hurled down to endless burnings. It is the last thing in the world he would think to complain of, that all sinners are not saved. Oh, it is a wonder of mercy that the whole world is not damned. And when he thinks of such a sinner's being saved, he feels a sense of gratitude that he never knew until he was a Christian.

II. HOW TRUE REPENTANCE IS SHOWN

I want to show you what the works of true repentance are and to make it so clear to your minds that you can know with certainty whether you have repented or not.

1. If your repentance is genuine, there is a conscious change of views and feeling in your mind about sin. Of this you will be just as conscious as you ever were of a change of views and feelings on any other subject. Now, can you say this? Do you know that on this point there has been a change in you and that old things are done away and all things have become new?

2. Where repentance is genuine, the inclination to repeat sin is gone. If you have truly repented, you do not now love sin. You do not now abstain from sin out of fear to avoid punishment, but you abstain because you hate it. How is this with you? Do you know that your inclination to commit sin is gone? Look at the sins you used to practice when you were impenitent — how do they appear to you? Do they look pleasant? Would you truly love to practice them again if you dared? If you do, if you have the inclination to sin remaining, you are only convicted. Your opinions of sin may be changed, but if the love of that sin remains, you are still an impenitent sinner.

3. Genuine repentance produces a reformation of conduct. I take this idea to be mainly intended in the text, where it says, "godly grief produces a repentance." Godly grief produces reformation of conduct.

Otherwise it is a repetition of the same idea, saying that repentance produces repentance. Instead, I believe the apostle was speaking of a change of mind such as produces a change of conduct, ending in salvation. Now, let me ask you, are you really reformed? Have you forsaken your sins? Or, are you practicing them still? If so, you are still a sinner. Though you may have changed your mind, if it has not produced a change of conduct, an actual reformation, it is not godly repentance.

4. Repentance, when true and genuine, leads to confession and restitution. The thief has not repented while he keeps the money he stole. He may have conviction, but no repentance. If he had repentance, he would go and give back the money. If you have cheated any one, and do not restore what you have unfairly taken, or if you have injured any one, and do not set about correcting the wrong you have done, you have not truly repented.

5. True repentance is a permanent change of character and conduct. The text says it is repentance that leads to salvation, "without regret." What else does the apostle mean by that expression but that true repentance is a change so deep and fundamental that the person never changes back again? The love of sin is truly abandoned. The individual who has truly repented has so changed his views and heart that he will not change back again, or go back to the love of sin. Bear this in mind now, all of you, that the truly penitent sinner exercises feelings of which he never will regret. The text says it is "leading to salvation." It goes right on to the very peace of heaven. The very reason why it ends in salvation is because it is without regret.

And here I must remark that you see why the doctrine of the Perseverance of the Saints is true, and what it means.[2] True repentance is such a thorough change of heart that the individual who performs it comes to hate sin so much that he will naturally persevere and not take back all his repentance and return to sin again.

---

[2] The Perseverance of the Saints is the fifth point of Calvinism that states the true believers always persevere in their faith to the very end. Though Finney believed in the doctrine of the Perseverance of the Saints, he was not an "Old Calvinist." His views are a blend of two main theologies. First, he drew heavily from the "New Divinity" Calvinists, a system of theology propounded by Jonathan Edwards and his followers. (See the book *Edwards on the Will* by Allen Guelzo for a scholarly examination of how Edwards' ideas influenced American theologians and ministers, including Finney.) Second, Finney's views are similar to those of "New Haven theology," a system propounded by the Congregationalist Nathaniel William Taylor, Professor of Theology at Yale University. Finney's blending of belief systems makes it difficult to neatly classify his theology into traditional schemes.

III. WHAT FALSE REPENTANCE IS

False repentance is said to be worldly, the grief of the world. It is grief for sin, arising from worldly considerations and motives connected with the present life. It at most has relevance to personal happiness in a future world, and has no regard to the true nature of sin.

1. It is not based on the change of mind I have described that belongs to true repentance. The change in false repentance is not on fundamental points. A person may see the evil consequences of sin in a worldly point of view, and it may fill him with dismay. He may see that it will greatly affect his character, or endanger his life. If some of his concealed conduct should be found out, he would be disgraced, and this may fill him with fear and distress. It is very common for people to have this kind of worldly grief when some worldly consideration is at the bottom of it all.

2. False repentance is based on selfishness. It may simply be a strong feeling of regret for what he has done because he sees the evil consequences of it for himself, because it makes him miserable, exposes him to the wrath of God, or injures his family or his friends. All this is pure selfishness. He may feel remorse of conscience — biting, consuming remorse — and no true repentance. It may extend to deep fear of the wrath of God and the pains of hell, and yet be purely selfish. All the while there may be no such thing as a hearty abhorrence of sin, and no feelings of the heart following the convictions of the mind, regarding the infinite evil of sin.

IV. HOW FALSE REPENTANCE IS SHOWN

1. False repentance leaves the heart unchanged. It leaves unbroken and unconquered the disposition of the heart to sin. The feelings on the nature of sin are not properly changed, and the individual still feels a desire for sin. He abstains from it, not from abhorrence of it, but from dread of the consequences of it.

2. False repentance produces death. It leads to hypocritical conceal-ment. The individual who has truly repented is willing to have it known that he has repented, and willing to have it known that he was a sinner. He who has only false repentance resorts to excuses and ly-ing to cover his sins, and is ashamed of his repentance. He will cover up his sins with a thousand apologies and excuses, trying to smooth them over, and lessen their enormity. If he speaks of his past conduct, he always does it in the softest and most favorable terms. You see a constant inclination to cover up his sin. This repentance leads to death.

How is it with you? Are you ashamed to have any person talk with you about your sins? Then your grief is only a worldly grief, and produces death. How often you see sinners avoiding conversation about their sins, and yet calling themselves seekers, and expecting to become Christians in that way. The same kind of grief is found in hell. No doubt all those wretched inhabitants of the pit want to get away from the eye of God. No such grief is found among the saints in heaven. Their grief is open, candid, full, and sincere. Such grief is not inconsistent with true happiness. The saints are full of happiness, and yet full of deep, undisguised, and flowing grief over sin. But this worldly grief is ashamed of itself, is miserable, and produces death.

3. False repentance produces only a partial reformation of conduct. The reformation that is produced by worldly grief extends only to those things of which the individual has been strongly convicted. The heart is not changed. You will see him avoid only those prominent sins about which he has been stirred.

Observe that young convert. If he is deceived, you will find that there is only a partial change in his conduct. He is reformed in certain things, but there are many things that are wrong that he continues to practice. If you become intimately acquainted with him, instead of finding him tremblingly aware of sin everywhere, and quick to detect it in everything that is contrary to the spirit of the gospel, you will find him, perhaps, strict and quick-sighted in regard to certain things, but loose in his conduct and lax in his views on other points, and very far from showing a Christian spirit in regard to all sin.

4. Ordinarily, the reformation produced by worldly grief is temporary even in those things that are reformed. The individual is continually relapsing into his old sins. The reason is that the disposition to sin is still there — it is only checked and restrained by fear. As soon as he has a hope and is in the church and gets bolstered up so that his fears are calmed, you see him gradually returning to his old sins. This was the problem with the house of Israel that made them so constantly return to their idolatry and other sins. They had only worldly grief. You see it now everywhere in the church. Individuals are reformed for a while and then relapse into their old sins. They love to call it getting cold in religion, backsliding, and the like. But the truth is, they have always loved sin. When the occasion offered, they returned to it, like the washed pig returned to its wallowing in the mud, because it was always a pig.

I want you to understand this point thoroughly. Here is the foundation of all those stops and starts in religion that you see so much of. People are awakened, convicted, and eventually they acquire hope and settle down in false security and then away they go. Perhaps they may keep on their guard enough to not be cast out of the church, but the foundations of sins are not broken up, and they return to their old ways. The woman that loved fashion loves it still, and gradually returns to her ribbons and trinkets. The man who loved money loves it still, and soon slides back into his old ways, dives into business, and pursues the world as eagerly and devotedly as he did before he joined the church.

Go through all the classes of society, and if you find thorough conversions, you will find that their most besetting sins before conversion are farthest from them now. The real convert is least likely to fall into his old besetting sin, because he detests it most. But if he is deceived and worldly minded, he is always tending back into the same sins. The fountain of sin was not broken up.

5. It is a forced reformation. The reformation produced by a false repentance, is not only a partial reformation, and a temporary reformation, but it is also forced and constrained. The reformation of one who has true repentance is from the heart. He no longer has an inclination to sin. In him the Bible promise is fulfilled. He actually finds that wisdom's ways are "ways of pleasantness, and all her paths are peace."[3] He experiences that the Savior's yoke is easy and his burden is light.[4] He has felt that God's commandments are not sad but joyous. "More to be desired are they than gold, even much fine gold; sweeter also than honey and drippings of the honeycomb."[5] But this false kind of repentance is very different: it is a legalistic repentance, the result of fear and not of love, a selfish repentance, anything but a free, voluntary, sincere change from sin to obedience. You will find, if there are any individuals here that have this kind of repentance, you are conscious that you do not abstain from sin by choice or because you hate it, but for other reasons. It is more because of the warnings of conscience, or the fear you shall lose your soul, or lose your hope, or lose your character, than from the abhorrence of sin or love for duty.

Such people always need to be urged to do their duty with a clear passage of scripture, or else they will evade duty and think there is no great harm in doing as they do. The reason is that they love their sins, and if there is not some clear command of God that they dare not fly in the face of, they will practice them. Not so with true repentance. If a thing seems contrary to the great law of love, the person who has

---

[3] Proverbs 3:17
[4] Matthew 11:30
[5] Psalm 19:10

true repentance will detest it and naturally avoid it, whether he has an clear command of God or not. Show me such a person, and I tell you he does not need a clear command to make him give up drinking or making or selling strong drink. He sees it is contrary to the great law of benevolence, and he truly detests it, and would no more do it than he would blaspheme God, steal, or commit any other abomination.

6. This false repentance leads to self-righteousness. The individual who has this repentance may know that Jesus Christ is the only Savior of sinners, and may profess to believe on him and to rely on him alone for salvation, but after all, he is actually placing ten times more reliance on his reformation than on Jesus Christ for his salvation. And if he would watch his own heart, he would know it is so. He may say he expects salvation by Christ, but in fact he is dwelling more on his reformation. His hope is based more on that than on the atonement of Christ, and he is really patching up a righteousness of his own.

7. It leads to false security. The individual supposes his worldly grief to be true repentance, and he trusts in it. It is a curious fact, that so far as I have been able to understand the state of mind of this class of people, they seem to take it for granted that Christ will save them because they have had grief because of their sins, although they are not conscious that they have ever felt any resting in Christ. They felt grief, and then they experienced relief and felt better, and now they expect to be saved by Christ, when their very consciousness will teach them that they have never felt a sincere reliance on Christ.

8. It hardens the heart. The individual who has worldly grief becomes harder in heart, in proportion to the number of times that he exercises such grief. If he has strong emotions of conviction, and his heart does not break up and flow out, the fountains of feeling are more and more dried up, and his heart more and more difficult to be reached. Take a real Christian, one who has truly repented, and every time you bring the truth to bear upon him to break him down before God, he becomes more and more soft, affected, melted, and broken down under God's blessed word, as long as he lives and to all eternity. His heart gets into the habit of following the convictions of his understanding, and he becomes as teachable as a little child.

Here is the grand distinction. Let churches, or individual members, who have only this worldly repentance, pass through a revival[6], and be woken up, and bustle about, and then grow cold again. Let this be repeated and you find them more and more difficult to be stirred, until eventually they become as hard as a millstone, and nothing can ever rally them to a revival again. In contrast are those churches and individuals who have true repentance. Let them go through successive revivals, and you find them growing more and more broken and tender until they get to such a state that if they hear the trumpet for a revival, they kindle and glow instantly, and are ready for the work.

9. It sears the conscience. People who falsely repent are liable at first to be distressed, whenever the truth is flashed upon their mind. But the real Christian is filled with peace at the very time that his tears are flowing from conviction of sin. And each repeated season of conviction makes him more and more watchful, tender, and careful, until his conscience becomes, like the apple of his eye, so tender that the very appearance of evil will offend it. But the other kind of sorrow, which does not lead to sincere renunciation of sin, leaves the heart harder than before, and eventually sears the conscience like with a hot iron. This sorrow produces death.

REMARKS

1. We learn from what has been said, one reason why there is so much spasmodic religion in the church. They have mistaken conviction for conversion, the grief of the world for that godly grief that produces repentance leading to salvation, without regret. I am convinced, after years of observation, that this is the true reason for the present deplorable state of the church all over the land.

2. We see why sinners under conviction feel as if it was a great cross to become Christians. They think it a great trial to give up their ungodly companions, and to give up their sins. If they had true repentance, they would not think it any cross to give up their sins. I remember how I used to feel, when I first saw young people becoming Christians and joining the church. I thought it was a good thing on the whole to have religion, because they would save their souls and get to heaven. But I thought it was a very sorrowful thing for them now. I never dreamed

---

[6] The theme of revival is a frequent one in this book. Much of this book is drawn from Finney's *Lectures on Revivals of Religion*, and most of Finney's ministry was dedicated to promoting revival in churches in America and England. At the famous "New Lebanon Convention," Finney and other ministers defined a revival as follows: "Revivals of true religion are the work of God's Spirit, by which, in a comparatively short period of time, many persons are convinced of sin, and brought to the exercise of repentance towards God, and faith in our Lord Jesus Christ."

then that these young people could be really happy now. I believe it is very common for people, who know that religion is good on the whole and good in the end, to think they cannot be happy in religion. This is because of a mistake about the true nature of repentance. They do not understand that true repentance leads to a disgust for those things that were formerly loved. Sinners do not see that when their young friends become true Christians, they feel disgust for their balls and parties, and sinful amusements and follies — the love for these things is crucified.

I once knew a young lady who was converted to God. Her father was a very proud worldly man. She used to be very fond of fashion, the dancing school, and balls. After she was converted, her father would force her to go to the dancing school. He used to go along with her, and force her to stand up and dance. She would go there and weep, and sometimes when she was standing up on the floor to dance, her feelings of disgust and grief would come over her so much that she would turn away and burst into tears. Here you see the cause of all that. She truly repented of these things, with a repentance without regret. Oh, how many related thoughts would such a scene recall to a Christian: compassion for her former merry companions, abhorrence of their giddy mirth. How she longed to be in the prayer meeting — how could she be happy dancing? Such is the mistake that the impenitent, or those who have only worldly grief fall into regarding the happiness of the real Christian.

3. Here you see what is the matter with those professing Christians who think it difficult to be very strict in religion. Such people are always apologizing for their sins, and pleading for certain practices that are not consistent with disciplined Christianity. It shows that they love sin still, and will go as far as they dare in it. If they were true Christians, they would detest it, turn from it, and would feel it difficult to be dragged to it.

4. You see the reason why some do not know what it is to enjoy Christianity. They are not cheerful and happy in religion. They are grieved because they have to break off from so many things they love, or because they have to give so much money. They are in the fire all the time. Instead of rejoicing in every opportunity of self-denial, and rejoicing in the clearest and most cutting exhibitions of truth, it is a great trial to them to be told their duty, when it opposes their inclinations and habits. The plain truth distresses them. Why? Because their hearts do not love to do duty. If they loved to do their duty, every ray of light that broke in upon their minds from heaven, pointing out their duty, would be welcomed, and make them more and more happy.

Whenever you see such people, if they feel cramped and distressed because the truth presses them, if their hearts do not yield and go along with the truth, the name of all such professing Christians is hypocrite. If you find that they are distressed like anxious sinners, and that the more you point out their sins the more they are distressed, be certain that they have never truly repented of their sins, nor given themselves up to be God's.

5. You see why many professed converts, who had very deep experiences at the time of their conversion, afterwards apostatize. They had deep convictions and great distress of mind, and afterwards they found relief and their joy was very great, and they were amazingly happy for a while. But eventually they decline, and then they apostatize. Some, who do not discriminate properly between true and false repentance, and who think there cannot be such "deep" exercises without divine power, call these cases of falling from grace. But the truth is, they went out from us because they were not of us.[7] They never had that repentance that kills and annihilates the disposition to sin.

6. See why backsliders are so miserable. There is a radical difference between a backslidden Christian and a hypocrite who has gone back from his profession of faith. The hypocrite loves the world, and enjoys sin when he returns to it. He may have some fears and some remorse, and some hesitation about the loss of character — but after all he enjoys sin. Not so with the backslidden Christian. He loses his first love, then he falls prey to temptation, and so he goes into sin. But he does not love it. It is always bitter to him — he feels unhappy and away from home. At the time, he indeed has no Spirit of God, no love of God working to keep him from sin, but he does not love sin. He is unhappy in sin and he feels that he is a wretch. He is as different from the hypocrite as can be. Such a person, when he leaves the love of God, may be delivered over to Satan for a time in order to destroy the flesh that the Spirit may be saved. But he can never again enjoy sin as he used to, or delight himself as he once could in the pleasures of the world. Never again can he drink sin like water. So long as he continues to wander, he is miserable. If there is such a person here tonight, you know it.

7. You see why convicted sinners are afraid to pledge themselves to give up their sins. They tell you they dare not promise to do it, because they are afraid they shall not keep the promise. There you have the reason. "They love sin." The drunkard knows that he loves rum, and though he may be forced to keep his promise and abstain from it, his appetite still craves it. So it is with the convicted sinner. He feels that

---

[7] See 1 John 2:19.

he loves sin, that his hold on sin has never been broken off, and he dares not promise.

8. See why some professing Christians are so opposed to pledges. It is on the same principle. They love their sins so much, they know their hearts will plead for indulgence, and they are afraid to promise to give them up. Hence many who profess to be Christians refuse to join the church. The secret reason is that they feel that their heart is still going after sin, and they dare not come under the obligations of the church-covenant. They do not want to be subject to the discipline of the church, in case they should sin. That person knows he is a hypocrite.

9. Those sinners who have worldly grief can now see where the difficulty lies, and what the reason is they are not converted. Their intellectual views of sin may be such that if their hearts agreed, they would be Christians. And perhaps they are thinking that this is true repentance. But if they were truly willing to give up sin, all sin, they would not hesitate to pledge themselves to it, and to have the whole world know that they had done it. If there are any such here, I ask you now to come forward and take these seats. If you are willing to give up sin, you are willing to promise to do it, and willing to have it known that you have done it. But if you resist conviction, and when your understanding is enlightened to see what you should do, your heart still goes after your sins, tremble, sinner, at the prospect before you. All your convictions will avail you nothing. They will only sink you deeper in hell for having resisted them.

If you are willing to give up your sins, you can give it the significance that I have named. But if you still love your sins and want to keep them, you can stay in your seats. And now, shall we go and tell God in prayer, that these sinners are unwilling to give up their sins, that though they are convinced they are wrong, they love their idols, and they will go after them? The Lord have mercy on them, for they are in a fearful situation.

Chapter 4

HOW TO REPENT

"Break up your fallow ground, for it is time to seek the LORD, *that he may come and rain righteousness on you."* (Hosea 10:12)

The Jews were a nation of farmers, and it is therefore common in the Scriptures to use illustrations from their occupation and to refer to scenes familiar to farmers and shepherds. The prophet Hosea addresses them as a nation of backsliders. He rebukes them for their idolatry, and threatens them with the judgments of God. Fallow ground is ground which has once been tilled, but which now lies waste, and needs to be broken up and softened, before it is ready to receive grain. I will show:

I. What it is to break up the fallow ground, in the sense of the text.

II. How it is to be performed.

I. WHAT IS IT TO BREAK UP THE FALLOW GROUND?

To break up the fallow ground is to break up your hearts, to prepare your minds to bring forth fruit unto God. The human mind is often compared in the Bible to ground, and the Word of God to seed sown in the ground. The fruit represents the actions and affections of those who receive it. To break up the fallow ground, therefore, is to bring the mind into such a state that it is fitted to receive the Word of God. Sometimes your hearts get matted down, hard and dry, until it is impossible to get fruit from them until they are broken up, softened, and fitted to receive the Word. It is this softening of the heart, so as to make it feel the truth, which the prophet calls breaking up your fallow ground.

II. HOW IS THE FALLOW GROUND TO BE BROKEN UP?

It is not by any direct efforts to feel. People fall into a mistake on this subject from not studying the laws of mind. People talk about religious feeling as if they could, by direct effort, call forth religious affection.[1] But this is not the way the mind acts. No person can make himself feel in this way, merely by trying to feel. The feelings of the mind are not directly under our control. We cannot directly will religious feelings. They are purely involuntary states of mind. They naturally and necessarily exist in the mind under certain circumstances that evoke them. But they can be controlled indirectly. Otherwise there would be no moral character in our feelings, if there were not a way to control them. One cannot say, "Now I will feel so-and-so towards such an object." But we can command our attention to it, and look at it intently, until the proper feeling arises. Let a man who is away from his family bring them up before his mind, and will he not feel? But it is not by saying to himself, "Now I will feel deeply for my family." A person can direct his attention to any object, about which he ought and wishes to feel, and in that way he will call into existence the proper emotions. Let a person bring his enemy before his mind, and his feelings of enmity will rise. So if a person thinks of God, and fastens his mind on any aspects of God's character, he will feel — emotions will come by the very laws of mind. If a person is a friend of God, let him contemplate God as a gracious and holy Being, and he will have emotions of friendship kindled in his mind. If a person is an enemy of God, only let him bring the true character of God before his mind, and fasten his attention on it, and then his bitter enmity will rise against God, or he will break down and give his heart to God.

If you mean to break up the fallow ground of your hearts, and make your minds feel on the subject of religion, you must go to work just as you would with any other subject. Instead of keeping your thoughts on everything else, and then imagining that by going to a few meetings you will get your feelings engaged, use common sense as you would

---

[1] The two key terms of this sentence, feeling and affection, are used interchangeably by Finney, but have different meanings than those used today. To understand feeling or affection merely as equivalent to emotion fails to capture the significance of these words. In the century before Finney, the great Christian preacher Jonathan Edwards heavily used the phrase "religious affection" and would influence many later writers. Edwards defined affections as "the more vigorous and sensible exercises of the inclination and will of the soul." Thus Finney also used the word affection, along with the term feeling, to represent the exercises and expressions of the will. It resembles the biblical word "heart." While feelings and affections include emotions, it has wider breadth and significance. As another example of these terms being confusing to today's reader, Finney sometimes talks about how a good Christian will raise the standard of feeling in a congregation. Such a sentence becomes meaningful in light of this definition of feeling.

on any other subject. It is just as easy to make your minds feel on the subject of religion as it is on any other. God has put these states of mind under your control. If people were as illogical about moving their limbs as they are about regulating their emotions, you would never have reached this meeting.

If you mean to break up the fallow ground of your hearts, you must begin by looking at your hearts. Examine and note the state of your minds, and see where you are. Many never seem to think about this. They pay no attention to their own hearts, and never know whether they are doing well in religion or not, whether they are gaining ground or going back, whether they are fruitful or lying waste. Now you must draw your attention away from other things, and look into this. Make a business of it. Do not be in a hurry. Examine thoroughly the state of your hearts, and see where you are: whether you are walking with God every day or with the devil, whether you are serving God or serving the devil most, whether you are under the dominion of the prince of darkness, or of the Lord Jesus Christ.

To do all this, you must set yourself to work to consider your sins. You must examine yourselves. Self-examination consists in looking at your lives, in considering your actions, in recalling the past, and learning its true character. Look back over your past history. Take up your individual sins one by one, and look at them. I do not mean that you should just cast a glance at your past life, and see that it has been full of sins, and then go to God and make a sort of general confession, and ask for pardon. That is not the way. You must take them up one by one. It will be a good thing to take a pen and paper, as you go over them, and write them down as they occur to you. Go over them as carefully as a merchant goes over his accounting books, and as often as a sin comes before your memory, add it to the list. General confessions of sin will never do. Your sins were committed one by one. As far as you can remember them, they should be reviewed and repented of one by one.[2]

Now begin, and take up first what are commonly, but improperly called Sins of Omission.

1. Ingratitude. Take this sin, for instance, and write down under that heading all the instances you can remember when you have received gifts from God for which you have never expressed gratitude. How many cases can you remember? Some remarkable providence, some wonderful turn of events, that saved you from ruin. Write down the instances of God's goodness to you when you were in sin, before your conversion, for which you have never been half thankful enough, and the numerous mercies you have received since. How long the catalogue of instances, where your ingratitude has been so blatant that you are forced to hide your face in confusion! Go on your knees and confess them one by one to God, and ask forgiveness. The very act of confession, by the laws of suggestion, will bring up others to your memory. Write these down. Go over them three or four times in this way, and see what an astonishing number of mercies there are for which you have never thanked God.

2. Lack of love to God. Think how grieved and alarmed you would be if you discovered any decrease of affection for you in your wife, husband, or children — if you saw another engrossing their hearts, and thoughts, and time. Perhaps in such a case you would practically die with a just and virtuous jealousy. Now, God calls himself a jealous God, have you not given your heart to other loves and infinitely offended him?

3. Neglect of the Bible. Put down the cases when for perhaps weeks, or longer, God's Word was not a pleasure. Some people, indeed, read over whole chapters in such a way that they could not tell what they

---

[2] This lecture, one of Finney's most famous, is an excellent example of his drawing from the example of Jonathan Edwards. In the tract *Christian Cautions: The Necessity of Self-examination*, Edwards exhorted his readers to systematically examine their lives for sin. The exercise that Finney is about to explain is very similar to that of Edwards in his tract. Edwards asked his readers to examine their lives for a set of sins that he described. Because Edwards believed in the necessity of living a holy life in order to be saved, this was an essential exercise of the Christian. As he writes in the tract, "Though men reform all other wicked practices, yet if they live in but one sinful way, which they do not forsake, it may prove their everlasting undoing" (Section I, Heading 2, Subheading 3). Since ignorance was no excuse, people were exhorted to proactively and diligently test their lives by the Bible. Edwards' Scriptural supports for this exercise included the following verses: Deuteronomy 4:9, Psalm 139:23-24, Proverbs 4:23, Matthew 26:41, Luke 21:34-36, 2 Corinthians 13:5, Ephesians 5:15, Hebrews 3:12-13.

had been reading. If so, no wonder that your Christian walk is such a miserable failure.

4. Unbelief. Recall the instances in which you have practically charged the God of truth with lying, by your unbelief of his clear promises and declarations. God has promised to give the Holy Spirit to them that ask him. Now, have you believed this? Have you expected him to answer? Have you not practically said in your hearts when you prayed for the Holy Spirit, "I do not believe that I shall receive?" If you have not believed nor expected to receive the blessing that God has clearly promised, you have charged him with lying.

5. Neglect of prayer. Think of the times when you have neglected secret prayer, family prayer, and prayer meetings, or have prayed in such a way as to offend God more grievously than to have omitted it altogether.

6. Neglect of the means of grace. When you have made trifling excuses to prevent your attending meetings, have neglected and poured contempt upon the means of salvation, merely from dislike of spiritual duties.

7. The manner in which you have performed those duties. That is, with lack of feeling and lack of faith, in a worldly frame of mind, so that your words were nothing but the mere chattering of a wretch who did not deserve God's least concern. Think of when you have fallen down upon your knees and "said your prayers" in such an unfeeling and apathetic manner that if you had been put under oath five minutes later, you could not have remembered what you had been praying for.

8. Lack of love for the souls of others. Look around at your friends and relatives, and remember how little compassion you have felt for them. You have stood by and seen them going right to hell, and it seems as though you did not care if they did go. How many days have there been, in which you did not make their condition the subject of a single fervent prayer, or demonstrate serious desire for their salvation?

9. Lack of care for nations without the gospel. Perhaps you have not cared enough for them to attempt to learn their condition, perhaps not even to read a missionary magazine. Look at this, and see how much you really care for the lost, and write down honestly the real amount of your feelings for them, and your desire for their salvation. Measure your desire for their salvation by the self-denial you practice, in giving of your resources to send them the gospel. Do you deny yourself even the hurtful superfluities of life, such as tea, coffee, and tobacco? Do you reduce your standard of living, and embrace subjecting yourself to any

inconvenience to save them? Do you daily pray for the lost in private? Are you saving something to put into the treasury of the Lord when you go up to pray? If you are not doing these things, and if your soul is not in agony for the poor ignorant lost, why are you such a hypocrite to pretend to be a Christian? Why, your profession is an insult to Jesus Christ!

10. **Neglect of family duties.** Think how you have lived before your family, how you have prayed, what an example you have set before them. What direct efforts do you habitually make for their spiritual good? What duty have you performed?

11. **Neglect of watchfulness over your own life.** In how many instances have you ignored your private duties, and have neither taken yourself to task, nor honestly made up your accounts with God! How often have you entirely neglected to watch your conduct, and having been off your guard, have sinned before the world, and before the church, and before God!

12. **Neglect of watch over your fellow believers.** How often have you broken your covenant that you would watch over them in the Lord! How little do you know or care about the state of their souls! And yet you are under a solemn oath to watch over them. What have you done to make yourself acquainted with them? In how many of them have you interested yourself, to know their spiritual state? Go over the list, and wherever you find there has been a neglect, write it down. How many times have you seen your fellow believers growing cold in religion, and have not spoken to them about it? You have seen them beginning to neglect one duty after another, and you did not reprove them, in a brotherly way. You have seen them falling into sin, and you let them go on. And yet you pretend to love them. What a hypocrite! Would you see your wife or child going into disgrace, or into the fire, and hold your peace? No, you would not. What do you then think of yourself, to pretend to love Christians and to love Christ, while you can see your fellow believers going into disgrace, and say nothing to them?

13. **Neglect of self-denial.** There are many professing Christians who are willing to do almost anything in religion that does not require self-denial. But when they are required to do anything that requires them to deny themselves — oh, that is too much! They think they are doing a great deal for God, and doing about as much as the Lord should reasonably ask. But they are not willing to deny themselves any comfort or convenience for the sake of serving the Lord. They will not willingly suffer hardship for the name of Christ. Nor will they deny

themselves the luxuries of life, to save a world from hell. They are so far from remembering that self-denial is a condition of discipleship that they do not know what self-denial is. They have never really denied themselves a ribbon or a pin for Christ and the gospel. Oh, how soon such professing Christians will be in hell! Some are giving from their abundance, and are giving much, and are ready to complain that others do not give more. However, in truth, they do not themselves give anything that they need, anything that they could enjoy if they kept it — they only give of their surplus wealth. Perhaps that poor woman, who puts in her mite[3], has exercised more self-denial than they have in giving thousands.

From these we now turn to Sins of Commission.

1. Worldly mindedness. What has been the state of your heart in regard to your worldly possessions? Have you looked at them as really yours — as if you had a right to use them as your own, according to your own will? If you have, write that down. If you have loved property, and pursued it for its own sake, or to gratify lust, ambition, a worldly spirit, or to acquire it for your families, you have sinned and must repent.

2. Pride. Recollect all the instances you can in which you have found yourself being proud. Vanity is a particular form of pride. How many times have you found yourself pursuing vanity about your dress and appearance? How many times have you thought more, put more effort, and spent more time about decorating your body to go to church than you have about preparing your mind for the worship of God? You have cared more how you appeared outwardly in the sight of mortals, than how your soul appeared in the sight of the heart-searching God. You have, in fact, set up yourself to be worshiped by them, rather than prepared to worship God yourself. You sought to divide the worship of God's house, to draw off the attention of God's people to look at your pretty appearance. It is in vain to pretend now that you do not care at all about having people look at you. Be honest about it. Would you take all this effort about your looks if every person were blind?

3. Envy. Look at the cases in which you were envious of those whom you thought were above you in any way. Or perhaps you have envied those who have been more talented or more useful than yourself. Have you not so envied some that you have been hurt to hear them praised? It has been more agreeable to you to dwell upon their faults than upon their virtues, upon their failures than upon their success. Be honest with yourself. If you have harbored this spirit of hell, repent deeply

---

[3] A reference to the woman in Mark 12:41-44.

before God, or he will never forgive you.

4. Criticizing. Think of instances in which you have had a bitter spirit, and spoken of Christians in a manner without charity and love. Charity requires you always to hope the best the situation will allow, and to offer the best explanation for any ambiguous conduct.

5. Slander. The times you have unnecessarily spoken behind people's backs of the faults, real or supposed, of members of the church or others. This is slander. You do not need to lie to be guilty of slander. To tell the truth with the intent to injure is to slander.

6. Levity. How often have you trifled before God as you would not have dared to trifle in the presence of an earthly ruler? You have either been an atheist and forgotten that there was a God, or have had less respect for him than you would for an earthly judge.

7. Lying. Understand now what lying is: any form of designed deception. If the deception is not designed, it is not lying. But if you intend to make an impression contrary to the plain truth, you lie. Put down all those cases you can remember. Do not call them by any soft name. God calls them LIES, and charges you with LYING, and you had better charge yourself correctly. How many are the falsehoods committed every day in business, and in social interactions, by words, and looks, and actions, designed to make an impression on others, for selfish reasons that is contrary to the truth!

8. Cheating. Write down all the cases in which you have done to an individual that which you would not like to have done to you. That is cheating. God has laid down a rule in the case, "Whatever you want others to do to you, do also to them."[4] That is the rule. And if you have not done so you are a cheat.

9. Hypocrisy. For instance, consider your prayers and confessions to God. Write down the instances in which you have prayed for things you did not really want. And the evidence is, that when you finished praying, you could not remember for what you had prayed. How many times have you confessed sins that you did not mean to break off, and when you had no solemn purpose not to repeat them?

10. Robbing God. Think of the instances in which you have wasted your time, squandering the hours that God gave you to serve him and save souls. Think of cases of vain amusements or foolish conversation, in reading novels or doing nothing, misapplying your talents and powers of mind, or squandering money on your lusts, or on things that you

---

[4] Matthew 7:12

did not need, and which did not contribute to your health, comfort, or usefulness. Perhaps some of you have spent God's money for tobacco. I will not speak of intoxicating drink, for I presume there is no professing Christian here that would drink it, and I hope there is not one that uses that filthy poison, tobacco. Think of a professing Christian using God's money to poison himself with tobacco!

11. Bad temper. Perhaps you have abused your wife, or your children, or your family, or servants, or neighbors. Write it all down.

12. Hindering others from being useful. Perhaps you have weakened their influence by accusations against them. You have not only robbed God of your own talents, but also tied the hands of somebody else. What a wicked servant is the person who not only wastes his own life but also hinders the rest! This is done sometimes by taking their time needlessly, sometimes by destroying Christian confidence in them. Thus you have played into the hands of Satan, and not only showed yourself an idle vagrant, but prevented others from working.

If you find you have committed a fault against an individual and that individual is within your reach, go and confess it immediately, and get that out of the way. If the individual you have injured is too far off for you to go and see, sit down and write the person a letter and confess the injury. If you have defrauded anybody, send the money, the full amount and the interest.

Go thoroughly to work in all this. Go now. Do not put it off — that will only make the matter worse. Confess to God those sins that have been committed against him, and to people those sins that have been committed against them. Do not think of getting off track by going around the stumbling blocks. Take them up out of the way. In breaking up your fallow ground, you must remove every obstruction. Things may be left that you think are small things, and you may wonder why you do not feel as you wish to feel in religion, when the reason is that your proud and carnal mind has covered up something that God requires you to confess and remove. Break up all the ground and turn it over. Do not "balk" at it, as the farmers say. Do not turn aside for little difficulties. Drive the plow right through them, aim deep, and turn the ground up, so that it may all be broken and soft, and fit to receive the seed and bear fruit "a hundredfold."

When you have thoroughly gone over your whole life history in this way, if you will then go over the ground a second time, and give your solemn and fixed attention to it, you will find that the things you have put down will remind you of other related and connected things of which you have been guilty. Then go over it a third time, and you will remember other things connected with these. And you will find in the end that you can remember an amount of history and particular actions, even in this life, which you did not think you would remember in eternity. Unless you take up your sins in this way, and consider them in detail, one by one, you cannot understand the amount of your sins. You should go over the list as thoroughly, and as carefully, and as solemnly, as you would if you were preparing yourself for the Judgment.

As you go over the catalogue of your sins, be sure to resolve upon present and entire reformation. Wherever you find anything wrong, resolve at once, in the strength of God, to sin no more in that way. It will be of no benefit to examine yourself, unless you determine to correct in every way that which you find wrong in heart, temperament, or conduct.

If you find as you go on with this duty that your mind is still clouded and unfocused, there must be some reason for the Spirit of God to depart from you. You have not been faithful and thorough. In the progress of such a work you must force yourself as a rational being up to this work, with the Bible before you, and try your heart until you do feel. You need not expect that God will work a miracle for you to break up your fallow ground. It is to be done by means.

Fasten your attention to the subject of your sins. You cannot thoroughly look at your sins for long and see how bad they are, without feeling, and feeling deeply. Experience fully proves the benefit of going over our history in this way. Set yourself to the work now. Resolve that you will not stop until you find that you can pray. You never will have the Spirit of God dwelling in you until you have unraveled this whole mystery of iniquity, and spread out your sins before God. Let there be this deep work of repentance and full confession, this breaking down before God, and you will have as much of the spirit of prayer as your body can bear. The reason why so few Christians know anything about the spirit of prayer is because they will not take the trouble to examine themselves properly, and so never know what it is to have their hearts completely broken up in this way.

You see that I have only begun to deal with this subject. I want to lay it out before you, in the course of these lectures, so that if you will begin and go on to do as I say, the results will be just as certain as they are when a farmer breaks up a fallow field, and softens it, and sows his grain. It will be so, if you will only begin in this way and keep on until all your hardened and callous hearts break up.

REMARKS

1. It will do no good to preach to you while your hearts are in this hardened, useless, and fallow state. The farmer might just as well sow his grain on the rock. It will bring forth no fruit. This is the reason why there are so many professing Christians in the church who are not bearing fruit, and why there is so much external showcase yet so little deep feeling. Look at the Sunday school, for instance, and see how much showcase there is and how little of the power of godliness. If you go on in this way the Word of God will continue to harden you, and you will grow worse and worse, just as the rain and snow on an old fallow field make the turf thicker and the lumps stronger.

2. See why so much preaching is wasted, and worse than wasted. It is because members of the church will not break up their fallow ground. A preacher may wear out his life, and do very little good, while there are so many "stony-ground" hearers, who have never had their fallow ground broken up. They are only half converted, and their religion is a change of opinion rather than a change of the feeling of their hearts. There is plenty of mechanical religion but very little that looks like deep heart-work.

3. Professing Christians should never satisfy themselves, or expect a revival, just by starting out of their slumbers, and blustering about, and talking to sinners. They must get their fallow ground broken up. It is utterly illogical to think of getting engaged in religion in this other way. If your fallow ground is broken up, then the way to get more feeling is to go out and see sinners on the road to hell, and talk to them, and guide inquiring souls, and you will experience more feeling. You may become excited without this breaking up of fallow ground. You may show a kind of zeal, but it will not last long, and it will not take hold of sinners, unless your hearts are broken up. The reason is that you go about it mechanically, and have not broken up your fallow ground.

4. And now, finally, will you break up your fallow ground? Will you enter upon the course now pointed out and persevere until you are thoroughly awake? If you fail here, if you do not do this, and get prepared, you can go no further with me. I have gone with you as far as it is of any use to go until your fallow ground is broken up. Now, you must make thorough work upon this point, or all I have further to say will do you little good. No, it will only harden and make you worse. If, when the next lecture-night arrives, it finds you with unbroken hearts, you should not expect to benefit from what I shall say. If you do not set about this work immediately I shall take it for granted that you do not mean to be revived, that you have forsaken your minister, and in-

tend to let him go up to battle alone. If you do not do this, I charge you with having forsaken Christ, with refusing to repent and "do the works you did at first"[5]. But if you will be prepared to enter into the work, I propose, God willing, in the next lecture, to lead you into the work of saving sinners.

---

[5] This phrase comes from Jesus' saying, "But I have this against you, that you have abandoned the love you had at first. Remember therefore from where you have fallen; repent, and do the works you did at first" (Revelation 2:4-5)

Part II

PRAYER

Chapter 5

PREVAILING PRAYER

"The effective fervent prayer of a righteous person avails much." (James 5:16*)

There are two kinds of means necessary to promote a revival: one to influence people, the other to influence God. The truth is employed to influence people, and prayer to move God. When I speak of moving God, I do not mean that prayer changes God's mind, or that his disposition or character is changed. But prayer produces a change in us that makes it consistent for God to act as it would not be consistent for him otherwise. When a sinner repents, that state of heart makes it proper for God to forgive him. God has always been ready to forgive him on that condition, so that when the sinner changes his heart and repents, it requires no change of heart in God to pardon him. It is the sinner's repentance that makes God's forgiveness proper, and is the occasion of God's acting as he does. So when Christians offer effective prayer, their state of heart renders it proper for God to answer them. He was never unwilling to bestow the blessing — on the condition that their heart was right, and offered the right kind of prayer.

Prayer is an essential link in the chain of causes that lead to a revival, as much as truth is. Some have zealously used truth to convert men, and laid very little stress on prayer. They have preached, talked, and distributed tracts with great zeal, and then wondered why they had so little success. The reason was that they forgot to use the other branch of the means, effective prayer. They overlooked the fact that truth by itself will never produce the effect, without the Spirit of God, and that the Spirit is given in answer to prayer.

Sometimes it happens that those who are the most engaged in employing truth are not the most engaged in prayer. This is always unfortunate. For unless they have the spirit of prayer (or unless some one else has), the truth by itself will do nothing but harden people in impenitence. Probably in the Day of Judgment it will be found that nothing is ever done by the truth, used ever so zealously, unless there is a spirit of prayer somewhere in connection with the presentation of truth.

Others err in the opposite direction. Not that they lay too much stress on prayer, but they overlook the fact that prayer might be offered forever, by itself, and nothing would be done. To expect the conversion of sinners by prayer alone, without the employment of truth, is to tempt God.

Our subject being Prevailing Prayer, I propose:

I. To show what is effective or prevailing prayer.

II. To state some of the most essential attributes of prevailing prayer.

III. To give some reasons why God requires this kind of prayer.

IV. To show that such prayer will avail much.

I. WHAT PREVAILING PRAYER IS

1. Effective, prevailing prayer, does not consist in benevolent desires alone. Benevolent desires are doubtless pleasing to God. Such desires pervade heaven and are found in all holy beings. But they are not prayer. People may have these desires as the angels and glorified spirits have them. But this is not the effective, prevailing prayer spoken of in the text. Prevailing prayer is something more than this.

2. Prevailing, or effective prayer, is that prayer which attains the blessing that it seeks. It is that prayer which effectively moves God. The very idea of effective prayer is that it achieves its goal.

II. ESSENTIAL ATTRIBUTES OF PREVAILING PRAYER

I cannot fully detail all the things that make up prevailing prayer. But I will mention some things that are essential to it, some things which a person must do in order to prevail in prayer.

1. A person must pray for a definite object. He need not expect to offer prevailing prayer if he prays at random, without any distinct or definite goal. He must have an object distinctly before his mind. I speak now of secret prayer. Many people go away into their rooms alone "to pray," simply because "they must say their prayers." The time comes when they are in the habit of going alone for prayer — in the morning, at noon, or at whatever time of day it may be. But instead

of having anything to say, any definite object before their mind, they fall down on their knees and pray for just what comes into their minds — for everything that floats in the imagination at the time. When they are finished, they can hardly describe what they have been praying for. This is not effective prayer. What should we think of anybody who should try to move a Legislature in this way, and should say, "Now it is winter, and the Legislature is in session, and it is time to send up petitions," and should go up to the Legislature and petition at random, without any definite object? Do you think such petitions would move the Legislature?

A person must have some definite object before his mind. One cannot pray effectively for a variety of objects at once. The mind is so constituted that it cannot fasten its desires intensely upon many things at the same time. All the examples of effective prayer recorded in the Bible are purposeful. Wherever you see that the blessing sought in prayer was attained, you will find that the prayer that was offered was for that definite goal.

2. Prayer, to be effective, must be in accordance with the revealed will of God. To pray for things contrary to the revealed will of God is to tempt God. There are three ways in which God's will is revealed to people for their guidance in prayer.

(a) By clear promises or predictions in the Bible, that he will give or do certain things, promises in regard to particular things, or in general terms, so that we may apply them to particular things. For instance, there is this promise, "Whatever you ask in prayer, believe that you have received it, and it will be yours" (Mark 11:24).

(b) Sometimes God reveals his will by his Providence. It would be impossible to reveal everything in the Bible. But God often makes it clear to those who have spiritual discernment that it is his will to grant particular blessings.

(c) By his Spirit. When God's people are at a loss what to pray for, agreeable to his will, his Spirit often instructs them. Where there is no particular revelation, and Providence leaves it unclear, and we do not know what to pray for, we are told that "the Spirit helps us in our weakness" and "the Spirit himself intercedes for us with groanings too deep for words" (Romans 8:26). A great deal has been said on the subject of praying in faith for things not revealed. It is objected that this doctrine implies a new revelation. I answer that, new or old, it is the very revelation that the LORD says he makes. It is clear here that the Spirit of God helps the people of God to pray according to the will of

God, when they themselves do not know what to pray for. "And he who searches hearts knows what is the mind of the Spirit, because the Spirit intercedes for the saints according to the will of God" (Romans 8:27). He leads Christians to pray for just those things, "with groanings too deep for words." When neither the Word nor Providence enables them to decide, let them be "filled with the Spirit," as God commands them to be. He says, "Be filled with the Spirit" (Ephesians 5:18). And he will lead their minds to those things that God is willing to grant.

3. To pray effectively you must pray with submission to the will of God. Do not confound submission with indifference. No two things are more different. I once knew an individual who came where there was a revival. He himself was cold, and did not enter into the spirit of it, and had no spirit of prayer. When he heard the believers pray as if they could not be denied, he was shocked at their boldness, and kept insisting on the importance of praying with submission. It was obvious that he confused submission with indifference.

Again, do not confuse submission in prayer with a general confidence that God will do what is right. It is proper to have this confidence that God will do right in all things. But this is different from submission. What I mean by submission in prayer is acquiescence in the revealed will of God. To submit to any command of God is to obey it. Submission to some possible, but secret, decree of God is not submission. To submit to any working of Providence is impossible until it comes. For we never can know what the event is to be, until it takes place.

Take a case: David, when his child was sick, was distressed, agonized in prayer, and refused to be comforted. He took it so much to heart that when the child died his servants were afraid to tell him. But as soon as he heard that the child was dead, he put aside his grief, arose, asked for food, and ate and drank as usual. While the child was alive he did not know what the will of God was, and so he fasted and prayed, and said, "Who knows whether the LORD will be gracious to me, that the child may live?" He did not know if his prayer and agony was the very thing on which it turned, whether the child was to live or not. He thought that if he humbled himself and begged God, perhaps God would spare him this blow. But as soon as God's will appeared, and the child was dead, he bowed like a saint. "I shall go to him, but he will not return to me" (2 Samuel 12:22-23). This was true submission. He reasoned correctly in the case. While he had no revelation of the will of God, he did not know if the child's recovery depended on his prayer. But when he had a revelation of the will of God, he submitted. While the will of God is not known, to submit, without prayer, is tempting God. For all you know, your offering the right kind of prayer may be the thing on which the event turns. In the case of an impenitent friend, the very condition on which he is to be saved from hell may be the fervency and persistence of your prayer for that individual.

4. Effective prayer for an object implies a desire for that object proportional with its importance. If a person truly desires any blessing, his desires will have some proportion to the greatness of the blessing. The desires of the Lord Jesus Christ for the blessing he prayed for were amazingly strong, amounting even to agony. If the desire for an object is strong, and it is a benevolent desire, and the object is not contrary to the will and providence of God, the presumption is that it will be granted. There are two reasons for this presumption:

(a) From the general benevolence of God. If it is a desirable object, it would be an act of benevolence of God to grant it. His general benevolence is presumptive evidence that he will grant it.

(b) If you find yourself moved with benevolent desires for any object, there is a strong presumption that the Spirit of God is inducing these very desires and stirring you up to pray for that object, so that it may be granted in answer to prayer. In such a case no degree of desire or persistence in prayer is improper. A Christian may come up and take hold of the hand of God. Observe the case of Jacob, when he exclaimed in an agony of desire, "I will not let you go unless you bless me" (Genesis 32:26). Was God displeased with his boldness and persistence? Not at all — he granted him the very thing he prayed for.

So it was in the case of Moses. God said to him, "Now therefore let me alone, that my wrath may burn hot against them and I may consume them, in order that I may make a great nation of you" (Exodus 32:10). What did Moses do? Did he stand aside and let God do as he said? No, his mind goes back to the Egyptians, and he thinks how they will triumph. "Why should the Egyptians say, 'With evil intent did he bring them out'? "[1] It seemed as if he took hold of the uplifted hand of God, to avoid the blow. Did God rebuke him and tell him he had no business to interfere? No, it seemed as if he was unable to deny anything with such bold urgency, and so Moses stood in the gap, and prevailed with God.

Prevailing prayer is often offered in the present day, when Christians have been wrought up to such a pitch of fervent urgency and such a holy boldness afterwards when they looked back upon it, they were frightened and amazed at themselves to think they should have dared

---

[1] Exodus 32:11

to exercise such boldness with God. And yet these prayers have prevailed, and obtained the blessing. And many of these people, with whom I am acquainted, are among the holiest people I know in the world.

5. Prayer, to be effective, must be offered from right motives. Prayer should not be selfish, but should be dictated by a supreme regard for the glory of God. A great deal is offered from pure selfishness. Women sometimes pray for their husbands, that they may be converted because they say, "It would be so much more pleasant to have my husband go to church with me." And they seem never to lift up their thoughts above self at all. They do not seem to think how their husbands are dishonoring God by their sins, or how God would be glorified in their conversion. So it is very often with parents. They cannot bear to think that their children should be lost. They pray for them very earnestly indeed. But if you talk with them upon the subject they are very tender about it and tell you how good their children are — how they respect religion, and how they are indeed, "almost Christians now." So they talk as if they were afraid you would hurt their children by simply telling them the truth. They do not think how such amiable and lovely children are dishonoring God by their sins. They are only thinking what a dreadful thing it will be for them to go to hell. Unless their thoughts rise higher than this, their prayers will never prevail with a holy God.

The temptation to selfish motives is so strong that there is reason to fear that many parental prayers never rise above the yearnings of parental tenderness. And that is the reason why so many prayers are not answered and why so many pious, praying parents have ungodly children. Much of the prayer for the non-Christian world seems to be based on no higher principle than sympathy. Missionary agents and others are dwelling almost exclusively upon the hundreds of millions of the lost going to hell, while little is said of their dishonoring God. This is a great evil, and until the church learns to have higher motives for prayer and missionary effort than sympathy for the lost, her prayers and efforts will never amount to much.

6. Prayer, to be effective, must be by the intercession of the Spirit. You never can expect to offer prayer according to the will of God without the Spirit. There must be a faith, such as is produced by the effective operation of the Holy Spirit.

7. It must be persevering prayer. As a general fact, Christians who have backslidden and lost the spirit of prayer, will not get at once into the habit of persevering prayer. Their minds are not in a right state, and

they cannot fix their thoughts to hold on the object of prayer until the blessing comes. If their minds were in that state in which they would persevere until the answer came, effective prayer might be offered at once. But they have to pray again and again, because their thoughts are so likely to wander away and are so easily diverted from the object.

Most Christians come up to prevailing prayer by a long process. Their minds gradually become filled with anxiety about an object, so that they will even go about their business breathing out their desires to God. Just as the mother whose child is sick goes around her house sighing as if her heart would break. And if she is a praying mother, her sighs are breathed out to God all day long. If she goes out of the room where her child is, her mind is still on it. If she is asleep, still her thoughts are on it, and she starts in her dreams, thinking that perhaps the child may be dying. Her whole mind is absorbed in that sick child. This is the state of mind in which Christians offer prevailing prayer.

Why did Jacob wrestle all night in prayer with God? He knew that he had done his brother Esau a great injury in stealing the birthright a long time before. And now he was informed that his injured brother was coming to meet him with an armed force, altogether too powerful to contend with. And there was great reason to suppose that Esau was coming with a purpose of revenge. There were two reasons then why Jacob should be distressed. The first was that he had done this great injury and had never made any reparation. The other was that Esau was coming with a force sufficient to crush him. Now what does he do? He first arranges everything in the best way he can to placate and meet his brother: sending his present first, then his property, then his family, putting those he loved farthest behind. And by this time his mind was so exercised that he could not contain himself. He goes away alone over the brook and pours out his very soul in an agony of prayer all night. And just as the day was breaking, the Angel of the Covenant said, "Let me go." Yet Jacob's whole being was agonized at the thought of giving up, and he cried out, "I will not let you go, unless you bless me." His soul was wrought up in agony, and he obtained the blessing, but he always bore the marks of it, and showed that his body had been greatly affected by this mental struggle. This is prevailing prayer.

Prayer is not effective unless it is offered up with an agony of desire. The apostle Paul speaks of it as a travail of the soul. Jesus Christ, when he was praying in the garden, was in such agony that "his sweat became like great drops of blood falling down to the ground" (Luke 22:44). I have never known a person sweat blood, but I have known a person pray until the blood started from his nose. And I have known people pray until they were all wet with perspiration, in the coldest weather in winter. I have known people pray for hours, until their strength was all exhausted with the agony of their minds. Such prayers prevailed with God.

This agony in prayer was prevalent in President Edwards' day, in the revivals that then took place.[2] It was one of the great stumbling blocks in those days to people who were opposed to the revival, that people used to pray until their body was overpowered with their feelings. I will give a paragraph of what President Edwards says on the subject, to let you see that this is not a new thing in the church, but has always prevailed wherever revivals prevailed with power. It is from his "Thoughts on Revival."[3]

> We cannot determine that God shall never give any person so much of a discovery of himself, not only as to weaken their bodies, but to take away their lives. It is supposed by very learned and judicious divines, that Moses' life was taken away in this way, and this has also been supposed to be the case with some other saints… If God gives a great increase of discoveries of himself, and of love to him, the benefit is infinitely greater than the calamity, though the life should presently be taken away…
>
> There is one particular kind of exercise in which many have been overpowered, which has been especially stumbling to some. That is, their deep distress for the souls of others… People may be allowed, from no higher a principle than common humanity, to be very deeply concerned, and greatly exercised in mind, at seeing others in great danger of, or being burned up in a house on fire. And it will be allowed to be equally reasonable, if they saw them in danger of a calamity ten times greater, to be still much more concerned, and so much more still, if the calamity was still vastly greater. Why then should it be thought unreasonable and looked upon with a very suspicious eye, as if it must come from some bad cause, when persons are extremely concerned at seeing others in very great danger of suffering the fierceness and wrath of almighty God to all eternity? Besides, it will doubtless be allowed that those that

---

[2] President Edwards is a reference to Jonathan Edwards, who served as President of Princeton University in 1758.

[3] From *Some Thoughts Concerning the Present Revival of Religion in New England* by Jonathan Edwards, Part I, Section II, Subheading II.

have great degrees of the Spirit of God, which is a Spirit of love, may well be supposed to have vastly more love and compassion to their fellow-creatures, than those that are influenced only by common humanity. Why should it be thought strange that those that are full of the Spirit of Christ should be proportionally in their love to souls, like Christ? He had so strong a love and concern for them, to be willing to drink the dregs of the cup of God's fury. At the same time that he offered up his blood for souls, he offered up also, as their High Priest, strong crying and tears[4], with an extreme agony, where the soul of Christ was in travail for the souls of the elect. Therefore, in saving them, he is said to see the *travail* of his soul. As such a spirit of love and concern for souls was the spirit of Christ, so it is that of the church. Therefore the church, in desiring and seeking that Christ might be brought forth in the souls of others, is represented as pregnant and "crying out in birth pains and the agony of giving birth" (Revelation 12:2). The spirit of those who have been in distress for the souls of others, so far as I can discern, seems not to be different from that of the apostle, who travailed for souls, and was ready to *wish himself accursed from Christ*, for others.[5] Nor from that of the Psalmist... "My eyes shed streams of tears, because people do not keep your law" (Psalm 119:136). Nor from that of the prophet Jeremiah, "My anguish, my anguish! I writhe in pain! Oh the walls of my heart! My heart is beating wildly; I cannot keep silent, for I hear the sound of the trumpet, the alarm of war" (Jeremiah 4:19). And so Jeremiah 9:1, 13:17, and Isaiah 22:4. We read of Mordecai, when he saw his people in danger of being destroyed with earthly destruction, that he "tore his clothes and put on sackcloth and ashes, and went out into the midst of the city, and he cried out with a loud and bitter cry" (Esther 4:1). And why then should persons be thought to be distracted when they cannot refrain from crying out, at the consideration of the misery of those that are going to eternal destruction?

I have quoted this to show that this was common in the great revivals of those days. It has always been so in all great revivals, and has been more or less common in proportion to the greatness, and extent, and

---

[4] Hebrews 5:7
[5] Romans 9:3

depth of the work. It was so in the great revivals in Scotland[6], and many people used to be overpowered, and some almost died, by the depth of their agony.

8. If you mean to pray effectively, you must pray a great deal. It was said of the Apostle James that after he was dead it was found that his knees were callous, like a camel's knees, by praying so much. Ah, here was the secret of the success of those early ministers! They had callous knees!

9. If you intend prayer to be effective, you must offer it in the name of Christ. You cannot come to God in your own name. You cannot plead your own merits. But you can come in a name that is always acceptable. You all know what it is to use the name of a person. If you should go to the bank with a draft or note, endorsed by John Jacob

---

[6] This would apply to John Livingstone, who spent the whole night prior to June 21, 1630 in prayer and conference, being designated the next day to preach at the Kirk of Shotts. He preached the next day on Ezekiel 36:25-26. After he preached for an hour and a half a few drops of rain dispersed the people. Livingstone, asking the people if they had any shelter from the storm of God's wrath, went on for another hour. About five hundred were converted on the spot. This revival was linked to another revival at the great meeting at Kilsyth on July 23, 1839. William Chalmers Burns, preaching on Psalm 110:3, retold the story of the Kirk of Shotts, and pressed immediate acceptance of Christ: "I felt my own soul moved in a manner so remarkable that I was led, like Mr. Livingstone, to plead with the unconverted instantly to close with God's offer of mercy... The power of the Lord's spirit became so mighty upon their souls as to carry all before it, like the 'rushing mighty wind' of Pentecost. Some were screaming out in agony. Others — and among these strong men — fell to the ground as if they had been dead. I was obliged to give out a psalm, our voices being mingled with the mourning groans of many prisoners sighing for deliverance."
So also, prayer prevailed at Cambuslang, Scotland in the revival under William Mc-Culloch and George Whitefield (1741-1742). When Whitefield reached Cambuslang he immediately preached to a vast congregation on a Tuesday at noon. At six o'clock he preached again, and a third time at nine. Then McCulloch took up the parable and preached until one in the morning, and still the people were unwilling to leave. So many were convicted, crying to God for mercy, that Whitefield described the scene as "a very field of battle." On the ensuing Communion Sunday, Whitefield preached to twenty thousand people; and again on the Monday, when, he said, "you might have seen thousands bathed in tears, some at the same time wringing their hands, others almost swooning, and others crying out and mourning over a pierced Savior. It was like the Passover in Josiah's time." On the voyage from London to Scotland, prior to this campaign, Whitefield had "spent most of his time on board ship in secret prayer." See Gledstone's "George Whitefield, M.A., Field Preacher." (This footnote taken from the original notes provided by the Fleming Revell Company.)

Astor[7], that would be giving you his name, and you know you could get the money from the bank just as well as he could himself. Now, Jesus Christ gives you the use of his name. And when you pray in the name of Christ, it means that you can prevail just as well as he could himself, and receive just as much as God's beloved Son would if he were to pray himself for the same things. But you must pray in faith.

10. You cannot prevail in prayer without renouncing all your sins. You must not only recall them to mind, and repent of them, but you must actually renounce them, and leave them off, and in the purpose of your heart renounce them all forever.

11. You must pray in faith. You must expect to obtain the things for which you ask. You need not look for an answer to prayer, if you pray without any expectation of obtaining it. You are not to form such expectations without any reason for them. In the cases I have supposed, there is a reason for the expectation. In case the thing is revealed in God's Word, if you pray without an expectation of receiving the blessings, you just make God a liar. If the will of God is indicated by his providence, you should depend on it, according to the clarity of the indication, so far as to expect the blessing if you pray for it. And if you are led by his Spirit to pray for certain things, you have as much reason to expect those things to be done as if God had revealed it in his Word.

But some say, "Will not this view of the leadings of the Spirit of God lead people into fanaticism?" I answer that I do not know but many may deceive themselves about this matter. Many have deceived themselves in regard to all the other points of religion. And if some people should think they are led by the Spirit of God, when it is nothing but their own imagination, is that any reason why those who know that they are led by the Spirit should not follow the Spirit? Many people suppose themselves to be converted when they are not. Is that any reason why we should not cling to the Lord Jesus Christ? Suppose some people are deceived in thinking they love God, is that any reason why the pious saint who knows he has the love of God shed abroad in his heart should not give expression to his feelings in songs of praise? Some may deceive themselves in thinking they are led by the Spirit of God. But there is no need of being deceived. If people follow impulses, it is their own fault. I do not want you to follow impulses. I want you to be sober-minded, and follow the sober, rational leadings of the Spirit of God. There are those who understand what I mean, and who know very well what it is to give themselves up to the Spirit of God in prayer.

---

[7] Astor (1763-1848), a famous businessman, was for a time the wealthiest person in the United States.

III. WHY GOD REQUIRES SUCH PRAYER

I will state some of the reasons why these things are essential to effective prayer. Why does God require such prayer, such strong desires, such agonizing supplications?

1. These strong desires illustrate the strength of God's feelings. They are like the real feelings of God for impenitent sinners. When I have seen, as I sometimes have, the amazing strength of love for souls that has been felt by Christians, I have been wonderfully impressed with the amazing love of God, and his desire for their salvation. The case of a certain woman, of whom I read, in a revival, made the greatest impression on my mind. She had such an unutterable compassion and love for souls that she actually panted for breath. What must be the strength of the desire that God feels, when his Spirit produces in Christians such amazing agony, such pangs of soul, such travail — God has chosen the best word to express it. It is travail — travail of the soul.

I have seen a man of as much strength of intellect and muscle as any man in the community fall down prostrate, absolutely overpowered by his unutterable desires for sinners. I know this is a stumbling block to many, and it always will be as long as there remain in the church so many blind and dull professing Christians. But I cannot doubt that these things are the work of the Spirit of God. Oh, that the whole church could be so filled with the Spirit as to travail in prayer, until a nation should be born in a day!

It is said in the Word of God, "as soon as Zion travailed, she gave birth" (Isaiah 66:8*). What does that mean? I asked a professor of religion this question once. He was taking exception to our ideas of effective prayer, and I asked what he supposed was meant by Zion's travailing. He said, "Oh, it means that as soon as the church shall walk together in the fellowship of the gospel, then it will be said that Zion travels! This walking together is called traveling." Not the same term, you see.

2. These strong desires that I have described are the natural results of great benevolence and clear views regarding the danger of sinners. It is perfectly reasonable that it should be so. If the women who are present should look up and see a family burning to death in a fire and hear their shrieks, and behold their agony, they would feel distressed, and it is very likely that many of them would faint with agony. And nobody would wonder at it, or say they were fools or crazy to feel so distressed at such an awful sight. It would be thought strange if there were not some expressions of powerful feeling. Why is it any wonder, then, if Christians should feel as I have described when they have clear views

of the state of sinners and the awful danger they are in? The fact is that those individuals who never have felt so have never felt much real benevolence, and their piety must be of a very superficial character. I do not mean to judge harshly, or to speak unkindly, but I state it as a simple matter of fact. People may talk about it as they please, but I know such piety is superficial. This is not criticizing, but plain truth.

People sometimes "wonder at Christians having such feelings." Wonder at what? Why, at the natural, logical, and necessary results of deep piety towards God, and deep benevolence towards humanity, in view of the great danger they see sinners to be in.

3. The soul of a Christian, when it is thus burdened, must have relief. God rolls this weight upon the soul of a Christian, for the purpose of bringing him nearer to himself. Christians are often so unbelieving that they will not exercise proper faith in God until he rolls this burden upon them so heavily that they cannot live under it, but must go to him for relief. It is like the case of many a convicted sinner. God is willing to receive him at once, if he will come right to him, with faith in Jesus Christ. But the sinner will not come. He hangs back, and struggles, and groans under the burden of his sins, and will not throw himself upon God, until his burden of conviction becomes so great that he can no longer live. When he is driven to desperation, and feels as if he were ready to sink into hell, he makes a mighty plunge, and throws himself upon God's mercy as his only hope. It was his duty to come before. God had no delight in his distress, for its own sake.

So, when professing Christians get loaded down with the weight of souls, they often pray again and again, and yet the burden is not gone nor their distress relieved, because they have never thrown it all upon God in faith. But they cannot get rid of the burden. So long as their benevolence continues, it will remain and increase. Unless they resist and quench the Holy Spirit, they can get no relief, until when they are eventually driven to an extreme, they make a desperate effort, roll the burden upon the Lord Jesus Christ, and exercise a childlike confidence in him. Then they feel relieved. Then they feel as if the soul they were praying for would be saved. The burden is gone, and God seems in kindness to soothe the mind with a sweet assurance that the blessing will be granted. Often, after a Christian has had this struggle, this agony in prayer, and has obtained relief in this way, you will find the sweetest and most heavenly affections flow out — the soul rests sweetly and gloriously in God, and rejoices "with joy that is inexpressible and filled with glory" (1 Peter 1:8).

Do any of you think that there are no such things now in the experience of believers? If I had time, I could show you, from President Edwards and other approved writers, cases and descriptions just like this. Do you ask why we never have such things here? I tell you it is not at all because you are so much wiser than Christians are in rural districts, or because you have so much more intelligence or more enlarged views of the nature of religion, or a more stable and well controlled piety. I tell you, no. Instead of priding yourselves in being free from such extravagances, you should hide your heads, because Christians in the city are so worldly, and have so much starch, and pride, and fashion, that they cannot come down to such spirituality as this. I wish it could be so. Oh, that there might be such a spirit in this city and in this church! I know it would make a commotion if we had such things done here. But I would not care. Let them say, if they please, that the folks in Chatham Chapel[8] are getting deranged. We need not be afraid of that, if we live near enough to God to enjoy his Spirit in the manner I have described.

4. These effects of the spirit of prayer upon the body are themselves no part of religion. It is only that the body is often so weak that the feelings of the soul overpower it. These bodily effects are not at all essential to prevailing prayer, but are only a natural result of highly excited emotions of the mind. It is not at all unusual for the body to be weakened, and even overcome, by any powerful emotion of the mind, on other subjects besides religion. The doorkeeper of Congress, in the time of the Revolution, fell down dead on receiving some highly cheering intelligence. I knew a woman in Rochester who was in a great agony of prayer for the conversion of her son-in-law. One morning he was at an anxious meeting[9], and she remained at home praying for him. At the close of the meeting he came home a convert, and she was so rejoiced that she fell down and died on the spot. It is no more strange that these effects should be produced by religion than by strong feeling on any

---

[8] The old Chatham Street Theater, New York, a popular place of blasphemy and vice, was purchased by a committee, including Lewis Tappan and other friends of Finney's. It was during the revivals of 1831 that two gentlemen called on the lease-holder and proposed to buy his lease. He said, "What for?" "For a church," they replied. "A w-h-a-t?" he inquired aghast. "A church," they reiterated. The astonished man broke into tears and exclaimed, "You may have it, and I will give you a thousand dollars towards it." When the house was consecrated to the service of God, Finney preached on "Who is on the Lord's side?" The bar was changed into a prayer-room and the first convert was an actor. Finney continued to preach there until the Broadway Tabernacle was built. (This footnote taken from the original notes provided by the Fleming Revell Company.)

[9] An anxious meeting is a meeting especially held for convicted (also called anxious) sinners. In this meeting, instructions are given as to how to obtain salvation.

other subject. It is not essential to prayer, but is the natural result of great efforts of the mind.

5. Doubtless one great reason why God requires the exercise of this agonizing prayer is, that it forms such a bond of union between Christ and the church. It creates a deep sympathy between them. It is as if Christ came and poured the overflow of his own benevolent heart into his people, and led them to sympathize and to cooperate with him as they never do in any other way. They feel just as Christ feels — so full of compassion for sinners that they cannot contain themselves. Thus it is often with those ministers who are successful in preaching to sinners. They often have such compassion and such overflowing desires for their salvation that these are shown in their speaking, and their preaching, just as though Jesus Christ spoke through them. The words come from their lips fresh and warm, as if from the very heart of Christ. I do not mean that he dictates their words, but he excites the feelings that give utterance to them. Then you see a movement in the hearers, as if Christ himself spoke through lips of clay.

6. This travailing in birth for souls creates also a remarkable bond of union between warm-hearted Christians and the young converts. Those who are converted appear very dear to the hearts that have had this spirit of prayer for them. The feeling is like that of a mother for her first-born. Paul expresses it beautifully when he says, "My little children!" His heart was warm and tender to them. "My little children, of whom I travail in birth again" — they had backslidden, and he has all the agonies of a parent over a wandering child — "I travail in birth again until Christ is formed in you" (Galatians 4:19*). In a revival, I have often noticed how those who had the spirit of prayer, loved the young converts. I know this is all so much algebra to those who have never felt it. But to those who have experienced the agony of wrestling, prevailing prayer, for the conversion of a soul, that soul, after it is converted, appears as dear as a child is to the mother. He has agonized for it, received it in answer to prayer, and can present it before the Lord Jesus Christ, saying, "Behold, I and the children whom the Lord has given me" (Isaiah 8:18. See also Hebrews 2:13).

7. Another reason why God requires this sort of prayer is, that it is the only way in which the church can be properly prepared to receive great blessings without being injured by them. When the church is thus prostrated in the dust before God, and is in the depth of agony in prayer, the blessing does them good. While at the same time, if they had received the blessing without this deep prostration of soul, it would have puffed them up with pride. But as it is, it increases their

holiness, their love, and their humility.

IV. SUCH PRAYER WILL AVAIL MUCH

The prophet Elijah mourned over the deteriorations of the house of Israel, and when he saw that no other means were likely to be effective, to prevent a perpetual going away into idolatry, he prayed that the judgments of God might come upon the guilty nation. He prayed that it might not rain, and God shut up the heavens for three years and six months, until the people were driven to the last extremity. And when he sees that it is time to relent what does he do? See him go up to the mountain and bow down in prayer. He wished to be alone. He told his servant to go seven times, while he was agonizing in prayer. The last time, the servant told him that a little cloud had appeared, like a man's hand, and he instantly arose from his knees — the blessing was obtained. The time had come for the calamity to be turned back. "Ah, but," you say, "Elijah was a prophet." Now, do not make this objection. They made it in the apostle's days, and what does the apostle say? Why he brought forward this very example, and the fact that Elijah was a human with the same passions as ourselves, as a case of prevailing prayer, and insisted that they should pray in the same way too (1 Kings 17:1; 18:41-45; James 5:17). John Knox was a man famous for his power in prayer, so that Queen Mary of England used to say that she feared his prayers more than all the armies of Europe. And events showed that she had reason to do it. He used to be in such an agony for the deliverance of his country, that he could not sleep. He had a place in his garden where he used to go to pray. One night he and several friends were praying together, and as they prayed, Knox spoke and said that deliverance had come. He could not tell what had happened, but he felt that something had taken place, for God had heard their prayers. What was it? Why, the next news they received was that Mary was dead!

Take a fact that was related to me by a minister. He said that in a certain town there had been no revival for many years, the church was nearly extinct, the youth were all unconverted, and desolation reigned unbroken. There lived in a retired part of the town, an elderly man, a blacksmith by trade, with so stammering a tongue that it was painful to hear him speak. On one Friday, as he was working alone in his shop, his mind was greatly stirred about the state of the church and of the impenitent. His agony became so great that he was induced to stop his work, lock the shop door, and spend the afternoon in prayer.

He prevailed, and on the Sabbath called on the minister and wanted him to appoint a "conference meeting." After some hesitation, the minister agreed, observing however, that he feared only few would attend. He arranged it for the same evening at a large private house. When evening came, more assembled than could be accommodated in the house. All were silent for a while until one sinner broke out in tears and asked, if anyone could pray, would he pray for him? Another followed, and another, and still another, until it was found that people from every quarter of the town were under deep conviction. And what was remarkable was, that they all dated their conviction at the hour that the old man was praying in his shop. A powerful revival followed. Thus this old stammering man prevailed, and as a prince had power with God.

REMARKS

1. A great deal of prayer is lost, and many people never prevail in prayer, because, when they have desires for particular blessings, they do not follow them up. They may have desires, benevolent and pure, which are excited by the Spirit of God. When they have them, they should persevere in prayer, for if they turn off their attention, they will quench the Spirit. When you find these holy desires in your minds:

(a) Do not quench the Spirit.

(b) Do not be diverted to other objects. Follow the leadings of the Spirit until you have offered that "effective fervent prayer" that "avails much" (James 5:16*).

2. Without the spirit of prayer, ministers will do only little good. A minister need not expect much success unless he prays for it. Sometimes others may have the spirit of prayer and obtain a blessing on his labors. Generally, however, those preachers are the most successful who have most of the spirit of prayer themselves.

3. Not only must ministers have the spirit of prayer, but it is necessary that the church should unite in offering that effective fervent prayer which can prevail with God. "This also I will let the house of Israel ask me to do for them" (Ezekiel 36:37).[10]

Now I have only to ask you, about what I have set forth, "Will you do it?" Have you done what I said to you at the last lecture? Have you gone over your sins, and confessed them, and got them all out of the way? Can you pray now? And will you join and offer prevailing prayer that the Spirit of God may come down here?

---

[10] The full verse reads, "Thus says the Lord GOD: This also I will let the house of Israel ask me to do for them: to increase their people like a flock." (Ezekiel 36:37)

Chapter 6

THE PRAYER OF FAITH

"Whatever you ask in prayer, believe that you have received it, and it will be yours." (Mark 11:24)

These words have been supposed by some to refer exclusively to the faith of miracles. But there is not the least evidence of this. The fact that the text was not intended by our Savior to refer exclusively to the faith of miracles is proved by its context. If you read the chapter, you will see that Christ and his apostles, as they returned from their place of rest in the morning, faint and hungry, saw a fig tree at a distance. It looked very beautiful, and doubtless gave signs of having fruit on it. But when they came near, they found nothing on it but leaves.

And [Jesus] said to it, "May no one ever eat fruit from you again." And his disciples heard it... As they passed by in the morning, they saw the fig tree withered away to its roots. And Peter remembered and said to him, "Rabbi, look! The fig tree that you cursed has withered." And Jesus answered them, "Have faith in God. Truly, I say to you, whoever says to this mountain, 'Be taken up and thrown into the sea,' and does not doubt in his heart, but believes that what he says will come to pass, it will be done for him." (Mark 11:14,20-23)

Then the words of the text follow, "Therefore I tell you, whatever you ask in prayer, believe that you have received it, and it will be yours."

Our Savior wanted to give his disciples instructions about the nature and power of prayer, and the necessity of strong faith in God. He therefore stated a very strong case, a miracle — one so great as the removal of a mountain into the sea. And he tells them, that if they exercise a proper faith in God, they might do such things. But his remarks are not to be limited to faith merely in regard to working miracles, because he goes on to say, "And whenever you stand praying, forgive, if you have anything against anyone, so that your Father also who is in heaven may forgive you your trespasses" (Mark 11:25).

Does that relate to miracles? When you pray, you must forgive. Is that required only when a person wishes to work a miracle? There are many other promises in the Bible related to this, and in nearly the same language, which have been similarly disregarded, supposing the promises refer to the faith employed in miracles. Just as if the faith of miracles was something different from faith in God!

In the last lecture I dwelt upon the subject of Prevailing Prayer. You will remember that I passed over the subject of faith in prayer very briefly, because I wished to reserve it for a separate discussion. The subject of the present lecture, then, is the Prayer of Faith. I propose to show:

I. That faith is a necessary condition of prevailing prayer.

II. What it is that we are to believe when we pray.

III. When we are obligated to exercise this faith, or to believe that we shall receive the thing we ask for.

IV. That this kind of faith in prayer always obtains the blessing sought.

V. To explain how we are to come into the state of mind in which we can exercise such faith.

VI. To answer several objections, which are sometimes alleged against these views of prayer.

I. FAITH A NECESSARY CONDITION

This fact will not be seriously doubted. There is such a thing as offering benevolent desires, which are acceptable to God as such, that do not include the exercise of faith regarding the actual receiving of those blessings. But such desires are not prevailing prayer, the prayer of faith. God may see fit to grant the things desired, as an act of kindness and love, but it would not be properly in answer to prayer. I am speaking now of the kind of faith that ensures the blessing. Do not understand me as saying that there is nothing in prayer that is acceptable to God, or that even obtains the blessing sometimes, without this kind of faith. But I am speaking of the faith that secures the very blessing it seeks. To prove that faith is necessary to prevailing prayer, it is only necessary to repeat what the apostle James clearly tells us, " If any of you lacks wisdom, let him ask God, who gives generously to all without reproach, and it will be given him. But let him ask in faith, with no doubting, for the one who doubts is like a wave of the sea that is driven and tossed by the wind" (James 1:5-6).

II. WHAT WE ARE TO BELIEVE WHEN WE PRAY

1. We are to believe in the existence of God. "Whoever would draw near to God must believe that he exists and that he rewards those who seek him" (Hebrews 11:6). There are many who believe in the existence of God, but do not believe in the efficacy of prayer. They profess to believe in God, but deny the necessity or influence of prayer.

2. We are to believe that we shall receive. Not something, or anything, but some particular thing we ask for. We are not to think that God is such a Being, that if we ask for a fish he will give us a serpent, or if we ask for bread, he will give us a stone. But he says, "whatever you ask in prayer, believe that you have received it, and it will be yours." With respect to the faith of miracles, it is obvious that the disciples were obligated to believe they should receive just what they asked for — that the very thing itself should come to pass. Now, what should people believe in regard to other blessings? Is it a mere loose idea, that if a person prays for a specific blessing, God will by some mysterious Sovereignty give something or another to him, or something to somebody else, somewhere? When a person prays for his children's conversion, is he to believe that either his children will be converted or somebody else's children — it is completely uncertain which? No, this is utter nonsense and highly dishonorable to God. We are to believe that we shall receive the very things that we ask for.

III. WHEN ARE WE OBLIGATED TO MAKE THIS PRAYER?

When are we obligated to believe that we shall have the very things we pray for? I answer, "when we have evidence of it." Faith must always have evidence. A person cannot believe a thing, unless he sees something that he supposes to be evidence. He is under no obligation to believe, and has no right to believe, something will be done, unless he has evidence. It is the height of fanaticism to believe without evidence. The kinds of evidence a person may have are the following:

1. Suppose that God has especially promised it. For instance, God says he is more ready to give his Holy Spirit to them that ask, than parents are to give bread to their children. Here we are obligated to believe that we shall receive it when we pray for it. You have no right to put an if, and say, "Lord, if it be your will, give us your Holy Spirit." This is to insult God. To put an "if" into God's promise, where God has put none, is equal to charging God with being insincere. It is like saying, "O

God, if you are sincere in making these promises, grant us the blessing we pray for."

I heard of a case where a young convert was used to teach a minister a solemn truth on the subject of prayer. She was from a very wicked family, but went to live at a minister's house. While there she was hopefully converted[1]. One day she went to the minister's study while he was there — something she was not in the habit of doing. He thought there must be something wrong with her. So he asked her to sit down, and kindly asked the state of her religious feelings. She then told him that she was distressed at the manner in which the older church members prayed for the Spirit. They would pray for the Holy Spirit to come, and would seem to be very sincere, and plead the promises of God, and then say, "O Lord, if it be your will, grant us these blessings for Christ's sake." She thought that saying, "If it be your will," when God had clearly promised it was questioning whether God was sincere in his promises. The minister tried to reason her out of it, and he succeeded in confusing her. But she was distressed and filled with grief and said, "I cannot argue the point with you, sir. But it is impressed on my mind that it is wrong, and dishonoring to God." And she went away, weeping with anguish. The minister saw she was not satisfied, and it led him to study the matter again. Finally he saw that it was putting an "if" where God had put none and where he had clearly revealed his will. He saw that it was an insult to God. Then he went and told his people they were obligated to believe that God was sincere when he made them a promise. And the spirit of prayer came down upon that church, and a most powerful revival followed.

2. Where there is a general promise in the Scriptures that you may reasonably apply to the particular case before you. If its real meaning includes the particular thing for which you pray, or if you can reasonably apply the principle of the promise to the case, there you have evidence. There are general promises and principles laid down in the Bible that Christians might make use of, if they would only think. Whenever you are in circumstances to which the promises or principles apply, there you are to use them. A parent finds this promise, "But the steadfast love of the LORD is from everlasting to everlasting on those who fear

---

[1] The expression "hopefully converted" was applied to those who professed faith and now lived consistent with Christian behavior. The expression can be found in Puritan writings such as those of Jonathan Edwards. It reflects a cautious attitude in which seeing someone profess faith and live a holy life is not enough to definitively say that person is a Christian (though it is minimally necessary). Since a person cannot know someone else's heart, the expression "hopefully converted" was used to effectively mean, "converted as far as can be determined."

him, and his righteousness to children's children, to those who keep his covenant and remember to do his commandments" (Psalm 103:17-18). Now, here is a promise made to those who possess a certain character. If any parent is conscious that this is his character, he has a rightful ground to apply it to himself and his family. If you have this character, you are obligated to make use of this promise in prayer, and believe it, even to your children's children.

I could go from one end of the Bible to the other, and produce an astonishing variety of texts that are applicable as promises. This would be enough to prove, that in whatever circumstances a child of God may be placed, God has provided in the Bible some promise, either general or particular, which he can apply, that is precisely suited to his case. Many of God's promises are very broad, to intentionally cover much ground. What can be broader than the promise in our text, "Whatever you ask in prayer"? What praying Christian is there who has not been surprised at the length and breadth and fullness of the promises of God when the Spirit has applied them to his heart? Who that lives a life of prayer has not wondered at his own blindness, in not having before seen and felt the extent of meaning and richness of those promises, when viewed under the light of the Spirit of God? At such times he has been astonished at his own ignorance, and found the Spirit applying the promises and declarations of the Bible in a sense in which he had never before dreamed of their being applicable.

The manner in which the apostles applied the promises, prophecies, and declarations of the Old Testament, places in a strong light the breadth of meaning, fullness, and richness of the Word of God. He that walks in the light of God's countenance and is filled with the Spirit of God as he should be will often make an application of promises to his own circumstances, and the circumstances of those for whom he prays, that a blind professor of religion would never dream of making.

3. Where there is any prophetic declaration that the thing prayed for is in the will of God. When it is plain from prophecy that the event is certainly to come, you are obligated to believe it, and to make it the ground for your special faith in prayer. If the time is not specified in the Bible, and there is no evidence from other sources, you are not obligated to believe that it shall take place immediately. But if the time is specified, or if the time may be learned from the study of the prophecies, and it appears to have arrived, then Christians are under obligation to understand and apply it, by offering the prayer of faith. For instance, take the case of Daniel, in regard to the return of the Jews from captivity. What does he say? "I, Daniel, perceived in the books

the number of years that, according to the word of the Lord to Jeremiah the prophet, must pass before the end of the desolations of Jerusalem, namely, seventy years" (Daniel 9:2). Here he learned from books, that is, he studied his Bible, and in that way understood that the length of the captivity was to be seventy years.

What does he do then? Does he sit down upon the promise, and say, "God has pledged himself to put an end to the captivity in seventy years, and the time has expired, and there is no need of doing anything"? Oh, no. He says, "Then I turned my face to the Lord God, seeking him by prayer and pleas for mercy with fasting and sackcloth and ashes" (Daniel 9:3). He set himself at once to pray that the thing might be accomplished. He prayed in faith. But what was he to believe? What he had learned from the prophecy. There are many prophecies yet unfulfilled, in the Bible, which Christians are obligated to understand, as far as they are capable of understanding them, and then make them the basis of believing prayer. Do not think, as some seem to do, that because a thing is foretold in prophecy it is not necessary to pray for it, or that it will come whether Christians pray for it or not. God says, in regard to this very class of events, which are revealed in prophecy, "This also I will let the house of Israel ask me to do for them" (Ezekiel 36:37).

4. When the signs of the times, or the providence of God, indicate that a particular blessing is about to be given, we are obligated to believe it. The Lord Jesus Christ blamed the Jews, and called them hypocrites, because they did not understand the indications of Providence. They could understand the signs of the weather, and see when it was about to rain, and when it would be fair weather. But they could not see from the signs of the times that the time had come for the Messiah to appear and build up the house of God. There are many professing Christians who are always stumbling and hanging back whenever anything to be done is proposed. They always say, "The time has not come — the time has not come," when there are others who pay attention to the signs of the times, and who have spiritual discernment to understand them. These pray in faith for the blessing and it comes.

5. When the Spirit of God is upon you, and excites strong desires for any blessing, you are obligated to pray for it in faith. You are obligated to infer, from the fact that you find yourself drawn to desire such a thing while in the exercise of such holy affections as the Spirit of God produces, that these desires are the work of the Spirit. People are not likely to desire with the right kind of desires unless the Spirit of God excites them. The apostle refers to these desires, excited by the Spirit,

where he says, "Likewise the Spirit helps us in our weakness. For we do not know what to pray for as we ought, but the Spirit himself intercedes for us with groanings too deep for words. And he who searches hearts knows what is the mind of the Spirit, because the Spirit intercedes for the saints according to the will of God" (Romans 8:26-27). Here, then, if you find yourself strongly drawn to desire a blessing, you are to understand it as an indication that God is willing to bestow that particular blessing, and so you are obligated to believe it. God does not trifle with his children. He does not go and excite in them a desire for one blessing, to turn them off with something else. But he excites the very desires he is willing to gratify. And when they feel such desires, they are obligated to follow them out until they get the blessing.

V. THIS KIND OF FAITH ALWAYS OBTAINS THE OBJECT

The text is clear here, to show that you shall receive the very thing prayed for. It does not say, "Believe that you have received it, and you will either have that or something else equivalent to it." To prove that this faith obtains the very blessing that is asked, I observe:

1. That otherwise we could never know whether our prayers were answered. We might continue praying and praying, long after the prayer was answered by some other blessing equivalent to the one for which we asked.

2. If we are not obligated to expect the very thing we ask for, it must be that the Spirit of God deceives us. Why should he excite us to desire a certain blessing when he means to grant something else?

3. What is the meaning of this passage, "which one of you, if his son asks him for bread, will give him a stone"? (Matthew 7:9). Does not our Savior rebuke the idea that prayer may be answered by giving something else? What encouragement do we have to pray for anything in particular, if we are to ask for one thing and receive another? Suppose a Christian should pray for a revival here — he would be answered by a revival in China! Or he might pray for a revival, and God would send cholera or an earthquake! All the history of the church shows that when God answers prayer he gives his people the very thing for which their prayers are offered. God grants other blessings, on both saints and sinners, which they do not pray for at all. He sends rain both upon the just and the unjust. But when he answers prayer, it is by doing what they ask him to do. To be sure, he often more than answers prayer. He grants them not only what they ask, but often connects other blessings with it.

4. Perhaps a difficulty may be felt about the prayers of Jesus Christ. People may ask, "Did not Jesus pray in the garden for the cup to be removed, and was his prayer answered?" I answer that this is no difficulty at all, for the prayer was answered. The cup he prayed to be delivered from was removed. This is what the apostle refers to when he says, "In the days of his flesh, Jesus offered up prayers and supplications, with loud cries and tears, to him who was able to save him from death, and he was heard because of his reverence" (Hebrews 5:7).

Some have supposed that he was praying against the cross, and begging to be delivered from dying on the cross! Did Christ ever shrink from the cross? Never. He came into the world with the purpose to die on the cross, and he never shrank from it. But he was afraid he should die in the garden before he came to the cross. The burden on his soul was so great, and produced such an agony that he felt as if he was at the point of dying. His soul was sorrowful even unto death. But the angel appeared to him, strengthening him. He received the very thing for which he asked.[2] As he says, "I knew that you always hear me" (John 11:42). But there is another case which is often brought up, that of the apostle Paul praying against the "thorn in the flesh." He says, "Three times I pleaded with the Lord about this, that it should leave me. But he said to me, 'My grace is sufficient for you, for my power is made perfect in weakness' " (2 Corinthians 12:7-9). It is the opinion of Dr. Clarke and others, that Paul's prayer was answered in the very thing for which he prayed — that "the thorn in the flesh, the messenger of Satan," of which he speaks was a false apostle who had distracted and perverted the church at Corinth. When Paul prayed against his influence, the Lord answering him by the assurance, "My grace is sufficient

---

[2] This interpretation is not commonly heard today, but there are at least three Scriptural supports for this view: 1) Mark links the cup to strength for enduring the hour. "[Jesus] fell on the ground and prayed that, if it were possible, the hour might pass from him. And he said, 'Abba, Father, all things are possible for you. Remove this cup from me. Yet not what I will, but what you will' " (Mark 14:35-36). 2) Luke's account puts the ministering angel immediately after Jesus' request, as if it were an answer to prayer. "And [Jesus] withdrew from them about a stone's throw, and knelt down and prayed, saying, 'Father, if you are willing, remove this cup from me. Nevertheless, not my will, but yours, be done.' And there appeared to him an angel from heaven, strengthening him" (Luke 22:41-43). Hence some commentators have suggested that Jesus was praying to be delivered from intense suffering at that hour in Gethsemane, which the angel relieved. 3) "In the days of his flesh, Jesus offered up prayers and supplications, with loud cries and tears, to him who was able to save him from death, and he was heard because of his reverence" (Hebrews 5:7). This verse seems to contradict the idea that Jesus prayed for deliverance from death but then was denied.

for you."

But suppose that Paul's prayer was not answered by the granting of the particular object for which he prayed. In order to make out this case as an exception to the prayer of faith, it is necessary to assume the very thing to be proved, that is, that the apostle prayed in faith. There is no reason to suppose that Paul would always pray in faith, any more than that any other Christian does. The very manner in which God answered him shows that it was not in faith. He virtually tells him, "That thorn is necessary for your sanctification, and to keep you from being exalted above measure. I sent it to you in love, and in faithfulness, and you have no business to pray that I should take it away. Leave it alone."

There is not only no evidence that Paul prayed in faith, but a strong presumption that he did not. From the record it is evident that he had nothing on which to build faith. There was no particular or general promise that could be applicable — no providence of God, no prophecy, no teaching of the Spirit, that God would remove this thorn. But the presumption was that God would not remove it, since he had given it for a particular purpose. The prayer appears to have been selfish, praying against a mere personal hindrance. This was not any personal suffering that hindered his usefulness, but on the contrary, it was given to him to increase his usefulness by keeping him humble. Because on some account he found it inconvenient and mortifying, he set himself to pray out of his own heart, evidently without being led to do so by the Spirit of God. Could Paul pray in faith without being led by the Spirit of God, any more than any other person? And will any one undertake to say that the Spirit of God led him to pray that this might be removed, when God himself had given it for a particular purpose that could be accomplished only as the "thorn" continued with him?

V. HOW WE ARE TO COME INTO THIS STATE OF MIND

How are we to have the state of mind in which we can offer such prayer? People often ask, "How shall I offer such prayer? Shall I say, 'Now I will pray in faith for such and such blessings'?" No, the human mind is not moved in this way. You might just as well say, "Now I will call up a spirit from the bottomless pit."

1. You must first obtain evidence that God will grant the blessing. How did Daniel make out to offer the prayer of faith? He searched the Scriptures. Now, you need not let your Bible lie on a shelf, and expect God to reveal his promises to you. "Search the Scriptures," and see where

you can get either a general or special promise, or a prophecy, on which you can plant your feet. Go through your Bible, and you will find it full of such precious promises, which you may plead in faith.

A notable case occurred in one of the towns in the western part of the state of New York where there was a revival. A certain clergyman came to visit the place, and heard a great deal said about the Prayer of Faith. He was staggered at what they said, for he had never regarded the subject in the light in which they did. He inquired about it of the minister that was laboring there. The minister requested him, in a kind spirit, to go home and take his Bible, look up the passages that refer to prayer, and go around to his most prayerful people and ask them how they understood these passages. He did so, going to his praying men and women, reading the passages, without note or comment, and asking what they thought. He found that their plain common sense had led them to understand these passages and to believe that they meant just what they said. This moved him. Then, the fact of his presenting the promises before their minds awakened the spirit of prayer in them, and a revival followed.

I could name many individuals who have set themselves to examine the Bible on this subject who, before they got half through with it, have been filled with the spirit of prayer. They found that God meant with his promises just what a plain, common sense person would understand them to mean. I advise you to try it. You have Bibles. Look them over, and whenever you find a promise that you can use, fasten it in your mind before you go on. You will not get through the Book without finding out that God's promises mean just what they say.

2. Cherish the good desires you have. Christians very often lose their good desires by not paying attention to this, and then their prayers are mere words, without any desire or sincerity at all. The least longing of desire must be cherished. If your body were likely to freeze, and you had even the least spark of fire, how you would cherish it! So, if you have the least desire for a blessing, be it ever so small, do not trifle it away. Do not lose good desires by levity, by criticizing, by worldly mindedness. Watch and pray.

3. Entire consecration to God is necessary for the prayer of faith. You must live a holy life, and consecrate everything to God — your time, talents, influence — all you have, and all you are, to be his entirely. Read the lives of pious people, and you will be struck with this fact, that they used to set apart times to renew their covenant, and dedicate themselves again to God. Whenever they have done so, a blessing has always followed immediately. If I had President Edwards' works here,

I could read passages showing how it was in his days.

4. You must persevere. You are not to pray for a thing once and then stop, and call that the prayer of faith. Look at Daniel. He prayed twenty-one days, and did not stop until he had obtained the blessing. He set his heart and his face to the Lord, to seek by prayer and supplications, with fasting, sackcloth, and ashes. He held on three weeks, and then the answer came. And why did not it come before? God sent an Archangel to bear the message, but the devil hindered him all this time. See what Christ says in the Parable of the Unjust Judge, and the Parable of the Loaves. What does he teach us in them? Why, that God will grant answers to prayer when it is persistent. "And will not God give justice to his elect, who cry to him day and night?" (Luke 18:7).

5. If you would pray in faith, be sure to walk every day with God. If you do, he will tell you what to pray for. Be filled with his Spirit, and he will give you objects enough to pray for. He will give you as much of the spirit of prayer as you have strength of body to handle.

A good man said to me, "Oh, I am dying for the lack of strength to pray! My body is crushed, the world is on me, and how can I stop praying?" I have known that man go to bed absolutely sick, for weakness and faintness, under the pressure. And I have known him pray as if he would do violence to Heaven, and then have seen the blessing come as plainly in answer to his prayer as if it were revealed, so that no person would doubt it any more than if God had spoken from heaven. Shall I tell you how he died? He prayed more and more. He used to take the map of the world before him, and pray, and look over the different countries and pray for them, until he died in his room, praying. Blessed man! His example brought shame to the ungodly, and carnal, unbelieving professors. But he was the favorite of Heaven, and a prevailing prince in prayer.

VI. OBJECTIONS BROUGHT AGAINST THIS DOCTRINE

1. "It leads to fanaticism and amounts to a new revelation." Why should this be a stumbling block? They must have evidence to believe, before they can offer the prayer of faith. And if God should give other evidence besides the senses, where is the objection? True, there is a sense in which this is a new revelation — it is making known something by his Spirit. But it is the very revelation that God has promised to give. It is just the one we are to expect, if the Bible is true. When we do not know what we should pray for, according to the will of God, his Spirit helps our weakness, and teaches us. Shall we deny the teaching of the Spirit?

2. It is often asked, "Is it our duty to offer the prayer of faith for the salvation of all people?" I answer, "No," for that is not according to the will of God. It is contrary to his revealed will. We have no evidence that all will be saved. We should feel benevolently to all and desire their salvation. But God has revealed that many of the human race shall be damned, and it cannot be a duty to believe that all shall be saved, in the face of a revelation to the contrary. In Christ's prayer, he clearly said, "I am not praying for the world but for those whom you have given me" (John 17:9).

3. But some ask, "If we were to offer this prayer for all people, would not all be saved?" I answer, "Yes, and so they would be saved, if they would all repent. But they will not."

4. But you ask, "For whom are we to pray this prayer? We want to know in what cases, for what people, and places, and at what times, we are to make the prayer of faith." I answer, as I have already answered, "When you have evidence — from promises, or prophecies, or providences, or the leadings of the Spirit — that God will do the things for which you pray."

5. "How is it that so many prayers of pious parents for their children are not answered? Did you not say there was a promise that pious parents may apply to their children? Why is it, then, that so many pious, praying parents have had impenitent children who have died in their sins?" Grant that it is so, what does it prove? "Let God be true though every one were a liar" (Romans 3:4). Which shall we believe: that God's promise has failed, or that these parents did not do their duty? Perhaps they did not believe the promise, or did not believe there was any such thing as the prayer of faith. Wherever you find a professing Christian who does not believe in any such prayer, you find, as a general rule, that he has children and others at home still in their sins.

6. "Will not these views lead to fanaticism? Will not many people think they are offering the prayer of faith when they are not?" That is the same objection that Unitarians make against the doctrine of regeneration: that many people think they have been born again when they have not. It is an argument against all spiritual religion of any kind. Some think they have it when they do not, and are fanatics. But there are those who know what the prayer of faith is, just as there are those who know what spiritual experience is, though it may stumble cold-hearted professors who do not know it. Even ministers often expose themselves to the rebuke that Christ gave to Nicodemus, "Are you the teacher of Israel and yet you do not understand these things?" (John

:10)

REMARKS

. People who have not known by experience what the prayer of faith s, have great reason to doubt their own piety. This is by no means ıncharitable. Let them examine themselves. It is to be feared that they ınderstand prayer as little as Nicodemus did the New Birth. They ıave not walked with God, and you cannot describe it to them, any nore than you can describe a beautiful painting to a blind man.

2. There is reason to believe that millions are in hell because professng Christians have not offered the prayer of faith. When they had promises under their eye, they have not had enough faith to use them. The signs of the times, and the indications of Providence, were favorıble, perhaps, and the Spirit of God prompted desires for their salvaion. There was enough evidence that God was ready to grant a blessng. If professors had only prayed in faith, God would have granted t.

3. You say, "This leaves the church under a great load of guilt." True, t does. No doubt many will stand up before God, covered all over with the blood of souls that have been lost from their lack of faith. The promises of God, accumulated in their Bibles, will stare them in the face, and weigh them down to hell.

4. Many professing Christians are so far from God, that talk to them ıbout the prayer of faith is unintelligible. Very often the greatest offense possible to them, is to preach about this kind of prayer.

5. I now want to ask professing Christians a few questions. Do you know what it is to pray in faith? Did you ever pray in this way? Have you ever prayed until your mind was assured the blessing would come — until you felt that rest in God, that confidence, as if you saw God come down from heaven to give it to you? If not, you should examine your foundation. How can you live without praying in faith? How do you live in view of your children, while you have no assurance that they will be converted? One would think you would go deranged. I knew a father who was a good man, but had erroneous views on the prayer of faith, and his whole family of children were grown up, without one of them being converted. After some time his son grew sick, and seemed about to die. The father prayed, but the son grew worse, and seemed sinking into the grave without hope. The father prayed, until his anguish was beyond words. He went at last and prayed (there seemed no prospect of his son surviving) so that he poured out his soul as if he would not be denied, until at last he got an assurance that his

son would not only live but be converted, and that not only this one but his whole family would be converted to God. He came into the house, and told his family his son would not die. They were astonished at him. "I tell you," he said, "he will not die. And no child of mine will ever die in his sins." That man's children were all converted years ago.

What do you think of that? Was that fanaticism? If you think so, it is because you know nothing about the matter. Do you pray this way? Do you live in such a manner that you can offer such prayer for your children? I know that the children of professing believers may sometimes be converted in answer to the prayers of somebody else. But should you live so? Do you dare trust in the prayers of others, when God calls you to sustain this important relation to your children?

Finally, see what combined effort is made to disregard the Bible. The wicked want to dispose those verses in the Bible that threaten them, and the church wants to dispose the verses of promises. And what is there left? Between them, they leave the Bible a blank. I ask it in love, "What is our Bible good for, if we do not lay hold of its precious promises and use them as the ground of our faith when we pray for the blessing of God?" You had better send your Bibles to the lost, where they will do some good, if you are not going to believe and use them. I have no evidence that there is much of this prayer now in this church or in this city. And what will become of them? What will become of your children? Your neighbors? The wicked?

Chapter 7

THE SPIRIT OF PRAYER

"Likewise the Spirit helps us in our weakness. For we do not know what to pray for as we ought, but the Spirit himself intercedes for us with groanings too deep for words. And he who searches hearts knows what is the mind of the Spirit, because the Spirit intercedes for the saints according to the will of God." (Romans 8:26-27)

In my last lecture I observed that one of the most important attributes of effective or prevailing prayer is faith. This was so extensive a subject that I reserved it for a separate discussion. And accordingly my last lecture was on the subject of faith in prayer, or as it is called, the Prayer of Faith. It was my intention to discuss the subject in a single lecture. But as I needed to condense so much on some points, it occurred to me and was mentioned by others, that there might be some questions that people would ask that should be answered more fully, especially as the subject is one on which there is so much confusion. One important purpose in preaching is to show the truth in such a way to answer the questions that would naturally arise to those who read the Bible with attention, and who want to know what it means, so that they can put it into practice. In explaining the text, I propose to show:[1]

I. What the Spirit does for us.

II. Why he does what the text declares him to do.

III. How he accomplishes it.

---

[1] This chapter is an abridgment of two lectures originally delivered by Finney. See the Appendix for details.

IV. The degree in which he influences the minds of those who are under his influence.

V. How his influences are to be distinguished from the influences of evil spirits, or from the suggestions of our own minds.

VI. How we are to obtain this agency of the Holy Spirit.

VII. Why many do not have the Spirit.

VIII. The consequences of having the Spirit.

IX. The consequences of not having the Spirit.

I. WHAT THE SPIRIT DOES

He intercedes for the saints. "He intercedes for us," and "helps us in our weakness," when "we do not know what to pray for as we ought." He helps Christians to pray "according to the will of God," or for the things that God desires them to pray for.

II. WHY IS THE HOLY SPIRIT THUS EMPLOYED?

Because of our ignorance. Because we do not know what we should pray for as we ought. We are so ignorant both of the will of God, revealed in the Bible, and of his unrevealed will that we could learn from his providence. People are very ignorant both of the promises and prophecies of the Bible, and blind to the providence of God. And they are even more in the dark about those points of which God has said nothing except by the leadings of his Spirit. I have named these four sources of evidence on which to ground faith in prayer — promises, prophecies, providences, and the Holy Spirit. When all other means fail to lead us to the knowledge of what we should pray for, the Spirit does it.

III. HOW DOES HE MAKE INTERCESSION?

In what manner does the Spirit operate, to help us in our weakness?

1. Not by superseding the use of our faculties. It is not by praying for us, while we do nothing. He prays for us by stirring our faculties. Not that he immediately suggests to us words, or guides our language. But he enlightens our minds, and makes the truth take hold of our souls. He leads us to consider the state of the church, and the condition of sinners around us. The manner in which he brings the truth before the mind, and keeps it there until it produces its effect, we cannot tell. But we can know at least this — that he leads us to a deep consideration of the state of things, and the natural and logical result of this is deep feeling. When the Spirit brings the truth before a person's mind there

is only one way in which the person can keep from feeling deeply. That is by turning away his thoughts to think of other things. Sinners, when the Spirit of God brings the truth before them, must feel. They feel wrong, as long as they remain impenitent. So, if a person is a Christian, and the Holy Spirit brings the subject into warm contact with his heart, it is just as impossible he should not be moved as it is that your hand should not feel pain if you put it into the fire. If the Spirit of God leads a person to dwell on matters intended to excite overpowering feelings regarding the salvation of souls, and he is not then moved, it proves that he has no love for souls, nothing of the Spirit of Christ, and knows nothing about Christian experience.

2. The Spirit makes the Christian feel the value of souls and the guilt and danger of sinners in their present condition. It is amazing how dull Christians often are about this. Even Christian parents let their children go right down to hell before their eyes, and scarcely seem to exercise a single feeling, or put forth an effort to save them. And why? Because they are so blind to what hell is, so unbelieving about the Bible, so ignorant of the precious promises that God has made to faithful parents. They grieve the Spirit of God away — and it is in vain to make them pray for their children, while the Spirit of God is away from them.

3. He leads Christians to understand and apply the promises of Scripture. It is amazing that in no age have Christians fully been able to apply the promises of Scripture to the events of life. This is not because the promises themselves are obscure. But there has always been an amazing inclination to overlook the Scriptures, as a source of light about the events of life. How astonished the apostles were at Christ's application of so many prophecies to himself! They seemed to be continually ready to exclaim, "Astonishing! Can it be so? We never understood it before!" Who, that has seen the way the apostles, influenced and inspired by the Holy Spirit, applied passages of the Old Testament to gospel times, has not been amazed at the richness of meaning which they found in the Scriptures? It has been this way with many a Christian. While deeply engaged in prayer he has seen that passages of Scripture are appropriate which he never thought before had any such application.

I once knew an individual who was in great spiritual darkness. He had secluded himself for prayer, resolved that he would not stop until he had found the Lord. He kneeled down and tried to pray. All was dark, and he could not pray. He rose from his knees, and stood for a while, but he could not give up, for he had promised that he would not let the sun go down before he had given himself to God. He knelt again, but his mind was dark, and his heart was as hard as before. He was nearly in despair, and said in agony, "I have grieved the Spirit of God away, and there is no promise for me. I am shut out from the presence of God." But his resolve was firm, and again he knelt down. He had said but a few words when this passage came into his mind, as fresh as if he had just read it, "You will seek me and find me when you seek me with all your heart" (Jeremiah 29:13, NIV). He saw that though this promise was in the Old Testament, and addressed to the Jews, it was still as applicable to him as to them. And it broke his heart, like the hammer of the Lord, in a moment. And he prayed, and rose up happy in God.[2]

This is often the case when professing Christians are praying for their children. Sometimes they pray, and are in confusion and doubt, feeling as if there were no foundation for faith, and no special promises for the children of believers. But while they have been pleading, God has shown them the full meaning of some promise, and their soul has rested on it as on his mighty arm. I once heard of a widow who was greatly concerned about her children until this passage was powerfully brought to her mind, "leave your fatherless children; I will keep them alive; and let your widows trust in me" (Jeremiah 49:11). She saw it had an extended meaning, and she was enabled to grasp it. She prevailed in prayer, and her children were converted. The Holy Spirit was sent into the world by the Savior to guide his people, and instruct them and bring things to their remembrance, as well as to convince the world of sin.

4. The Spirit leads Christians to desire and pray for things of which nothing is specifically said in the Word of God. Take the case of an individual. The fact that God is willing to save is a general truth. So it is a general truth that he is willing to answer prayer. But how shall I know the will of God for that individual? Can I pray in faith according to the will of God for the conversion and salvation of that individual, or not? Here the Spirit comes to lead the minds of God's people to pray for those individuals, and at those times, when God is prepared to bless them. When we do not know what to pray for, the Holy Spirit leads the mind to dwell on some object, to consider its situation, to realize its value, and to feel for it, and pray, and "travail in birth," until the person is converted. This sort of experience, I know, is less common in cities than it is in some parts of the country, because of the vast number

---

[2] This story is actually Charles Finney's own conversion experience. This occurred in a grove of trees nearby his house where he went to pray, having resolved not to leave until he had given his heart to the Lord.

of things that in cities divert attention and grieve the Spirit.

I have had much opportunity to know how it has been in some districts. I was acquainted with an individual who used to keep a list of people for whom he was especially concerned. I have had the opportunity to know many people for whom he became thus interested who were immediately converted. I have seen him pray for people on his list when he was literally in agony for them, and have sometimes known him to call on someone else to help him pray for such a person. I have known his mind to fasten on an individual of hardened, abandoned character, and who could not be reached in any ordinary way. In a town in a north part of this State, where there was a revival, there was a certain individual who was a most violent and offensive opponent. He kept a tavern, and used to enjoy swearing at a furious rate whenever there were Christians within hearing, in order to hurt their feelings. He was so bad that one man said he believed he should have to sell his place, or give it away, and move out of town, because he could not live near a man who swore this way. This good man of whom I am speaking passed through the town, and, hearing of the case, was very grieved and distressed for the individual. He took him on his praying list. The case weighed on his mind when he was asleep and when he was awake. He kept thinking about the ungodly man, and praying for him for days. And, the first we knew of it, the tavern keeper came into a meeting, confessed his sins, and poured out his soul. His bar immediately became the place where they held prayer meetings. In this manner the Spirit of God leads individual Christians to pray for things that they would not pray for. Thus they pray for things "according to the will of God."

Great evil has been done by saying that this kind of influence amounts to a new revelation. Many people will be so afraid of it, if they hear it called a new revelation, that they will not stop to ask what it means, or whether or not the Scriptures teach it. The plain truth of the matter is that the Spirit leads a person to pray. If God leads a person to pray for an individual, the inference from the Bible is, that God intends to save that individual. If we find, by comparing our state of mind with the Bible, that we are led by the Spirit to pray for an individual, we have good evidence to believe that God is prepared to bless him.

5. The Spirit gives Christians a spiritual discernment about the movements and developments of Providence. They sometimes almost seem to prophesy. No doubt people may be deluded, and sometimes are, by leaning to their own understanding when they think the Spirit leads them. But there is no doubt that a Christian may be made to discern

clearly the signs of the times, so as to understand from Providence what to expect, and thus to pray for it in faith. Thus they are often led to expect a revival, and to pray for it in faith, when nobody else can see the least signs of it.

There was a woman in New Jersey, in a place where there had been a revival. She was sure there was going to be another. She wanted to have "conference meetings" appointed. But the minister and elders saw nothing to encourage it, and would do nothing. She saw they were blind, and so she went forward, and got a carpenter to make seats for her, for she said she would have meetings in her own house — there was certainly going to be a revival. She had barely opened her doors for meetings before the Spirit of God came down with great power, and these sleepy church members found themselves immediately surrounded with convicted sinners. They could only say, "Surely the LORD is in this place, and I did not know it" (Genesis 28:16). The reason why such persons as this praying woman understand the indication of God's will is not because of superior wisdom, but because the Spirit of God leads them to see the signs of the times. And this is not by revelation, but they are led to see a converging of providences to a single point that produces in them a confident expectation of a certain result.

IV. THE DEGREE OF INFLUENCE

In what degree are we to expect the Spirit of God to affect the minds of believers? The text says, "The Spirit himself intercedes for us with groanings too deep for words." I understand the meaning of this to be that the Spirit excites desires too great to be spoken except with groans — making the soul too full to speak its feelings with words, so that the person can only groan them out to God, who understands the language of the heart.

V. DISTINGUISHING THE INFLUENCES

How are we to know whether it is the Spirit of God that influences our minds, or not?

1. Not by feeling some external influence applied to us. We are not to expect to feel our minds in direct physical contact with God. If this happened, we know of no way in which it can be made perceptible. We know that we control our minds freely, and that our thoughts focus on something that captures our interest. But we are not to expect a miracle, such as a perceptible leading by the hand, hearing something whispered in the ear, or seeing a miraculous manifestation of the will of God.

Individuals often grieve the Spirit away, because they do not harbor him and cherish his influences. Sinners often do this ignorantly. They suppose that if they were under conviction by the Spirit, they should have mysterious feelings — a shock would come upon them that they could not mistake. Many Christians are so ignorant of the Spirit's influences, and have thought so little about having his assistance in prayer, that when they have such influences they do not know it, and so do not yield to them, and cherish them. We perceive nothing under the Spirit's influence, only the movement of our own minds. There is nothing else that can be felt. We merely know that our thoughts are intensely focused on a certain subject.

Christians are often unnecessarily misled and distressed on this point because they are afraid they do not have the Spirit of God. They feel intensely, but they do know not what makes them feel. They are distressed about sinners. But should they not be distressed, when they think of their condition? Now the truth is, the very fact that you are thinking upon them is evidence that the Spirit of God is leading you. Do you not know that most of the time these things do not affect you this way? Most of the time you do not think much about the case of sinners. You know their salvation is always equally important. Even when you are not busy, your mind lacks any feeling for them. But now, although you may be busy with other things, you think, you pray, and feel intensely for them, even while you are about business that at other times would occupy all your thoughts. Now, almost every thought you have is, "God have mercy upon them!" Why is this? Why, their case is placed in a strong light before your mind. Do you ask what it is that leads your mind to exercise benevolent feelings for sinners, and to agonize in prayer for them? What can it be but the Spirit of God? There are no devils that would lead you this way. If your feelings are truly benevolent, you should consider it as the Holy Spirit leading you to pray for things according to the will of God.

2. "Test the spirits" by the Bible. People are sometimes led away by strange fantasies and crazy impulses. If you compare them faithfully with the Bible, you never need to be led astray. You can always know whether your feelings are produced by the Spirit's influences by comparing your desires with the character of Christianity, as described in the Bible. The Bible commands you to "test the spirits." "Beloved, do not believe every spirit, but test the spirits to see whether they are from God" (1 John 4:1).

VI. HOW SHALL WE GET THIS INFLUENCE OF THE SPIRIT?

1. It must be sought by fervent, believing prayer. Christ says, "If you

then, who are evil, know how to give good gifts to your children, how much more will the heavenly Father give the Holy Spirit to those who ask him!" (Luke 11:13) Does anyone say, I have prayed for it, and it does not come? It is because you do not pray correctly. "You ask and do not receive, because you ask wrongly, to spend it on your passions" (James 4:3). You do not pray from right motives. A professing Christian, a leading member in a church, once asked a minister what he thought of his situation. He had been praying week after week for the Spirit, and had not found any benefit. The minister asked what his motive was in praying. He replied that, "he wanted to be happy." He knew those who had the Spirit were happy, and he wanted the enjoyment they had. Why, the devil himself might pray so! That is mere selfishness. The man, when this was shown to him, at first turned away in anger. He saw that he had never known what it was to pray. He was convinced that he was a hypocrite, and that his prayers were all selfish, dictated only by a desire for his own happiness. David prayed that God would sustain him by his Spirit, that he might teach transgressors and turn sinners to God.[3] A Christian should pray for the Spirit to be more useful to God and glorify him more, not to personally be happier. This man saw clearly where he had been in error, and he was converted. Perhaps many here have been making just the same mistake. You should examine if your prayers are not tinted with selfishness.

2. Use the means adapted to stir your minds on the subject and to keep your attention fixed there. If a person prays for the Spirit, and then diverts his mind to other objects — if he uses no other means, but goes away to worldly objects, he tempts God. The person swings loose from his object, and it would be a miracle if he should get what he prays for. How is a sinner to get conviction? Why, by thinking of his sins. That is the way for a Christian to obtain deep feeling — by thinking about the object. God is not going to pour these things on you without any effort of your own. You must cherish the slightest impressions. Take the Bible, and go over the passages that show the condition and prospects of the world. Look at the world, look at your children and your neighbors, and see their condition while they remain in sin. Then, persevere in prayer and effort until you obtain the blessing of the Spirit of God to dwell in you. This was the way, doubtless, that Dr. Watts came to have the feelings that he has described in his hymn:

> My thoughts on awful subjects dwell,
> Damnation and the dead;

---

[3] Psalm 51:11-13

What horrors seize the guilty soul
Upon a dying bed!

Look, as it were, through a telescope that will bring far objects to your sight. Look into hell, and hear them groan. Then turn the glass upwards and look into heaven, and see the saints there, in their white robes, and hear them sing the song of redeeming love. Ask yourself, "Is it possible that I should prevail with God to elevate the sinner there?" Do this, and if you are not a wicked person and a stranger to God, you will soon have as much of the spirit of prayer as your body can bear.

3. Aim to obey perfectly the written law. In other words, have no fellowship with sin. Aim at being entirely above the world, "You therefore must be perfect, as your heavenly Father is perfect" (Matthew 5:48). If you sin at all, let it be your daily grief. The one who does not aim at this intends to live in sin. Such an individual need not expect God's blessing, for this person is not sincere in desiring to keep all his commandments.

VII. WHY MANY DO NOT HAVE THE SPIRIT

1. It may be that you live a hypocritical life. Your prayers are not sincere. Not only is your religion a mere outward show, without any heart, but you are insincere in your interactions with others. Thus you do many things to grieve the Spirit, so that he cannot dwell with you.

A minister was once living with a certain family, and the lady of the house was constantly complaining that she did not "enjoy" religion, and nothing seemed to help her. One day some ladies visited her, and insisting that she was very offended because they had not visited before, she urged them to stay and spend the day, and declared she could not agree to let them go. They excused themselves, and left the house. As soon as they were gone she told her servant that she wondered why these people had so little sense to be always troubling her and taking up her time! The minister heard it, immediately rebuked her, and told her she should understand why she did not "enjoy" religion. It was because she was in the daily habit of insincerity that amounted to downright lying. And the Spirit of truth could not dwell in such a heart.

2. Others have so much levity that the Spirit will not dwell with them. The Spirit of God is solemn and serious, and will not dwell with those who give way to thoughtless levity.

3. Others are so proud that they cannot have the Spirit. They are so fond of dress, high life, accessories, fashion, etc., that it is no wonder

they are not filled with the Spirit. And yet such people will pretend to be at a loss to know why it is that they do not "enjoy" religion!

4. Some are so worldly-minded, love property so much, and are trying so hard to get rich, that they cannot have the Spirit. How can he dwell with them when all their thoughts are on things of the world, and all their powers absorbed in obtaining wealth? And when they get money they are troubled if pressed by conscience to do something with it for the conversion of the world. They show how much they love the world in all their interactions with others. Little things show it. They will bargain down a poor man, who is doing a little piece of work for them, to the lowest penny. If they are dealing on a large scale, very likely they will be liberal and fair, because it is to their advantage. But if it is a person they do care not about: a laborer, a mechanic, or a servant — they will grind him down to the last fraction, no matter what the work is really worth. They actually pretend to make it a matter of conscience that they cannot possibly give any more. Now, they would be ashamed to deal this way with people of their own rank, because it would be public and hurt their reputation. But God knows it, and has it all written down, that they are covetous and unfair in their dealings, and will not do right except when it is for their interest. Now, how can such professing Christians have the Spirit of God? It is impossible.

5. Others do not fully confess and forsake their sins, and so cannot enjoy the Spirit's presence. They will perhaps confess their sins in general terms and are always ready to acknowledge that they are sinners. Or they will confess partially some particular sins. But they do it reservedly, proudly, guardedly, as if they were afraid they should say a little more than is necessary, when they confess to others. They do it in a way that shows that, instead of flowing from a candid heart, the confession is extracted from them by conscience gripping them. If they have injured any one, they will make a partial retraction, which is hard-hearted, cruel, and hypocritical, and then they will ask, "Now brother, are you satisfied?" We know that it is very difficult for a person who has been wronged to say in such a case that he is not satisfied even if the confession is cold and heartless. But I tell you that God is not satisfied. He knows whether you have made a full and honest confession, and taken all the blame that belongs to you. If your confessions have been forced and extracted from you, do you suppose you can cheat God? "Whoever conceals his transgressions will not prosper, but he who confesses and forsakes them will obtain mercy" (Proverbs 28:13). "He who humbles himself will be exalted" (Luke 14:11). Unless you come down, and confess your sins honestly, and compensate where you have done injury, you have no right to expect the spirit of

prayer.

6. Others are neglecting some known duty, and that is the reason why they do not have the Spirit. Someone does not pray with his family, though he knows he should do so, and yet he is trying to get the spirit of prayer! There is many a young man who feels in his heart he should prepare for the ministry, but who does not have the spirit of prayer because he has some worldly goal in view which prevents his devoting himself to the work. He knows his duty, refuses to do it, and yet is praying for direction from the Spirit of God! He cannot have it.

Another has neglected to make an outward profession of faith. He knows his duty, but he refuses to join the church. He once had the spirit of prayer but, neglecting his duty, he grieved the Spirit away. And now he thinks, if he could once more enjoy the light of God's face and have his feelings renewed, he would do his duty and join the church. And so he is trying to bring God over on his terms, to grant him his presence. He should not expect it. You will live and die in darkness, unless you are willing first to do your duty, before God manifests himself as reconciled to you. It is in vain to say you will come forward if God will first show you the light of his face. He never will do it as long as you live. He will let you die without it, if you refuse to do your duty.

I have known women who felt that they should talk to their unconverted husbands and pray with them. But they neglected it, and so they entered darkness. They knew their duty and refused to do it. They "went around it," and lost the spirit of prayer.

If you have neglected any known duty, and thus lost the spirit of prayer, you must yield first. God has a controversy with you. You have refused obedience to God, and you must retract. You may have forgotten it, but God has not. You must set yourself to recall it to mind and repent. God never will yield or grant you his Spirit until you repent. Were I omniscient, I could call the names of the individuals in this congregation who have neglected some known duty or committed some sin that they have not repented of. Now they are praying for the spirit of prayer, but they cannot succeed in obtaining it.

7. Perhaps you have resisted the Spirit of God. Perhaps you are in the habit of resisting the Spirit. You resist conviction. In preaching, when something has been said that involved your situation, your heart has risen up against it. Many are willing to hear clear and convicting preaching, so long as they can apply it all to other people. A spirit of contempt for humankind makes them take satisfaction in hearing oth-

ers searched and rebuked. But, if the truth touches them, they directly cry out that the preaching is "personal" and "abusive." Is this your case?

8. The fact is that you do not, on the whole, desire the Spirit. This is true in every case in which you do not have the Spirit. Let me be clear here. I want you to carefully distinguish this possibility. Nothing is more common than for people to desire something for certain reasons, yet not to choose it after considering everything. A person may see in a shop window an article that he desires to purchase. So he goes in and asks the price, thinks about it a little, yet in the end decides not to purchase it. He desires the article but does not like the price, so that in the end he prefers not to purchase it. People may desire the Spirit of God from a consideration of the comfort and joy that he brings. If you know from former experience what it is to commune with God, and how sweet it is to immerse in penitence and to be filled with the Spirit, you cannot help but want a return of those joys. And you may determine to pray earnestly for it, and to pray for a revival of religion. But, on the whole, you are unwilling it should come. You have so much to do that you cannot attend to it. Or it will require so many sacrifices that you cannot bear to have it. There are some things you are not willing to give up. You find that if you wish to have the Spirit of God dwell with you, you must lead a different life. You must give up the world, you must make sacrifices, you must break off from your worldly associates, and make confession of your sins. And so, on the whole, you do not wish to have the Spirit come, unless he will agree to dwell with you and let you live as you please. But that he will never do.

VIII. THE CONSEQUENCES OF HAVING THE SPIRIT

1. You will be called eccentric, and you will probably deserve it. You will probably be truly eccentric. I never knew a person who was filled with the Spirit that was not called eccentric. And the reason is that such people are unlike other folk. There is therefore the best of reasons why such persons should appear eccentric. They take different views, are moved by different motives, and led by a different spirit. You should expect such remarks. How often I have heard the remark about various persons, "He is a good man — but he is rather eccentric." I have sometimes asked for particular details. What does his eccentricity consist in? I hear the list, and it amounts to this — that he is spiritual. Be resolved for this, to be called "eccentric." Now there is such a thing as pretended eccentricity. That is horrible! But there is such a thing as being so deeply permeated with the Spirit of God that you will appear

strange and eccentric to those who cannot understand the reasons for your conduct.

2. If you have much of the Spirit of God, it is not unlikely you will be thought deranged by many. We judge people to be deranged when they act differently from what we think is good judgment and common sense, and when they come to conclusions for which we can see no good reasons. Paul was accused of being deranged by those who did not understand the views under which he acted. No doubt Festus thought that Paul was crazy, and that "great learning had driven him out of his mind." But Paul said, "I am not out of my mind, most excellent Festus" (Acts 26:24-25). His conduct was so strange, so unusual, that Festus thought it must be insanity. But the truth simply was, Paul understood the subject so clearly that he threw his whole soul into it. Festus and the rest were entirely ignorant about the motivations that drove him. This is by no means uncommon. Many people have appeared to the unspiritual as if they were deranged. Yet they saw good reasons for doing what they did. God was leading their minds to act in such a way that those who were not spiritual could not understand the reasons.

3. If you have the Spirit of God, you must expect to feel great distress about the condition of the church and the world. Some spiritual epicureans ask for the Spirit because they think he will make them so perfectly happy. Some people think that spiritual Christians are always free from sorrow. There never was a greater mistake. Read your Bibles, and see how the prophets and apostles were always groaning and distressed in view of the state of the church and of the world. The apostle Paul said he was "always carrying in the body the death of Jesus" (2 Corinthians 4:10). "I protest," he said, "I die every day" (1 Corinthians 15:31). You will know what it is to sympathize with the Lord Jesus Christ, and be baptized with the baptism that he was baptized with. Oh, how he agonized when looking at the state of sinners! How he travailed in soul for their salvation! The more you have of his spirit, the more clearly you will see the condition of sinners, and the more deeply you will be distressed about them. Many times you will feel as if you could not live in light of their situation — your distress will be unspeakable.

4. You will be often grieved with the state of the ministry. Some years ago I met a woman belonging to one of the churches in this city. I asked her about the state of religion here. She seemed unwilling to say much about it, made some general remarks, and then choked up, her eyes filled with tears, and she said, "Oh, our minister's mind seems to be

very dark!" Spiritual Christians often feel like this and often weep over it. I have seen much of it, having often found Christians who wept and groaned in secret, contemplating the ignorance in the minds of ministers in regard to religion, worldliness, and fear of man. But they dared not speak of it lest they should be denounced and threatened, and perhaps cast out of the church. I do not say these things critically, to reproach my brethren, but because they are true. And ministers should know that nothing is more common than for spiritual Christians to feel burdened and distressed at the state of the ministry. I do not wish to stir up any wrong feelings towards ministers. But it should be known that Christians do often get spiritual views of things, their souls are kindled up, and then they find that their minister does not share their feelings. They find he is far below where he should be, and spiritually is far below some of the members of his church.

This is one of the most prominent and deeply deplorable evils of the present day. The piety of the ministry, though real, is so superficial, that in many cases the spiritual people of the church feel that ministers cannot sympathize with them. The preaching does not meet their needs and it does not feed them. The ministers do not have deep enough religious experience to know how to search and wake up the church, how to help those under temptation, to support the weak, and to direct the strong. When a minister has gone with a church as far as his experience in spiritual matters goes, there he stops. Until he has a renewed experience, until he is reconverted, his heart broken up again, and he steps forward in the divine life and Christian experience, he will help them no more. He may preach sound doctrine, but so may an unconverted minister. But his preaching will lack that searching power, that practical bearing, that anointing, which alone will reach the case of a spiritually minded Christian. It is a fact over which the church is groaning, that the piety of young men suffers so much in the course of their education, that when they enter the ministry, however much intellectual furniture they may possess, they are in a state of spiritual babyhood. They need nursing and feeding, instead of trying to feed the church of God.

5. If you have much of the Spirit of God, you must know you will have much opposition, both in the church and the world. Very likely the leaders in the church will oppose you. There has always been opposition in the church. So it was when Christ was on earth. If you are far above their state of feeling, church members will oppose you. Anyone who lives a godly life in Christ Jesus will be persecuted (2 Timothy 3:12). Often the elders and even the minister will oppose you, if you are filled with the Spirit of God.

6. You must expect very frequent and agonizing conflicts with Satan. Satan has very little trouble from those Christians who are not spiritual, but lukewarm, slothful, and worldly minded. Such people do not understand what is said about spiritual conflicts. Perhaps they will smile when such things are mentioned. And so the devil leaves them alone. They do not disturb him, nor he them. But spiritual Christians he knows very well are doing him a vast injury, and therefore he sets himself against them. Such Christians often have terrible conflicts. They have temptations that they never thought of before: blasphemous thoughts, atheism, suggestions to do deeds of wickedness, to destroy their own lives, and the like. And if you are spiritual you may expect these terrible conflicts.

7. But, you will have peace with God. If the church, and sinners, and the devil, oppose you, there will be One with whom you will have peace. Let you who are called to these trials, conflicts, and temptations, and who groan, pray, and weep, remember this consideration. Your peace, so far as your feelings towards God are concerned, will flow like a river.

8. You will likewise have peace of conscience if the Spirit leads you. You will not be constantly prodded and kept on the rack by a guilty conscience. Your conscience will be calm and quiet, unruffled as the summer's lake.

9. If filled with the Spirit, you will be useful. You cannot help being useful. Even if you were sick and unable to go out of your room, or to talk, and saw nobody, you would be ten times more useful than a hundred of those common sort of Christians who have no spirituality. To give you an idea of this, I will relate an anecdote. A pious man in the western part of this State was suffering from tuberculosis. He was a poor man and was ill for years. An unconverted merchant in the place, who had a kind heart, used to send him now and then some things for his comfort, or for his family. He felt grateful for the kindness, but could offer nothing in return, as he wanted to do. Eventually he determined that the best return he could make would be to pray for the man's salvation. So he began to pray, his soul kindled, and he got hold of God. No revival was taking place there, but, eventually to the astonishment of everyone, this merchant came right out on the Lord's side. The fire kindled all over the place, a powerful revival followed, and many were converted.

This poor man lingered in this way for several years, and died. After his death, I visited the place, and his widow put his diary into my hands. Among other entries was this, "I am acquainted with about thirty ministers and churches." He then went on to set apart certain hours in the day and week to pray for each of these ministers and churches, and also certain seasons for praying for different missionary stations. Then followed, under different dates, such facts as these, "Today I have been enabled to offer what I call the prayer of faith for the outpouring of the Spirit on church A, and I trust in God that there will soon be a revival there." Under another date he had written, "I have today been able to offer what I call the prayer of faith for church B, and trust that there will soon be a revival there." Thus he had gone over a great number of churches, recording the fact that he had prayed for them in faith that a revival might soon prevail among them.

Of the missionary stations, if I remember right, he mentioned in particular one at Ceylon. I believe the last place mentioned in his diary, for which he offered the prayer of faith, was the place in which he lived. Not long after, the revival commenced, and spread over the region of country, nearly, I believe, if not quite, in the order in which the places had been mentioned in his diary. In due time news came from Ceylon that there was a revival of religion there. The revival in his own town did not begin until after his death. His wife told me that he was so exercised in prayer during his sickness, that she often feared he would "pray himself to death." The revival was exceedingly powerful in the whole region, and the fact that it was about to prevail had not been hidden from this servant of the Lord. According to his Word, "the secret of the LORD is with those who fear him" (Psalm 25:14*). Thus, this man, too feeble to go out of his house, was yet more useful to the world and the church of God than all the heartless professing believers in the country. Standing between God and the desolations of Zion, and pouring out his heart in believing prayer, he had "struggled with God and with men, and had prevailed" (Genesis 32:28*).

IX. THE CONSEQUENCES OF NOT BEING FILLED WITH THE SPIRIT

1. You will often doubt, and reasonably so, whether you are a Christian. You will have doubts, and you should have them, because the children of God are led by the Spirit of God. If you are not led by the Spirit, what reason do you have to think that you are a child of God? You will try to make a little evidence go a long way to increase your hopes. But you cannot do it, unless your conscience is seared, like with a hot iron. You cannot help being often plunged into painful doubt about your state (Romans 8:9, 2 Corinthians 13:5).

2. You will always be unsettled in your views about the prayer of faith. The prayer of faith is something so spiritual, so much a matter of ex-

perience and not of speculation, that unless you are spiritual you will not understand it fully. You may talk a great deal about the prayer of faith, and for a while become thoroughly convinced about it. But you will never feel settled enough on it to keep the same attitude about it, and in a little while you will be completely uncertain again. I know of a remarkable example in a fellow minister. He told me, "When I have the Spirit of God and enjoy his presence, I believe firmly in the prayer of faith. But when I do not have him, I find myself doubting whether there is any such thing, and my mind is full of objections." I know, from my own experience, what this is, and when I hear people objecting to the view of prayer that I have presented in these lectures, I understand very well what their difficulty is. I have often found it impossible to satisfy their minds, while they are so far from God, when at the same time, they would understand it themselves without argument with some personal experience.

3. If you do not have the Spirit, you will be very likely to stumble by seeing those who have him. You will doubt the propriety of their conduct. If they seem to be motivated much more than yourself, you will be likely to call it "animal feeling." You will perhaps doubt their sincerity when they say they have such feelings. You will say, "I don't know what to make of this brother. He seems to be very pious, but I do not understand him — I think he has a great deal of animal feeling." Thus you will be trying to criticize them, for the purpose of justifying yourself.

4. You will have a good reputation with the impenitent and with carnal professing believers. They will praise you, as "a rational, orthodox, consistent Christian." You will have just the mindset to walk with them, because you are agreed.

5. You will be much troubled with fears about fanaticism. Whenever there are revivals, you will see in them "a strong tendency to fanaticism," and will be full of fears and anxiety.

6. You will be a cause for shame to Christianity. The impenitent will sometimes praise you because you are so much like them, and sometimes laugh about you because you are such a hypocrite.

7. You will know only little about the Bible.

8. If you die without the Spirit, you will fall into hell. There can be no doubt about this. Without the Spirit you will never be prepared for heaven.

REMARKS

1. Christians are as guilty for not having the Spirit as sinners are for not repenting. In fact, they are even more guilty. As they have more light, they are even more guilty.

2. All beings have a right to complain of Christians who do not have the Spirit. You are not doing work for God, and the Lord has a right to complain. He has placed his Spirit at your disposal, and if you do not have the Spirit, God has a right to hold you responsible for all the good you might otherwise do. You are sinning against heaven, because you should be adding to the happy ranks of the redeemed. Sinners, the church, and ministers, all have a right to complain.

3. You are an obstacle to the work of the Lord. It is in vain for a minister to try to work in spite of you. Ministers often groan and struggle and wear themselves out in vain, trying to do good where there are people who live so that they do not have the Spirit of God. If the Spirit is poured out, the church will immediately grieve him away. Thus, you may tie the hands and break the heart of your minister, wear him down, and perhaps kill him, because you will not be filled with the Spirit.

4. Do not tempt God by "waiting" for his Spirit, while using no means to obtain his presence.

5. If you intend to have the Spirit, you must be childlike, and yield to his influences — being just as easily moved as air. If he is drawing you to prayer, you must quit everything to yield to his gentle efforts. No doubt you have sometimes felt a desire to pray for some object, and you have put it off and resisted, until God left you. If you wish him to remain, you must yield to his softest leadings, watch to learn what he would have you do and yield yourself to his guidance.

6. Christians should be willing to make any sacrifice to enjoy the presence of the Spirit. A woman in high society who was a professing Christian said, "I must either give up hearing this minister preach, or I must give up my merry company." She gave up the preaching and stayed away. How different from another case — that of a woman in the same social standing — who heard the same minister preach, and went home resolved to abandon her merry and worldly manner of life. She changed her whole manner of dress, of accessories, of living, and of conversation. Her merry and worldly friends were soon willing to leave her to the enjoyment of communion with God and free to spend her time in doing good.

7. You see from this, that it must be very difficult for those in fashionable life to go to heaven. What a calamity to be in such circles! Who

can enjoy the presence of God in them? See how crazy those are who are scrambling to get up to these social circles, expanding their houses, changing their style of living, their dress, and their furniture. It is like climbing up to the masthead to be thrown off into the ocean. To enjoy God, you must come down, not go up there. God is not there, among all the starch and flattery of high life.

8. Many professing Christians are as ignorant of spirituality as Nicodemus was of the New Birth. They are ignorant, and I fear unconverted. If anyone talks to them about the spirit of prayer, it is all algebra to them. The case of these professing believers is awful. How different was the character of the apostles! Read the history of their lives, read their letters, and you will see that they were always spiritual and walked daily with God. But now how little is there of such religion! "When the Son of Man comes, will he find faith on earth?" (Luke 18:8) Put some of these professing believers to work in a revival, and they do not know what to do, for they have no energy, no skills and make no impression. When will professing Christians set themselves to work, filled with the Spirit? If I could see this church filled with the Spirit, I would ask nothing more to influence the many minds around us. Not two weeks would pass before the revival would spread all over this city.

9. Why do you suppose that so little stress is laid on the influences of the Spirit in prayer, when so much is said about his influences in conversion? Many people are amazingly afraid the Spirit's influences will be left out. They lay great stress on the Spirit's influences in converting sinners. But how little is said, how little is printed, about his influence in prayer! How little complaining there is that people do not make enough of the Spirit's influence in leading Christians to pray according to the will of God! Let it never be forgotten that no Christian ever prays correctly, unless led by the Spirit.

10. I have dwelt more on this subject, because I want to have it made so plain that you will be careful not to grieve the Spirit. I want you to have high ideas of the Holy Spirit, and to feel that nothing good will be done without his influences. No praying or preaching will be of any use without him. If Jesus Christ were to come down here and preach to sinners, not one would be converted without the Spirit. Be careful, then, not to grieve him away, by slighting or neglecting his heavenly influences when he invites you to pray.

11. In praying for an object, it is necessary to persevere until you obtain it. Oh, with what eagerness Christians sometimes pursue a sinner in their prayers, when the Spirit of God has fixed their desires on him! No

miser pursues gold with so fixed a determination.

12. The fear of being led by impulses has done great injury, by not being properly considered. A person's mind may be led by an *ignis fatuus*[4]. But we do wrong if we let the fear of impulses lead us to resist the good impulses of the Holy Spirit. No wonder Christians do not have the spirit of prayer, if they are unwilling to take the trouble to distinguish, but will reject or resist all leadings of invisible agents. A great deal has recklessly been spoken on the subject of fanaticism, and that causes many minds to reject the leadings of the Spirit of God. "For all who are led by the Spirit of God are sons of God" (Romans 8:14). And it is our duty to "test the spirits to see whether they are from God" (1 John 4:1). We should insist on a close scrutiny, and an accurate discrimination. There must be such a thing as being led by the Spirit. And when we are convinced it is of God, we should be sure to follow on, with full confidence that he will not lead us wrong.

13. We see from this subject the absurdity of using set forms of prayer. The very idea of using a form rejects, of course, the leadings of the Spirit. Nothing more destroys the spirit of prayer, and entirely confuses the mind as to what prayer is, than to use forms. Forms of prayer are not only absurd in themselves, but they are the very device of the devil to destroy the spirit and break the power of prayer. It is of no use to say the form is a good one. Prayer does not consist in words. And it does not matter what the words are if the heart is not led by the Spirit of God. If the desire is not kindled, the thoughts directed, and the whole current of feeling produced and led by the Spirit of God, it is not prayer. And set forms are best designed to keep an individual from correctly praying.

14. The subject provides a test of character. "The Spirit intercedes," for whom? For the saints. If you are truly a saint, you know by experience what it is to be moved in this way. If you do not, it is because you have grieved the Spirit of God so that he will not lead you. You live in such a manner that this Holy Comforter will not dwell with you, nor give you the spirit of prayer. If this is so, you must repent. Do not stop to settle whether you are a Christian or not, but repent, as if you never had repented. I do not assume that you are a Christian. So go, like a humble sinner, and pour out your heart to the Lord. You never can have the spirit of prayer in any other way.

15. If people do not know the spirit of prayer, they are very likely to

---

[4] Literally, a "foolish fire." A term given to mysterious lights that trick travelers at night.

be unbelieving in regard to the results of prayer. They do not see what takes place, or do not see the connection, or do not see the evidence. They are not expecting spiritual blessings. When sinners are convicted, they conclude that such are merely frightened by terrible preaching. And when people are converted, they feel no confidence, saying, "We will see how they turn out."

16. Those who have the spirit of prayer know when the blessing comes. It was this way when Jesus Christ appeared. Those ungodly religious scholars did not know him. Why? Because they were not praying for the redemption of Israel. But Simeon and Anna knew him. Why? Take note of what they said, how they prayed, and how they lived. They were praying in faith, and so they were not surprised when Jesus came (Luke 2:25-38). So it is with the Christians of whom I speak. If sinners are convicted or converted, they are not surprised. They are expecting just such things. They know God when he comes, because they are looking out for his visits.

17. There are three classes of people in the church who are prone to error, or have left the truth out of view, on this subject.

(a) Those who place great reliance on prayer, and use no other means. They are alarmed at any special means, and talk about your "working up a revival."

(b) More than these are those who use means, and pray, but never think about the influences of the Spirit in prayer. They talk about prayer for the Spirit, and feel the importance of the Spirit in the conversion to sinners, but do not realize the importance of the Spirit in prayer. And their prayers are all cold talk, nothing that anybody can feel, or that can take hold of God.

(c) Those who have certain strange notions about the Sovereignty of God, and are waiting for God to convert the world without prayer or means.

There must be in the church a deeper sense of the need of the spirit of prayer. The fact is that generally, those who use means most diligently, and make the most strenuous efforts for the salvation of people, and who have the most correct notions of how means should be used for converting sinners, also pray most for the Spirit of God, and wrestle most with God for his blessing. And what is the result? Let facts speak, and say whether these people do or do not pray, and whether the Spirit of God does not testify to their prayers, and follow their labors with his power.

18. Nothing will produce an excitement and opposition so quickly as the spirit of prayer. If any person should feel burdened with the case of sinners and groan in his prayer, some become nervous, and he is visited at once with rebuke and opposition! From my soul I hate all pretense of feeling where none exists, and all attempts to work one's self up into feeling by groans. But I feel obligated to defend the position, that there is such a thing as being in a state of mind in which there is only one way to keep from groaning, and that is by resisting the Holy Spirit. I was once present where this subject was discussed. It was said that, "groaning should be frowned upon." The question was asked in reply whether God could produce such a state of feeling. Then abstaining from groaning would be impossible. The answer was, "Yes, but he never does." Then the apostle Paul was greatly deceived when he wrote about groanings too deep for words. Edwards was deceived when he wrote his book about revivals. Revivals are all in error. Now, no one who reviews the history of the church will adopt such a sentiment. I do not like this attempt to shut out, stifle, or limit the spirit of prayer. I would sooner cut off my right hand than rebuke the spirit of prayer, as I have heard of its being done by saying, "Do not let me hear any more groaning!"

I hardly know where to end this subject. I should like to discuss it a month, indeed, until the whole church could understand it, so as to pray the prayer of faith. Beloved, I want to ask you, do you believe all this? Or do you wonder how I should talk this way? Perhaps some of you have had some glimpses of these things. Now, will you give yourselves up to prayer, and live so as to have the spirit of prayer, and have the Spirit with you all the time? Oh, for a praying church! I once knew a minister who had a revival fourteen winters in succession. I did not know how to account for it, until I saw one of his members get up in a prayer meeting and make a confession. He said, "Brethren, I have been long in the habit of praying every Saturday night until after midnight, for the descent of the Holy Spirit among us. And now, brethren," and he began to weep, "I confess that I have neglected it for two or three weeks." The secret was out. That minister had a praying church. Brethren, in my present state of health, I find it impossible to pray as much as I have been in the habit of doing, and yet continue to preach. It overcomes my strength. Now, shall I only pray, and stop preaching? That will not do. Now, will you not, who are in health, throw yourselves into this work, bear this burden, and give yourselves to prayer, until God shall pour out his blessing upon us?

Chapter 8

MEETINGS FOR PRAYER

"Again I say to you, if two of you agree on earth about anything they ask, it will be done for them by my Father in heaven." (Matthew 18:19)

Thus far, in treating of the subject of prayer, I have limited my remarks to secret prayer. I am now to speak of social prayer, or prayer offered in company, where two or more are united in praying. Such meetings have been common since the time of Christ, and it is probable that God's people have always been in the habit of making united supplication, whenever they have had the privilege. The propriety of the practice will not be questioned here. I do not need to dwell now on the duty of social prayer. Nor is it my intent to discuss the question, whether any two Christians agreeing to ask any blessing, will be sure to obtain it. My object is to make some remarks on meetings for prayer, noting:

I. The purposes of prayer meetings.

II. The manner of conducting them.

III. Several things that will defeat the purpose of holding them.

I. THE PURPOSES OF PRAYER MEETINGS

1. One purpose of gathering several persons together for united prayer is to promote union among Christians. Nothing tends more to cement the hearts of Christians than praying together. Never do they love one another so much as when they witness the outpouring of each other's hearts in prayer. Their spirituality creates a feeling of union and confidence, very important to the prosperity of the church. It is doubtful whether Christians can ever be divided, if they are in the habit of really

praying together. Hard feelings and differences among themselves are eliminated by uniting in prayer. The great goal is gained, if you can bring them really to unite in prayer. If this can be done, the difficultie vanish.

2. To extend the spirit of prayer. God has so made us, and such is the economy of his grace, that we are sympathetic beings, and communi cate our feelings to one another. A minister, for instance, will often breathe his own feelings into his congregation. The Spirit of God that inspires his soul makes use of his feelings to influence his hearers, jus as much as the Spirit makes use of the words he preaches. So God makes use of the feelings of Christians. Nothing is more deliberate to create a spirit of prayer than to unite in social prayer with one who has the spirit himself, unless this one should be so far ahead that his prayer will repel the rest. His prayer will awaken them, if they are no so far behind as to revolt at it and resist it. If they are anywhere near the standard of his feelings, his spirit will kindle, and burn, and spread all around. One individual who obtains the spirit of prayer will often stir a whole church, and extend the same spirit through the whole, so that a general revival follows.

3. Another grand purpose of social prayer is to move God. Not that it changes the mind and feelings of God. When we speak of "moving" God, as I have said in a former lecture, we do not mean that prayer changes the will of God. But when Christians offer the right kind of prayer, they are in such a state of mind that it becomes proper for God to grant a blessing. They are then prepared to receive it, and he gives because he is always the same, and always ready and happy to show mercy. When Christians are united, and praying as they should, God opens the windows of heaven, and pours out his blessing until there is not room to receive it (Malachi 3:10).[1]

---

[1] "When God has something very great to accomplish for his church," says Jonathan Edwards, "it is his will that there should precede it, the extraordinary prayers of his people, as is clear by Ezekiel 36:37 taken with the context. And it is revealed that when God is about to accomplish great things for his church, he will begin by remarkably pouring out the spirit of grace and supplication (Zechariah 12:10). If we are not to expect that the devil should go out of a particular person that is under demon possession without extraordinary prayer, or prayer and fasting, how much less should we expect to have him cast out of the land and the world without it! I should think the people of God in this land would be in the way of their duty to do three times as much fasting and prayer as they do" (*Thoughts on the Revival*, Part 5). As previously mentioned, Finney was very influenced by the writings of Edwards. He read them in the house of Dr. Aiken of Utica, who said that Finney "often spoke of them with rapture." (This footnote taken from the original notes provided by the Fleming Revell Company.)

4. Another important purpose of prayer meetings is the conviction and conversion of sinners. When properly conducted, they are eminently suited to produce this effect. Sinners are likely to be solemn when they hear Christians pray. Where there is a spirit of prayer, sinners will be affected. An ungodly man, a universalist, once said about a certain minister, "I can handle his preaching very well, but when he prays, I feel filled with awe — as if God were coming down upon me." Sinners are often convicted by hearing prayer. A young man of distinguished talents said about a certain minister to whom, before his conversion, he had been very much opposed, "As soon as he began to pray, I began to be convicted. If he had continued to pray much longer, I should not have been able to hold myself back from Christ." Just as soon as Christians begin to pray as they should, sinners then know that Christians do pray, and begin to feel awe. They do not understand what spirituality is, because they have no experience of it. But when such prayer is offered, they know there is something in it. They know God is in it, and it brings them near to God. It makes them feel reverently solemn, and they cannot bear it. And not only is it suited to impress the minds of sinners, but when Christians pray in faith, the Spirit of God is poured out and sinners are melted down and converted on the spot.

II. THE MANNER OF CONDUCTING PRAYER MEETINGS

1. It is often good to open a prayer meeting by reading a short portion of the Word of God, especially if the person leading the meeting can call to mind any portion that will be applicable to the object or occasion, and that is moving and to the point. If the person has no passage that is applicable, it is better not read any at all. Do not drag in the Word of God to make up part of the meeting as a mere matter of form. This is an insult to God. It is not good to read any more than is applicable to the subject before the meeting or the occasion. Some people think it is always necessary to read a whole chapter, though it may be very long and have a variety of subjects. It is just as wise to read a whole chapter as it would be for a minister to take a whole chapter for his text, when his goal was to make some particular truth bear on the minds of his audience. The purpose of a prayer meeting should be to bring Christians to the point, to pray for a definite object. Wandering over a large field hinders and destroys this goal.

2. It is proper that the person who leads should make some short and appropriate remarks, calculated to explain the nature of prayer, and the encouragements we have to pray, and to bring the object to be prayed for directly before the minds of the people.

A person can no more pray without having his thoughts concentrated than he can do anything else. The person leading should therefore see to this, by bringing up before their minds the object for which they came to pray. If they came to pray for any object, he can do this. And if they did not, they had better go home. It is of no use to stay there and mock God by pretending to pray when they have nothing on earth to pray for.

After stating the object, the leader should bring up some promise or some principle, as the ground of encouragement to expect an answer to their prayers. If there is any indication of Providence, or any promise, or any principle in the Divine government, that provides a ground of faith, let him call it to mind, and not let them be talking out of their own hearts at random, without knowing any solid reason for expecting an answer. One reason why prayer meetings generally accomplish so little is because there is so little common sense used in them. Instead of looking around for some solid footing on which to rest their faith, people come together and pour forth words, and neither know nor care whether they have any reason to expect an answer. If they are going to pray about anything concerning which there can be any doubt or any mistake, in regard to the ground of faith, they should be shown the reason there is for believing that their prayers will be heard and answered. It is easy to see that, unless something like this is done, three-fourths of them will have no idea of what they are doing, or of the ground on which they should expect to receive what they pray for.

3. In calling on persons to pray it is always desirable to let things take their own course, wherever it is safe. If it can be left so with safety, let those pray who are most inclined to pray. It sometimes happens that even those who are ordinarily the most spiritual, and most proper to be called on, are not at the time in a suitable frame of mind. They may be cold and worldly, and only freeze the meeting. But if you let those pray who desire to pray, you avoid this. But often this cannot be done with safety, especially in large cities, where a prayer meeting might be liable to be interrupted by those who have no business to pray — some fanatic or crazy person, some hypocrite or enemy, who would only make a noise. In most places, however, the course may be taken with perfect safety. Give up the meeting to the Spirit of God. Those who desire to pray, let them pray. If the leader sees anything that needs to be set right, let him remark, freely and kindly, and put it right, and then go on again. Only he should be careful to time his remarks, so as not to interrupt the flow of feeling, or to chill the meeting, or to turn the thoughts of the people from the proper subject.

4. If it is necessary to name the individuals who are to pray, it is best

to call first on those who are most spiritual. If you do not know who they are, then choose those whom you would naturally suppose to be most "alive." If they pray at the outset, they will be likely to spread the spirit of prayer through the meeting, and elevate the tone of the whole. Otherwise, if you call on those who are cold and lifeless, they will be likely to diffuse a chill. The only hope of having a productive prayer meeting is when at least a part of the church is spiritual, and infuses its spirit into the rest. This is the very reason why it is often best to let things take their course, for then those who have the most feeling are likely to pray first, and give character to the meeting.

5. The prayers should always be very short. When individuals pray a long time they forget that they are only the mouth of the congregation, and that the congregation cannot be expected to feel united in prayer, if they are long and tedious, and go all around the world, and pray for everything they can think of. Commonly, those who pray a long time in a meeting do so, not because they have the spirit of prayer, but because they have not. Some people will spin out a long prayer in telling God who and what he is, or they pray out a whole system of divinity. Some preach, others exhort the people — until everyone wishes they would stop, and God certainly also wishes this. They should keep to the point, and pray for what they came to pray for, and not follow the imagination of their own foolish hearts all over the universe.

6. Each one should pray for one object. It is good for every individual to have one object for prayer. Two or more may pray for the same thing, or each for a separate object. If the meeting is convened to pray for some specific thing, let them all pray for that. If its object is more general, let them select their subjects, according to their interests. If one feels particularly inclined to pray for the church, let him do it. If the next person feels inclined to pray for the church, he may do so too. Perhaps the next will feel inclined to pray for sinners. Let him do it, and as soon as he has finished let him stop. Whenever a person has deep feeling, he always feels on some particular point, and if he prays about that, he will speak out of the abundance of his heart, and then he will naturally stop when he is done.

7. If, in the course of the meeting, it becomes necessary to change the object of prayer, let the leader state the fact, and explain it in a few words. If the object is to pray for the church, or for backsliders, or sinners, or the lost, let him state it plainly, and then present it before them, until he brings them to think and feel deeply before they pray. Then he should state the grounds on which they may rest their faith to obtain the blessings for which they pray, if any such statement is

needed, and thus lead them right up to the throne and let them take hold of the hand of God. This is according to the nature of the mind. People always do it for themselves when they pray in secret, if they really mean to pray to any purpose. And so it should be in prayer meetings.

8. It is important that the time should be fully occupied, so as not to leave long periods of silence, which make a bad impression and chill the meeting. I know that sometimes churches have seasons of silent prayer. But in those cases they should be specially requested to pray in silence, so that everyone knows why they are silent. This often has a very powerful effect, where the whole congregation spends a few moments in silence, while all lift up their thoughts to God. This is very different from having long intervals of silence because there is no one to pray. Every one feels that such a silence is like the cold damp of death over the meeting.

9. It is exceedingly important that the meeting leader should press sinners who may be present to immediate repentance. The leader should earnestly urge the Christians who are present, to pray in such a way as to make sinners feel that they are expected to repent immediately. This tends to inspire Christians with compassion and love for souls. The remarks made to sinners are often like pouring fire upon the hearts of Christians, to awaken them to prayer and effort for the conversion of the unsaved. Let them see and feel the guilt and danger of sinners among them, and then they will pray.

III. THINGS THAT MAY DEFEAT THE PRAYER MEETING

1. When there is an unhappy lack of confidence in the leader, there is no hope of any good. Whatever may be the cause, whether he is to blame or not, the very fact that he leads the meeting will dampen it, and prevent all good. I have seen it in churches, where there was some offensive elder or deacon (perhaps correctly deemed offensive, perhaps not) set to lead, and the meeting would die under his influence. If there is a lack of confidence in regard to his piety, or in his ability, or in his judgment, or in anything connected with the meeting, everything he says or does will fall to the ground. The same thing often takes place where the church has lost confidence in the minister.

2. Where the leader lacks spirituality, there will be a dryness and coldness in his remarks and prayers. Everything will indicate his lack of anointing, and his whole influence will be the very opposite of what it should be. I have known churches where a prayer meeting could not be sustained, and the reason was not obvious, but those who under-

tood the state of things knew that the leader was so notorious for his lack of spirituality that he would inevitably freeze a prayer meeting to death. In many churches the elders are so far from being spiritual men that they always freeze a prayer meeting. And at the same time they are often amazingly jealous for their dignity, and cannot bear to have anybody else lead the meeting. If any member that is spiritual takes the lead, they will confront him, saying, "Why, you are not an elder. You should not lead a prayer meeting in the presence of an elder!" And thus they stand in the way, while the whole church is suffering under their ruinous influence.

A person who knows he is not in a spiritual frame of mind has no business to conduct a prayer meeting — he will kill it. There are two reasons. First, he will have no spiritual discernment, and will know neither what to do, nor when to do it. A person who is spiritual can see the movements of Providence, and can feel the Spirit of God, and understand what he is leading them to pray for, so as to time his goals, and take advantage of the state of feeling among Christians. He will not overthrow all the feeling in a meeting by introducing things that are out of place or ill-timed. He has spiritual discernment to understand the leadings of the Spirit, and his workings on those who pray. Suppose an individual leads who is not spiritual, that there are two or three prayers, and the spirit of prayer arises, but the leader, having no spiritual discernment to see it, makes some remarks on another point, or reads a piece out of some book that is as far from the feeling of the meeting as the North Pole! What they are called to pray for may be just as evident to the praying people present as if the Son of God himself had come into the meeting and named the goal. But the leader will overthrow it all, because he is so obtuse that he does not understand the directions of the meeting.

And then, if the leader is not spiritual, he will very likely be dull and dry in his remarks, and in all his efforts. He will give out a long hymn in a dreamy manner, and then read a long passage of Scripture, in a tone so cold that he will spread a wintry atmosphere over the meeting, and it will be dull, as long as his cold heart is placed in front of the whole thing.

3. A lack of suitable talents in the leader. If he is lacking in the talents that make a meeting useful, if he can say nothing, or if his remarks are so random as to produce levity or contempt, or if they have nothing in them that will impress the mind, or are not guided by good sense, or are not appropriate, he will injure the meeting. A person may be pious, but so weak that his prayers do not edify, but rather disgust. When this

is so, he had better keep silent.

4. Sometimes the benefit of a prayer meeting is defeated by a bad spiri in the leader. For instance, where there is a revival with great opposi tion, if a leader gets up in a prayer meeting and talks about example of opposition, thus diverting the meeting away from the goal, he doe not know whose side he is on. Its effect is always ruinous to a praye meeting. Let a minister in a revival come out and preach against the op position, and he will inevitably destroy the revival, and turn the heart of Christians away from their proper object. Let the person who is se to lead the church be careful to guard his own spirit, lest he should mis lead the church, and spread a wrong attitude. The same will be true if anyone who is called upon to speak or pray, introduces in his re marks or prayers anything controversial, unreasonable, unscriptural ridiculous, or irrelevant. Any of these things will quench the tende breathings of the spirit of prayer, and destroy the meeting.

5. Persons coming late to the meeting. This is a very great hindrance When people have begun to pray, and their attention is fixed, and they have shut their eyes and closed their ears, to keep out everything from their minds, in the midst of a prayer somebody will come bolting ir and walk through the room. Some will look up, and all have thei minds interrupted for the moment. Then they all get fixed again, and another comes in, and so on. I suppose the devil would not care how many Christians went to a prayer meeting, if they would only go after the meeting had begun. He would be glad to have ever so many go "scattering along" in such a way, dodging in very piously and distract ingly.

6. When people make cold prayers and cold confessions of sin, they are sure to quench the spirit of prayer. When the influences of the Spirit are enjoyed, in the midst of the warm expressions that are flowing forth, let an individual come in who is cold, and pour out his cold breath like the damp of death, and it will make every Christian who has any feeling want to get out of the meeting.

7. In some places it is common to begin a prayer meeting by reading a long portion of Scripture. Then the deacon or elder gives out a long hymn. Next, they sing it. Then he prays a long prayer, praying for the Jews, and the fullness of the Gentiles, and many other objects that have nothing to do with the occasion of the meeting. After that perhaps he reads a long extract from some book or magazine. Then they have another long hymn and another long prayer, and then they go home.

I once heard an elder say that a church had kept up a prayer meeting so many years, and yet had experienced no revival. The truth was, that the officers of the church had been accustomed to carry on the meetings in just such a dignified way, and their dignity would not allow anything to be changed. No wonder there was no revival! Such prayer meetings are enough to hinder a revival. And if ever revivals should begin, the prayer meeting would destroy them. There was a prayer meeting once in this city, as I have been told, where there appeared to be some feeling, and someone very reasonably proposed that they should have two or three prayers in succession, without rising from their knees. One dignified man present opposed it, and said that they never had done this, and he hoped there would be no innovations! He did not approve of innovations. That was the end of the revival! Such people have their prayer meetings stereotyped, and are determined not to change their habit, whether they receive blessing or not. To allow any such thing would be "a new measure," and they never like new measures!

8. A great deal of singing often hurts a prayer meeting. The agonizing spirit of prayer does not lead people to sing. There is a time for everything: a time to sing, and a time to pray. But if I know what it is to travail in birth for souls, Christians never feel less like singing than when they have the spirit of prayer for sinners.

When singing is introduced in a prayer meeting, the hymns should be short, and so selected as to bring out something solemn. It should have some striking words, such as the Judgment Hymn, or others intended to produce an effect on sinners. It should produce a deep impression on the minds of Christians, but not that joyful kind of singing that makes everybody feel comfortable, and turns off the mind from the object of the prayer meeting.

I once heard a celebrated organist produce a remarkable effect in an extended meeting. The organ was powerful, and the double bass pipes were thunderous. The hymn was given out that had these lines:

> See the storm of vengeance gathering
> over the path you dare to tread;
> Hear the awful thunder rolling,
> Loud and louder o'er your head.

When he came to these words, we first heard the distant roar of thunder, then it grew nearer and louder, until at the word "louder," there was a crash that seemed almost to overpower the congregation. Such things in their proper place do good. But common singing dissipates feeling. It should always not take away feeling, but deepen it.

Often a prayer meeting is hurt by calling on the young converts to sing joyful hymns. This is highly improper in a prayer meeting. It is no time for them to let feeling flow away in joyful singing, while so many sinners around them, and their own former companions, are going down to hell. A revival is often put down by the church and the minister giving themselves up to singing with young converts. Thus, by stopping to rejoice when they should feel more and more deeply for sinners, they grieve away the Spirit of God, and they soon find that their agony and travail of soul are gone.

9. Introducing subjects of controversy into prayer will defeat a prayer meeting. Nothing of a controversial nature should be introduced into prayer, unless it is the object of the meeting to settle that thing. Otherwise, let Christians come together in their prayer meetings, on the broad ground of offering united prayer for a common object. And let controversies be settled somewhere else.

10. If individuals refuse to pray when they are called to, it injures a prayer meeting. Some say they cannot pray in their families. They have no excuse. God will take none. They have tongues to talk to their neighbors, and can talk to God if they have any heart for it. God says he will pour out his fury on the families that do not call on his name. I could mention many facts to show that God curses those who refuse to pray when they should. Until professing Christians repent of this sin, and take up this cross (if they choose to call praying "a cross"), they should not expect a blessing.

11. Prayer meetings are often too long. They should always be dismissed while Christians have feeling, and not be spun out until all feeling is exhausted, and the spirit of prayer is gone.

12. Heartless confessions injure a meeting. People confess their sins but do not forsake them. Every week they will make the same confession. Why, they have no intention to forsake their sins! It shows plainly that they do not mean to reform. All their religion consists in these confessions. Instead of getting a blessing from God they will get only a curse.

13. Harm is also done when Christians spend all the time in praying for themselves. They should have done this in their own homes. When they come to a prayer meeting, they should be prepared to offer effective intercessions for others. If Christians pray at home as they should, they will feel like praying for sinners. If, however, their private prayers

are exclusively for themselves, they will not get the spirit of prayer. I have known people to be alone for days to pray for themselves, and never get any energy because their prayers were all selfish. But if such people will just forget themselves, and move their hearts outward and pray for others, it will wake up such a feeling that they will be able to pour forth their hearts in prayer. And then they can go to work for souls.

14. A lack of union in prayer damages the meeting. When one leads, the others do not follow, because they are thinking of something else. Their hearts do not unite and say, "Amen." It is as bad as if one person should make a petition and another object against it. It is as though one asks God to do something, and the others ask him not to do it, or to do something else.

15. Neglect of secret prayer is yet another hindrance. Christians who do not pray in secret cannot unite with power in a prayer meeting, and cannot have the spirit of prayer.

REMARKS

1. A badly conducted prayer meeting often does more hurt than good. In many churches, the general manner of conducting prayer meetings is such that Christians do not have the least idea of the purpose or the power of such meetings. It is such as tends to keep down rather than to promote pious feeling and the spirit of prayer.

2. A prayer meeting is a measurement of the state of religion in a church. If the prayer meeting is neglected, or the spirit of prayer is not manifested, you know of course that religion is in a low condition. Let me go into the prayer meeting, and I can always see the state of religion that prevails in the church.

3. Every minister should know that if the prayer meetings are neglected, all his labors are in vain. Unless he can get Christians to attend the prayer meetings, all else that he can do will not improve the state of religion.

4. A great responsibility rests on the one who leads a prayer meeting. If the meeting is not what it should be, if it does not elevate the state of religion, the person should go seriously to work and see what is wrong, and get the spirit of prayer, and prepare to make remarks designed to do good and set things right. A leader has no business to lead prayer meetings if not prepared, both in head and heart, to do this.

5. Prayer meetings are the most difficult meetings to sustain — as indeed they ought to be. They are so spiritual that unless the leader is

very prepared, both in heart and mind, they will dwindle. It is in vain for the leader to complain that members of the church do not attend. In nine cases out of ten it is the leader's fault that they do not attend. If he felt as he should, they would find the meeting so interesting that they would naturally attend. If he is so cold, and dull, and lacking in spirituality so as to freeze everything, no wonder people do not come to the meeting. Church officers often complain and scold because people do not come to the prayer meeting, when the truth is they themselves are so cold that they freeze to death everybody who does come.

6. Prayer meetings are most important meetings for the church. It is highly important for Christians to sustain the prayer meetings, in order to (a) promote union, (b) increase brotherly love, (c) cultivate Christian confidence, (d) promote their own growth in grace, and (e) cherish and advance spirituality.

7. Prayer meetings should be numerous in the church and designed to exercise the gifts of every member — man or woman. Everyone should have the opportunity to pray and express heart feelings. The sectional prayer meetings are designed to do this. And if they are too large to permit it, let them be divided, so as to bring the entire mass into the work, to exercise all gifts, and spread union, confidence, and brotherly love, through the whole.

8. It is important that impenitent sinners should attend prayer meetings. If none come of their own accord, go out and invite them. Christians should take great trouble to persuade their impenitent friends and neighbors to come to prayer meetings. They can pray better for impenitent sinners when they have them right before their eyes. I have known women's prayer meetings to exclude sinners from the meetings. The reason was that they were so proud that they were ashamed to pray before sinners. What a spirit! Such prayers will do no good. They insult God. You have not done enough, by any means, when you have gone to the prayer meeting yourself. You cannot pray if you have invited no sinner to go. If all the members have neglected their duty so, and have gone to the prayer meeting, and taken no sinners along with them, no subjects of prayer — what have they come for?

9. The great goal of all the means of grace is to aim directly at the conversion of sinners. You should pray that they be converted there. Do not pray that they may be merely awakened and convicted, but that they may be converted on the spot. No one should either pray or make any remarks, as if he expected a single sinner would go away without giving his heart to God. You should all make the impression on his mind, that NOW he must submit. And if you do this, while you are yet

peaking, God will hear.

f Christians made it clear that they had really set their hearts on the
onversion of sinners, and were bent upon it, and prayed as they should,
here would rarely be a prayer meeting held without souls being con-
'erted, and sometimes every sinner in the room. That is the very time,
f ever, when sinners should be converted in answer to those prayers.
 do not doubt but that you may have sinners converted in every sec-
ional prayer meeting, if you do your duty. Take them there — take
'our families, your friends, or your neighbors there with that intent.
3ive them the proper instruction, if they need instruction, and pray
or them as you should, and you will save their souls. If you do your
luty in a right manner, rely on the fact that God will not keep back his
)lessing, but the work will be done.

Part III

WITNESSING

Chapter 9

HOW TO TESTIFY TO THE GOSPEL

" 'You are my witnesses,' declares the LORD, *'and my servant whom I have chosen.' " (Isaiah 43:10)*

In the text it is affirmed that the children of God are his witnesses. In several preceding lectures I have been dwelling on the subject of prayer, or on that class of means for the promotion of a revival, which is intended to move God to pour out his Spirit. I am now to commence the other class, dealing with the means to be used for the conviction and conversion of sinners.

It is true, in general, that persons are affected by the subject of religion in proportion to their conviction of its truth. Lack of attention to religion is the main reason why so little is felt concerning it. No being can look at the great truths of religion and not feel deeply concerning them. The devil cannot. He believes and trembles. Angels in heaven feel, in view of these things. God feels! An intellectual conviction of truth is always accompanied with feeling of some kind.

One grand purpose God has in leaving Christians in the world after their conversion is that they may be witnesses for God. They are to call the attention of thoughtless people to the subject, and make them see the difference in the character and destiny of those who believe the gospel and those who reject it. This lack of attention is the main challenge in promoting religion. And what the Spirit of God does is to awaken the attention of people to the subject of their sin and the plan of salvation. Miracles have sometimes been used to arrest the attention of sinners, and in this way miracles may become instrumental in conversion — although conversion is not itself a miracle, nor do miracles themselves ever convert anybody. They may be the means of awakening. Miracles are not always effective even in that. And if continued or made common, they would soon lose their power. What is wanted in the world is something that can be a sort of omnipresent miracle, able not only to arrest attention but also to keep it, and keep the mind in warm contact with the truth, until it yields.

Hence we see why God has scattered his children everywhere, in families and among the nations. He never would want them to be altogether in one place, however agreeable it might be to their feelings. He wishes them scattered. When the church at Jerusalem herded together, neglecting to go forth as Christ had commanded and to spread the gospel all over the world, God let loose a persecution upon them and scattered them abroad, and then they "went everywhere preaching the Word" (Acts 8:4*).

In examining the text, I will ask:

I. On what particular points Christians are to testify for God.

II. The manner in which they are to testify.

I. ON WHAT POINTS ARE CHRISTIANS TO TESTIFY?

Generally, they are to testify to the truth of the Bible. They are competent witnesses to this, for they have experience of its truth. The experienced Christian has no more need of external evidence to prove the truth of the Bible to his mind, than he has to prove his own existence. The whole plan of salvation is so fully spread out and settled in his conviction, that to try to reason him out of his belief in the Bible would be as impossible as to reason him out of the belief in his own existence. People have tried to awaken a doubt of the existence of the physical world, but they cannot succeed. No one can doubt the existence of the physical world. To doubt it is against his own consciousness. You may use arguments that he cannot answer, and may puzzle and perplex him, and shut his mouth. He may be no logician or philosopher, and may not be able to detect your fallacies. But, what he knows, he knows.

So it is in religion. The Christian is conscious that the Bible is true. The mere child in religion knows by his experience the truth of the Bible. A person may hear objections from infidels that he never thought of, and that he cannot answer, and he may be confounded. But he cannot be driven from his ground. He will say, "I cannot answer you, but I

now the Bible is true." It is as if a man should look in a mirror, and
ay, "That is my face." The question is put to him, "How do you know
: is your face?" "Why," he replies, "by its looks." So when a Christian
ees himself described in the Bible, he sees the likeness to be so exact,
hat he knows it is true.

More particularly, Christians are to testify to:[1]

. The immortality of the soul. This is clearly revealed in the Bible.

.. The vanity and unsatisfying nature of all earthly things.

. The satisfying nature and glorious sufficiency of Christianity.

. The guilt and danger of sinners. On this point they can speak from
xperience as well as from the Word of God. They have seen their own
ins, and they understand more of the nature of sin, and the guilt and
langer of sinners.

. The reality of hell, as a place of eternal punishment for the wicked.

. The love of Christ for sinners.

. The necessity of a holy life, if we think of ever getting to heaven.

. The necessity of self-denial, and of living above the world[2].

. The necessity of meekness, heavenly-mindedness, humility, and in-
egrity.

.0. The necessity of an entire renovation of character and life, for all
vho would enter heaven.

These are the subjects on which they are to be witnesses for God. And
hey are obligated to testify in such a way as to constrain people to
believe the truth.

I. HOW ARE CHRISTIANS TO TESTIFY?

By precept and example. On every proper occasion by their lips, but
mainly by their lives. Christians have no right to be silent with their
ips. They should "correct, rebuke and encourage — with great pa-
:ience and careful instruction" (2 Timothy 4:2, NIV). But their main
nfluence as witnesses is by their example.

---

[1] Here Finney lists those aspects of the gospel that can primarily be demonstrated in
action, as explained in the next section. The doctrinal content of the gospel (such as
repentance, faith in Christ, and the atonement) is covered in subsequent chapters.

[2] "Living above the world" is an expression Finney uses to convey living a life radically different from the world. It conveys a life of holiness, and living "unstained
from the world" (James 1:27).

They are required to be witnesses in this way, because example teaches with so much greater force than precept. This is universally known, "Actions speak louder than words." But where both precept and example are brought to bear, the greatest amount of influence is brought to bear upon the mind. As to how they are to testify to the truth of the points specified, they should live in their daily walk and conversation as if they believed the Bible.

1. As if they believed the soul to be immortal, and as if they believed that death was not the end of their existence, but the entrance into an unchanging state. They should live to make this impression upon all around them. It is easy to see that precept without example will do no good. All the arguments in the world will not convince humankind that you really believe this, unless you live as if you believe it. Your reasoning may be unanswerable, but if you do not live accordingly, your practice will defeat your arguments. They will say you are an ingenious philosopher, or a talented debater, and perhaps admit that they cannot answer you. But then they will say, it is evident that your reasoning is all false, and that you know it is all false, because your life contradicts your theory. Or they will say that, if it is true, you do not believe it. And so all the influence of your testimony goes to the other side.

2. Against the vanity and unsatisfying nature of the things of this world. The failure to testify in this is the great stumbling block in the way of humankind. Here the testimony of God's children is needed more than anywhere else. People are so struck with the objects of sense, and so constantly occupied with them, that they are very likely to shut out eternity from their minds. A small object that is held close to the eye may shut out the distant ocean. The things of the world that are near appear so magnified in their minds, so that they overlook everything else. One important purpose in keeping Christians in the world is to practically teach people on this point. But suppose professing Christians teach the vanity of earthly things by precept, and contradict it in practice? Suppose the women are just as fond of dress, and just as particular in observing all the fashions, and the men as eager to have fine houses and transportation, as the people of the world. Who does not see that it would be quite ridiculous for them to testify with their lips, that this world is all vanity, and its joys unsatisfying and empty? People feel the absurdity, and this shuts the lips of Christians. They are ashamed to speak to their neighbors, while they cumber themselves with these trinkets, because their daily conduct testifies, to everybody, the very opposite. How it would look for certain church members, men or women, to go about among the common people, and talk to them

about the vanity of the world! Who would believe what they said?

3. To the satisfying nature of religion. Christians are obligated to show, by their conduct, that they are actually satisfied with the enjoyments of religion, without the pomps and vanities of the world, that the joys of religion and communion with God keep them above the world. They are to show that this world is not their home. Their profession is that heaven is a reality and that they expect to dwell there forever. But suppose they contradict this by their conduct, and live in such a way as to prove that they cannot be happy unless they have a full share of the fashion and show of the world. As for going to heaven, they would much rather remain on earth than die and go there! What does the world think, when it sees a professing Christian just as afraid to die as an infidel? Such Christians commit perjury — they swear to a lie, since their testimony amounts to conveying that there is nothing in religion for which a person can afford to live above the world.

4. Regarding the guilt and danger of sinners. Christians are obligated to warn sinners of their awful condition, and exhort them to flee from the wrath to come, and lay hold of everlasting life. But who does not know that the manner of doing this is everything? Sinners are often struck under conviction by the very manner of doing a thing. There was a man once very much opposed to a certain preacher. On being asked to give some reason, he replied, "I cannot bear to hear him, for he says the word 'HELL' in such a way that it rings in my ears for a long time afterwards." He was displeased with the very thing that made the power of speaking that word. The manner may be such as to convey an idea directly opposite to the meaning of the words. A man may tell you that your house is on fire in such a way as to make directly the opposite impression, and you will take it for granted that it is not your house that is on fire. The watchman might cry out, "Fire! Fire!" in such a way that everybody would think he was either drunk or talking in his sleep.

Go to a sinner, and talk with him about his guilt and danger. If in your manner you make an impression that does not correspond to your words, you in effect bear testimony the other way, and tell him he is in no danger. If the sinner believes at all that he is in danger of hell, it is completely for reasons other than your saying so. If you live in such a way as to show that you do not feel compassion for sinners around you, if you show no tenderness, by your eyes, your features, your voice, if your manner is not solemn and earnest, how can they believe you are sincere?

Woman, suppose you tell your unconverted husband, in an easy, laughing way, "My dear, I believe you are going to hell," will he believe you? If your life is merry and trifling, you show that you either do not believe there is a hell, or that you wish to have him go there, and are trying to avoid every serious impression from his mind. Do you have children that are unconverted? Suppose you never say anything to them about religion, or when you talk to them it is in a cold, hard, dry way, conveying the impression that you have no feeling in the matter. Do you suppose they believe you? They do not see the same coldness in you in regard to other things. They are in the habit of seeing the mother in your eye, and in the tones of your voice, your emphasis, and the like, and feeling the warmth of a mother's heart as it flows out from your lips on all that concerns them. If, then, when you talk to them on the subject of religion, you are cold and trifling, can they suppose that you believe it? If your behavior before your child is this apathetic, heartless, prayerless spirit, and then you talk to him about the importance of religion, the child will go away and laugh, to think you should try to persuade him there is a hell.

5. To the love of Christ. You are to bear witness to the reality of the love of Christ, by the regard you show for his precepts, his honor, his kingdom. You should act as if you believed that he died for the sins of the whole world, and as if you blamed sinners for rejecting his great salvation. This is the only legitimate way in which you can impress sinners with the love of Christ. Christians, instead of this, often live so as to make the impression on sinners that Christ is so compassionate that they have very little to fear from him. I have been amazed to see how a certain class of professing Christians want ministers to be always preaching about the love of Christ. If a minister urges Christians to be holy, and to labor for Christ, they call it "legalistic" preaching. They say they want to hear the gospel. Well, suppose you present the love of Christ. How will they bear testimony in their lives? How will they show that they believe it? Why, by conformity to the world they will testify, point-blank, that they do not believe a word of it. They care nothing at all for the love of Christ, except to have it for a cover-up, that they can talk about it and so conceal their sins. They have no sympathy with his compassion, and no belief in it as a reality, and no concern for the feelings of Christ that fill his mind when he sees the condition of sinners.

6. To the necessity of holiness in order to enter heaven. They must live holy lives.[3] The idea has so long prevailed that we "cannot be perfect here," that many professing Christians do not seriously aim

---

[3] See Hebrews 12:14.

at a sinless life. They cannot honestly say that they even so much as really meant to live without sin. They drift along before the tide, in a loose, sinful, unhappy, and detestable manner, at which, the devil undoubtedly laughs, because it is, of all ways, the surest path to hell.

7. To the necessity of self-denial, humility, and heavenly-mindedness. Christians should show, by their own example, what the religious walk is which is expected of people. That is the most powerful preaching, after all, and the most likely to have influence on the impenitent, which shows them the great difference between themselves and Christians. Many people seem to think they can make people become religious best by bringing religion down to their standard. As if the nearer you bring religion to the world, the more likely the world will be to embrace it. As distant the poles of the earth are apart, all this is as far from the truth about making Christians. But it is always the policy of carnal professing Christians. And they think they are displaying wonderful wisdom and prudence, by taking so much trouble not to scare people at the mighty strictness and holiness of the gospel. They argue that if you show religion to people as requiring such a great change in their manner of life, such new habits, such a separation from their old associates — why, you will drive them all away. This seems plausible at first sight. But it is not true. Let professing Christians live in this lax and easy way, and sinners say, "Why, I do not see but that I am about right, or at least so near right that it is impossible God should send me to hell only for the difference between me and these professing Christians. It is true, they do a little more than I do. They go to the Communion table, and pray in their families, and a few such little things, but these details cannot make any such great difference as between heaven and hell." No, the true way is, to show Christianity and the world in strong contrast, or you can never make sinners feel the necessity of a change. Until the necessity of this fundamental change is embodied and held forth in strong light, by example, how can you make people believe they are going to be sent to hell if they are not wholly transformed in heart and life?

This is not only true in theory, but it has been proved by the history of the world. Now, I was reading a letter from a missionary in the East, who wrote something like, "a missionary must live like nobility, and so recommend his religion to the respect of the natives." He advocated a show of superiority to thus impress them with respect! Is this the way to convert the world? No. You can no more convert the world in this way than by blowing a ram's horn. What did the Jesuits[4] do? They went out among the people in the daily practice of self-denial, teaching, and preaching, and praying, and laboring, mingling with every caste, and bringing their instructions to the capacity of every individual. In that way their religion spread over the vast empire of Japan. I am not saying anything about the religion they taught. I speak only of their following the true policy of missions, in showing by their lives a wide contrast with a worldly spirit. If Christians attempt to accommodate religion to human worldliness, they make the salvation of the world impossible. How can you make people believe that self-denial and separation from the world are necessary, unless you practice them?

8. Again, they are to testify by meekness, humility, and heavenly-mindedness. The people of God should always show a temperament like the Son of God, who, when he was abused, did not abuse in return. If a professor of religion is irritable, ready to resent an injury, to fly into an outburst, and to take the same measures as the world does to get compensation, by going to law and the like — how is he to make people believe there is any reality in a change of heart! He cannot recommend religion while he has such a spirit.

If you are in the habit of resenting hurtful conduct, if you do not bear it meekly, and put the best light on it, you contradict the gospel. Some people always show a bad spirit, quick to put the worst light upon what is done, and to snap back at any little thing. This shows a great lack of that love which "bears all things, believes all things, hopes all things, endures all things" (1 Corinthians 13:7). But if a person always shows meekness under injuries, it will confound opposition. Nothing makes so solemn an impression upon sinners, and bears down with such tremendous weight on their consciences, as seeing a Christian, truly Christ-like, bearing affronts and injuries with the meekness of a lamb. It cuts like a two-edged sword.

I will mention a case to illustrate this. A young man abused a minister to his face, and insulted him in an unprecedented manner. The minister possessed his soul in patience, and spoke mildly in reply, telling him the truth pointedly, but yet in a very kind manner. This only made him angrier, and he went away in a rage, declaring that he was "not going to stay and bear this abuse," as if it were the minister, instead of

---

[4] The Jesuits (the Society of Jesus) were an order founded by Ignatius of Loyola in 1540. They forsook worldly fashion and material wealth, devoting themselves to missionary activity, education, and service to the poor. They were an extremely successful group, who collectively spread their religion all over the world, including South America and Asia.

imself, that had been scolding. The sinner went away, but with the arrows of the Almighty in his heart. In less than half an hour he followed ne minister to his home in intolerable agony, wept, begged forgiveess, broke down before God, and yielded up his heart to Christ. This alm and mild manner was more overwhelming to him than a thouand arguments. Now, if that minister had been thrown off his guard, nd answered harshly, no doubt he would have ruined the soul of that oung man. How many of you have defeated every future effort you nay make with your impenitent friends or neighbors, in some such vay as this? On some occasion you have been so easily angered that our words now fall on deaf ears, and you have laid a stumbling block ver which that sinner will stumble into hell. If you have done it in ny instance, do not sleep until you have done all you can to correct he mischief.

. Finally, they are to testify to the necessity for complete honesty in a Christian. Oh, what a field opens here for remark! It extends to all the reas of life. Christians need to show the strictest regard to integrity in very aspect of business, and in all their interactions with their fellow eople. If every Christian would pay strict regard to honesty, and alvays be conscientious to do exactly right, it would make a powerful mpression on the minds of people as to the reality of religious principle.

A lady was once buying some eggs in a store, and the clerk miscounted nd gave her one more than the number. She saw it at the time, but said nothing, and after she got home it troubled her. Feeling that she had cted wrongly, she went back to the young man and confessed it, and aid the difference. The impression of her conscientious integrity went o his heart like a sword. It was a great sin in her in concealing the niscount, because the temptation was so small. For if she would cheat him out of an egg, it showed that she would cheat him out of his whole tore, if she could do it without being found out. But her prompt and humble confession showed an honest conscience.

I am happy to say, there are some people who conduct their business on this principle of integrity. The wicked hate them for it, railing against them, and shouting in bars that they will never buy goods from these individuals. But then they will go right away and buy from them, because they know they will be honestly dealt with. Suppose that all Christians could be equally trusted: what would be the consequence? Christians would run away with the business of the city. The Christians would soon do the business of the world. Some professing Christians make the argument that if they do not do business upon the common principle, of stating one price and taking another, they cannot compete with people of the world. This is all false — false in logic, false in history. Only make it your invariable rule to do right, and do business upon principle, and you control the market. The ungodly will be obliged to conform to your standard. It is perfectly in the power of Christians to regulate the commerce of the world, if they will only themselves maintain perfect integrity.

Again, if Christians will do the same in politics they will sway the destinies of nations, without involving themselves at all in the evil and corrupting strife of parties. Only let Christians generally determine to not vote for someone who is dishonest, or without pure morals. Only let it be known that Christians are united in this, whatever may be their difference in political sentiments, and no person would run for election who was not of such character. In three years it would be talked about in taverns, and published in newspapers, when any person was a candidate for office, "What a good man he is — how moral — how pious!" and the like. And any political party would no more set up a known Sabbath-breaker, or a gambler, or a profane swearer, or a rum-seller, as their candidate for office, than they would set up the devil himself for President of the United States. The carnal policy of many professing Christians, who undertake to correct politics by such means as wicked people employ, and who are determined to vote with a party, let the candidate be ever so profligate, is all wrong — wrong in principle, contrary to logic and common sense, and ruinous to the best interests of humankind. The dishonesty of the church is cursing the world. I am not going to preach a political sermon, but I want to show you that if you mean to impress people favorably toward your religion by your lives, you must be honest, strictly honest, in business, politics, and everything you do. What do you suppose those ungodly politicians, who know themselves to be playing a dishonest game in carrying an election, think of your religion, when they see you uniting with them? They know you are a hypocrite!

REMARKS

1. It is unreasonable for professing Christians to wonder at the thoughtlessness of sinners. Everything considered, the apathy of sinners is not a surprise. We are affected by testimony, and only by that testimony which is received by our minds. Sinners are so taken up with business, pleasure, and the things of the world, that they will not examine the Bible to find what Christianity is. Their feelings are excited only on worldly subjects, because these only are brought into warm contact with their minds. The things of the world therefore make a strong im-

pression. But there is so little to make an impression on their minds in respect to eternity, and to bring religion home to them, that they do not feel on the subject. If they examined the subject, they would feel. But they do not examine it, nor think upon it, nor care for it. And they never will, unless God's witnesses rise up and testify. But since most professing Christians live testifying to the contrary, how can we expect that sinners will feel rightly upon the subject? Nearly all the influence that comes to their minds tends to make them feel the other way. God has left his cause here before the human race, and left his witnesses to testify in his behalf. Behold, they turn around and testify to the contrary! Is it any wonder that sinners are apathetic?

2. We see why it is that preaching does so little good, and how it is that so many sinners get hardened to the gospel. Sinners that live under the gospel are often supposed to be hardened, but only let the church wake up and act consistently, and they will feel. If the church were to live one week as if they believed the Bible, sinners would melt down before them. Suppose I were a lawyer, and should go into court and explain my client's case. I make my statements, say what I expect to prove, and then call my witnesses. The first witness takes his oath, and then rises up and contradicts me to my face. What good will all my pleading do? I might address the jury for a month, and be as eloquent as Cicero, but so long as my witnesses contradict me, all my pleading will do no good. It is the same with a minister who is preaching in the midst of a cold, obtuse, and God-dishonoring church. In vain he holds up to view the great truths of religion, when every member of the church is ready to witness that he lies. Why, in such a church, the very manner of the people in going out of the aisles contradicts the sermon. They press out as cheerful and as easy, bowing to one another, and whispering together, as if nothing were the matter. If the devil should come in and see the state of things, he would think he could not improve the business for his interest.

Yet there are ministers who will go on in this way for years, preaching to a people who by their lives contradict every word that is said. And these ministers think it their duty to do so. Duty! For a minister to preach to a church that is undoing all his work, contradicting all his testimony, and that will not change! No. Let him shake off the dust from his feet for a testimony, and go to the lost, or to new settlements. The man is wasting his energies, and wearing out his life, and just rocking the cradle for a sleepy church, which is testifying to sinners that there is no danger. Their whole lives are a practical assertion that the Bible is not true. Shall ministers continue to wear themselves out so? Probably not less than ninety-nine percent of the preaching in this country is lost, because it is contradicted by the church. Not one truth in a hundred that is preached takes effect, because the lives of the professing Christians declare that it is not so.

3. It is evident that the standard of Christian living must be raised, or the world will never be converted. If we had, scattered all over the world, a minister for every five hundred souls, every child in a Sunday school, and every young person in a Bible class, you might have the entire setup you want. But if the church members should contradict the truth by their lives, no revival would be produced.

They never will have a revival in any place while the whole church in effect testifies against the minister. Often it is the case that where there is the most preaching, there is the least religion, because the church contradicts the preaching. I never knew means fail to produce a revival where Christians live consistently. One of the first things is to raise the standard of religion, so as to embody the truth of the gospel in the sight of all people. Unless ministers can get their people to wake up, and act as if religion were true, and back their testimony by their lives, the attempt to promote a revival will be in vain.

Many churches are depending on their minister to do everything. When he preaches, they will say, "What a great sermon that was! He is an excellent minister. Such preaching must do good. We shall have a revival soon, no doubt." And all the while they are contradicting the preaching by their lives. I tell you, if they are depending on preaching alone to carry on the work, they must fail. Let an apostle rise from the dead, or an angel come down from heaven and preach, without the church to witness for God, it would have no effect. The novelty might produce a certain kind of interest for a time, but as soon as the novelty was gone, the preaching would have no saving effect, while contradicted by the witnesses.

4. Every Christian makes an impression by his conduct, and witnesses either for one side or the other. His looks, dress, whole demeanor, make a constant impression on one side or the other. He cannot help testifying for or against religion. He is either gathering with Christ, or scattering abroad. At every step you tread on chords that will vibrate to all eternity. Every time you move, you touch keys whose sound will echo all over the hills and valleys of heaven, and through all the dark caverns and vaults of hell. Every movement of your lives, you are exerting a tremendous influence that will effect the immortal interests of souls all around you. Are you asleep, while all your conduct is exerting such an influence?

Are you going to walk in the street? Be careful how you dress. What is that on your head? What does that gaudy ribbon, and those ornaments upon your dress, say to every one who meets you? They make the impression that you wish to be thought pretty. Be careful! You might just as well write on your clothes, "No truth in Christianity!" These fashions say, "Give me dress, give me fashion, give me flattery, and I am happy!" The world understands this testimony as you walk the streets. You are living "letters, known and read by all" (2 Corinthians 3:2*). If you show pride, levity, bad temper, it is like tearing open the wounds of the Savior. How Christ might weep to see professing believers going about displaying his cause to contempt at the corners of streets. The "women should adorn themselves in respectable apparel, with modesty and self-control, not with braided hair and gold or pearls or costly attire, but with what is proper for women who profess godliness — with good works" (1 Timothy 2:9-10). Only let them act consistently, and their conduct will convict the world — heaven will rejoice and hell groan at their influence. But oh, let them display vanity, try to be pretty, bow down to the goddess of fashion, fill their ears with ornaments, and their fingers with rings, let them put feathers in their hats and clasps upon their arms, lace themselves up until they can hardly breathe, let them put on their necklaces, "walking and flirting" (Isaiah 3:18*)[5], and their influence is reversed. Heaven puts on the robes of mourning, and hell may hold a jubilee!

5. It is easy to see why revivals do not prevail in a great city. How can they? Just look at God's witnesses, and see what they are testifying to! They seem to be agreed together to tempt the Spirit of the Lord, and to lie to the Holy Spirit! They make their vows to God, to consecrate themselves wholly to him, then they go bowing down at the shrine of fashion — and next they wonder why there are no revivals! It would be more than a miracle to have a revival under such circumstances. How can a revival prevail here? Do you suppose I have such a vain imagination of my own ability, as to think I can promote a revival merely by my preaching, while you live on as you do? Do you not know that so

---

[5] The full Isaiah passage reads, "The LORD says, 'The women of Zion are haughty, walking along with outstretched necks, flirting with their eyes, tripping along with mincing steps, with ornaments jingling on their ankles. Therefore the Lord will bring sores on the heads of the women of Zion; the LORD will make their scalps bald.' In that day the Lord will snatch away their finery: the bangles and headbands and crescent necklaces, the earrings and bracelets and veils, the headdresses and ankle chains and sashes, the perfume bottles and charms, the signet rings and nose rings, the fine robes and the capes and cloaks, the purses and mirrors, and the linen garments and tiaras and shawls." (Isaiah 3:16-23, NIV)

far as your influence goes, many of you are preventing a revival? Your spirit and behavior produce an influence on the world against Christianity. How shall the world believe religion, when the witnesses are not agreed among themselves? You contradict yourselves, you contradict one another, you contradict your minister, and the result of the whole testimony is, there is no need of being pious.

Do you believe the things I have been preaching are true, or are they the ravings of a disturbed mind? If they are true, do you recognize the fact that they have reference to you? Perhaps you say, "I wish some of the rich churches could hear it!" But I am not preaching to them, I am preaching to you. My responsibility is to you, and my fruits must come from you. Now, are you contradicting it? What is the testimony on the page of the record that is now sealed for the Judgment, concerning this day? Have you manifested a sympathy with the Son of God, when his heart is bleeding in view of the desolations of Zion? Have your children, your clerks, your servants seen it to be so? Have they seen a solemnity on your face, and tears in your eyes, in view of perishing souls?

Finally, I remark that God and all moral beings have great reason to complain of this false testimony. There is reason to complain that God's witnesses turn and testify point-blank against him. They declare by their conduct that there is no truth in the gospel. Heaven might weep and hell rejoice to see this. Oh, how guilty! Here you are, going to the Judgment, red all over with blood. Sinners are to meet you there, those who have seen how you live, many of them already dead, and many others whom you will never see again upon earth. What an influence you have had! Perhaps hundreds of souls will meet you in the Judgment Day and curse you (if they are allowed to speak) for leading them to hell, by denying the truth of the gospel in practice. What will become of this city, and of the world, when the church is united in practice to testify that God is a liar? They testify by their lives, that if they make a living and live a moral life, that enough of Christianity. Oh, what a doctrine of devils is that! It is enough to ruin the whole human race!

Chapter 10

TO WIN SOULS REQUIRES WISDOM

"Whoever wins souls is wise." (Proverbs 11:30*)

The most common definition of wisdom is that it is the choice of the best end and the selection of the most appropriate means for the accomplishment of that end. "Whoever wins souls," God says, "is wise." The object of this lecture is to help Christians to accomplish that infinitely desirable end, the salvation of souls. I shall confine my attention to the private efforts of individuals for the conversion and salvation of others. In giving some directions to help private Christians in this work, I propose to show:

. How they should deal with apathetic sinners.

I. How they should deal with awakened sinners.

II. How they should deal with convicted sinners.

. DEALING WITH APATHETIC SINNERS

1. In regard to the time. It is important that you should select a proper time to try to make a serious impression on the mind of an apathetic sinner. If you fail to select the most proper time, you will likely be defeated. You may say that it is your duty at all times to warn sinners, and try to awaken them to think of their souls. And so it is. Yet if you do not pay due regard to the time and opportunity, your hope of success may be very doubtful.

a) It is desirable, if possible, to address an apathetic person when he is not occupied with other tasks. The more his attention is occupied with

something else, the more difficult it will be to awaken him to religion.
People who are apathetic and indifferent to religion are often offended,
rather than benefited, by being called off from important business. For
instance, a minister perhaps goes to visit the family of a merchant, or
mechanic, or farmer, and finds the person absorbed in his business.
Perhaps he calls him off from his work when it is urgent, and the person is uneasy and irritable, and feels as if it were an intrusion. In such
a case, there is little room to expect any good. It is true that religion is
infinitely more important than all his worldly business, and he should
postpone everything for the salvation of his soul, yet he does not feel it.
If he did, he would no longer be an apathetic sinner. Therefore he regards it as unjustifiable, and gets offended. You must take him as you
find him, an apathetic, impenitent sinner, and deal with him accordingly. He is absorbed in other things and very likely to be offended if
you select such a time to call his attention to religion.

(b) It is important to talk to a person, if possible, when he is not strongly
excited about another subject. Otherwise he will be in an unfit frame
of mind to be addressed on the subject of religion. The stronger that
excitement is, the more likely that you will do no good. You may possibly reach him. Persons have had their minds arrested and turned to
religion in the midst of a powerful excitement on other subjects. But it
is not likely.

(c) Be sure that the person is perfectly sober. It used to be more common for people to drink spirits every day, and become intoxicated. Precisely in proportion as they are so, they are unfit to be approached on
the subject of religion. If they have been drinking beer, or cider, or
wine, so that you can smell their breath, there is but little chance of
producing any lasting effect on them. I have had professing Christians
bring to me persons whom they supposed were under conviction (people under alcohol are very fond of talking upon religion). But as soon
as I came near enough to smell the breath of such people, I have asked,
"Why do you bring this drunken man to me?" They have replied,
"Why, he is not drunk, he has only been drinking a little." Well, that
little has made him a little drunk! It is exceedingly rare for a person to
be truly convicted who has had any intoxicating liquor.

(d) If possible, where you wish to converse with a person on the subject
of salvation, take him when he is in a good temperament. If you find
him in a bad mood, he will probably get angry and abuse you. Better
leave him alone for that time, or you will be likely to quench the Spirit.
It is possible you may be able to talk in such a way as to cool his temper,
but it is not likely. The truth is, people hate God, and though their

hatred may be dormant, it is easily excited. If you bring God fully before their minds when they are already excited with anger, it will be so much easier to stir their hatred to open violence.

e) If possible, always take an opportunity to converse with apathetic sinners when they are alone. Most people are too proud to be conversed with freely about themselves in the presence of others, even their own family. A person in such circumstances will brace up all his powers to defend himself, while, if he were alone, he would melt down under the truth. He will resist the truth or try to laugh it off, for fear that if he should show any feeling, someone will go and report that he is thinking seriously about religion.

In visiting families, instead of calling all the family together at the same time to be talked to, the better way is to see them all, one at a time. There was a case of this kind. Several young ladies, of a proud, merry, and fashionable character, lived together in a fashionable family. Two men were hoping to bring the subject of Christianity before them, but were at a loss how to accomplish it. The men worried that the ladies would combine to resist every serious impression. After a while, they invited one of the young ladies by name. She came down, and they conversed with her on the subject of her salvation. Being alone, she not only treated them politely, but also seemed to receive the truth with seriousness. A day or two later, in the same way they invited another, and then another, and so on, until they had talked with each one separately. In a little while the ladies were all, I believe, hopefully converted. The impression made on one was followed up with the others so that not one was left to have a bad influence on the rest.

There was a pious woman who ran a boardinghouse for young gentlemen. She had twenty-one or two of them in her house, and at length she became very anxious for their salvation. She made it a subject of prayer, but saw no seriousness among them. Eventually she saw that something must be done besides praying, and yet she did not know what to do. One morning, after breakfast, as the rest were leaving, she asked one of them to wait a few minutes. She took him aside, and conversed with him tenderly on the subject of religion, and prayed with him. She followed up the impression she made, and soon he was hopefully converted. Then she spoke to another, and so on, taking one at a time, and letting none of the rest know what was going on, so as not to alarm them, until all these young men were converted to God. Now, if she had brought the subject before the group, they likely would have ridiculed it, or perhaps they would have been offended and left the house, and then she could have had no further influence over them.

But taking one alone, and treating him respectfully and kindly, he had no such motive for the resistance that comes in the presence of others.

(f) Try to seize an opportunity to converse with an apathetic sinner, when the events of Providence seem to favor your intent. If any particular event occurs that makes a serious impression, be sure to use the occasion faithfully.

(g) Seize the earliest opportunity to converse with those around you who are apathetic. Do not put it off, thinking a better opportunity will come. You must seek an opportunity, and if none occurs, make one. Appoint a time or place to have a conversation with your friend or neighbor where you can speak freely. Send a note or go to the person intentionally. Make it look like a matter of business — as if you were sincere in trying to promote his soul's salvation. Then he will feel that it is a matter of importance, at least in your eyes. Follow it up until you succeed, or become convinced that, for the time being, nothing more can be done.

(h) If you have any feeling for a particular individual, take an opportunity to converse with that individual while this feeling continues. If it is a truly benevolent feeling, you have reason to believe the Spirit of God is moving you to desire the salvation of his soul, and that God is ready to bless your efforts for his conversion. In such a case, make it the subject of special and urgent prayer, and seek an early opportunity to pour out all your heart to him and bring him to Christ.

2. In regard to the manner of doing all this:

(a) When you approach an apathetic individual, be sure to treat him kindly. Let him see that you address him, not because you seek a quarrel with him, but because you love his soul, and desire his best good in time and eternity. If you are harsh and overbearing in your manner, you will probably offend him, and drive him farther off from the way of life.

(b) Be solemn. Avoid all lightness of manner or language. Levity will produce anything but a right impression. You should feel that you are doing a very solemn work, which is going to affect the character of your friend or neighbor, and probably determine his destiny for eternity. Who could trifle and use levity in such circumstances, if his heart were sincere?

(c) Be respectful. Some suppose it is necessary to be abrupt, rude, and coarse, in their interactions with the apathetic and impenitent. No mistake can be greater. The apostle Peter has given us a better rule on he subject, where he says to have, "sympathy, brotherly love, a tender heart, and a humble mind. Do not repay evil for evil or reviling for reviling, but on the contrary, bless" (1 Peter 3:8-9). A rude and coarse style of speaking will only create an unfavorable opinion both of yourself and of your religion.

(d) Be sure to be very plain. Do not tolerate yourself to cover up any circumstance of the person's character, and his relations to God. Lay it all open, not for the purpose of offending or wounding him, but because it is necessary. Before you can cure a wound, you must probe it to the bottom. Keep back none of the truth, but let it come out plainly before him.

(e) Be sure to address his conscience. Unless you address the conscience pointedly, you get no hold of the mind at all.

(f) Bring the great and fundamental truths to bear upon the person's mind. Sinners are very likely to run off upon some excuse, or some subordinate point, especially one of sectarianism. For instance, if the person has a Presbyterian background, he will try to turn the conversation on the points of difference between Presbyterians and Methodists. Do not talk with him on any such point. Tell him the present business is to save his soul, and not to settle controversial questions in theology. Hold him to the great fundamental points, by which he must be saved or lost.

(g) Be very patient. If he has a real difficulty in his mind, be very patient until you find out what it is, and then clear it up. If what he alleges is a petty objection, make him see its pettiness. Do not try to answer it by argument, but show him that he is not sincere. It is not worthwhile to spend your time in arguing against a petty objection. Make him feel that he is committing sin to raise it, and thus enlist his conscience on your side.

(h) Be careful to guard your own spirit. There are many people who do not have good enough temperaments to talk with a person who is very opposed to Christianity. And such a person wants no better triumph than to see you angry. He will go away exulting because he has "made one of these saints mad."

(i) If the sinner is inclined to entrench himself against God, be careful not to take his side in anything. If he says he cannot do his duty, do not take sides with him, or say anything to condone his falsehood. Do not tell him he cannot, or help him to maintain himself in the controversy against his Maker. Sometimes an apathetic sinner will begin finding fault with Christians. Do not side with him against Christians. Just tell him that he does not have to answer for their sins — he had better see to his own concerns. If you agree with him, he feels that he has you on his side. Show him that it is a wicked and critical spirit that prompts him to make these remarks, and not a regard for the honor of the religion or the laws of Jesus Christ.

(j) Bring up the individual's particular sins. Talking in general terms against sin will produce no results. You must make a person feel that you mean him. A minister who cannot make his hearers feel that he means them cannot expect to accomplish much. Some people are very careful to avoid mentioning the particular sins of which they know the individual to be guilty, for fear of hurting his feelings. This is wrong. If you know his history, bring up his particular sins kindly, but plainly — not to give offense, but to awaken the conscience, and give full force to the truth.

(k) It is generally best to be short, and not spin out what we have to say. Move the attention as soon as you can to the very point. Say a few things and press them home, and bring the matter to a choice. If possible, get them to repent and give themselves to Christ at the time. This is the real issue. Carefully avoid making an impression that you do not wish them to repent NOW.

(l) If possible, when you talk with sinners, be sure to pray with them. If you talk with them, and leave them without praying, you leave your work undone.

II. THE MANNER OF DEALING WITH AWAKENED SINNERS

Be careful to distinguish between an awakened sinner, and one who is under conviction. When you find a person who feels a little on the subject of religion, do not take it for granted that he is convicted of sin, and thus omit to use means to show him his sin. Persons are often awakened by some providential circumstance such as sickness, thunderstorm, pestilence, death in the family, disappointment, etc., or directly by the Spirit of God. Their ears are open, and they are ready to hear about Christianity with attention and seriousness, and some feeling. If you find a person awakened, no matter by what means, lose no time to pour in light upon his mind. Do not be afraid, but show him the breadth of the divine law, and the exceeding strictness of its precepts. Make him see how it condemns his thoughts and life. Search out his heart, find what is there, and bring it up before his mind, as far as you can. If possible, melt him down on the spot. When once you have got a sinner's attention, very often his conviction and conversion are the work of a few moments. You can sometimes do more in five minutes, man in years — or a whole lifetime, while he is apathetic or indifferent.

I have been amazed at the conduct of those cruel parents, and other heads of families, who will let an awakened sinner be in their families for days and weeks, and not say a word to him on the subject. They say, "If the Spirit of God has begun a work in him, he will certainly carry it on!" Perhaps the person is anxious to talk, finds Christians as often as possible, expecting they will converse with him, and they do not say a word. Amazing! Such a person should be found immediately, as soon as he is awakened, and a blaze of light poured into his mind without delay. Whenever you have reason to believe that a person within your reach is awakened, do not sleep until you have poured in the light upon his mind, and have tried to bring him to immediate repentance. This is the time to press the subject with effect.

In revivals, I have often seen Christians who were constantly on the lookout to see if any persons appeared to be awakened. As soon as they saw any one begin to show feeling under preaching they would take note, and as soon as the meeting was over invite him to a room, and talk and pray with him — if possible not leaving him until he was converted.

A remarkable case like this occurred in a town at the West. A merchant came there from far away to buy goods. It was a time of powerful revival, but he was determined to keep out of its influence and so he would not go to any meetings. Eventually he found everyone so engaged in religion that it encountered him at every turn. He got annoyed, and vowed that he would go home. There was so much religion there, he said, that he could do no business and would not stay. So he booked his seat for the coach, which was to leave at four o'clock the next morning. As he spoke of going away, a gentleman where he was staying, one of the young converts, asked him if he would not go to a meeting once before he left town. He finally agreed and went to the meeting. The sermon took hold of his mind, but not with sufficient power to bring him into the kingdom. He returned to his lodgings, and called the landlord to bring his bill. The landlord, who had himself recently experienced Christianity, saw that he was agitated. He accordingly spoke to him on the subject of religion, and the man burst into tears. The landlord immediately called in three or four young converts, and they prayed, and exhorted him. At four o'clock in the morning, when the coach came, he went on his way rejoicing in God! When he got home he called his family together, confessed to them his past sins, acknowledged his determination to live differently, and prayed with them for the first time. It was so unexpected that it was soon known abroad. People began to ask questions, and a revival broke out in the place. Now, suppose these Christians had been unconcerned, as some are, and let the man go away, slightly affected? It is unlikely he ever could have been saved. Such opportunities are often lost forever when the favorable moment is passed.

III. THE MANNER OF DEALING WITH CONVICTED SINNERS

By a convicted sinner, I mean one who feels himself condemned by the law of God, as a guilty sinner. He has enough instruction to understand something of the extent of God's law, and he sees and feels his guilty state, and knows what his remedy is. To deal with these people often requires great wisdom.

1. When a person is convicted, but not converted, and remains in an anxious state, there is generally some specific reason for it. In such cases it does no good to exhort him to repent, or to explain the law to him. He knows all that. He understands these general points, but still he does not repent. There must be some particular difficulty to overcome. You may preach, pray, and exhort, until doomsday, and not gain anything.

You must then set yourself to discover what that particular difficulty is. A physician, when called to a patient, and finds him sick with a particular disease, first administers the general remedies that are applicable to that disease. If they produce no effect, and the disease still continues, he must examine the case, and learn the constitution of the individual, and his habits, diet, manner of living, etc., and see why the medicine does not take effect. So it is with the case of a sinner convicted but not converted. If your ordinary instructions and exhortations fail, there must be a difficulty. The individual himself often knows the particular difficulty, though he keeps it concealed. Sometimes, however, it is something that has escaped even his own observation.

(a) Sometimes the individual has some idol, something that he loves more than God, which prevents him from giving himself up. You must search out and see what it is that he will not give up. Perhaps it is wealth, perhaps some earthly friend, perhaps playful fashion or merry company, or some favorite amusement. At any rate, there is something on which his heart is so set that he will not yield to God.

(b) Perhaps he has done an injury to some individual that calls for compensation, and he is unwilling to confess it, or to make a fair recompense. Now, until he confesses and forsakes this sin, he can find no mercy. If he has injured the person in property or character, or has abused him, he must make it up. Tell him frankly that there is no hope or him until he is willing to confess it, and to do what is right. Perhaps he has defrauded somebody in trade, or taken some unfair advantage, contrary to the golden rule, and is unwilling to make satisfaction. This is a very common sin among merchants and men of business. I have known many sad instances, where people have grieved away the Spirit of God, or else have nearly been driven to absolute despair, because they were unwilling to make compensation where they have done such things. Now it is obvious that such persons never can have forgiveness until they make restitution.

(c) Sometimes there is some particular sin that he will not forsake. He pretends it is only a small one, or tries to persuade himself it is no sin at all. No matter how small it is, he can never get into the kingdom of God until he gives it up. Sometimes an individual has seen it to be a sin to use tobacco, and he can never find true peace until he gives it up. Perhaps he sees it as a small sin. But God knows nothing about small sins in such a case. What is the sin? It is injuring your health, and setting a bad example. You are taking God's money, which you are obligated to use in his service, and spending it for tobacco. What would a merchant say if he found one of his clerks in the habit of going to the money drawer, and taking enough money to provide him with cigars? Would he call it a small offense? No, he would say the clerk deserved to be sent to the State prison. I mention this particular sin, because I have found it to be one of the things to which people who are convicted will hold on, although they know it to be wrong, and then wonder why they do not find peace.

(d) They may have entrenched themselves somewhere, and in regard to some particular point they are determined not to yield. For instance, they may have taken strong ground that they will not do a particular thing. I knew a man who was determined not to go into a certain grove to pray. Several other people during the revival had gone into the grove, and there, by prayer and meditation, given themselves to God. His own clerk had been converted there. The lawyer himself was awakened, but he was determined that he would not go into that grove. He had powerful convictions, and went on for weeks in this way, with no relief. He tried to make God believe that it was not pride that kept him from Christ. So, when he was going home from a meeting he would kneel down in the street and pray. And not only that, but he would look around for a mud puddle in the street, in which he might kneel, to show that he was not proud. He once prayed all night in his parlor — but he would not go into the grove. His distress was so great and he was so angry with God that he was strongly tempted to kill himself and actually threw away his knife for fear he should cut his throat. At length he concluded he would go into the grove and pray. As soon as he got there he was converted, and poured out his full heart to God.[1]

So, individuals are sometimes entrenched in a determination that they will not go to a particular meeting: perhaps the inquiry meeting, or some prayer meeting. Or they will not have a certain person to pray with them, or they will not take a particular seat, such as the "anxious seat."[2] They say they can be converted just as well without yielding this point, for religion does not consist in going to a particular meeting, or taking a particular attitude in prayer, or a particular seat. This is true, but by taking this ground they make it the material point. And so long as they are entrenched there, and determined to bring God to their terms, they never can be converted. Sinners will often yield anything else, and do anything else, and do anything in the world, but yield the point upon which they have taken a stand against God. They cannot be humbled, until they yield this point, whatever it is. And if, without yielding, they get a hope, it will be a false hope.

(e) Perhaps he has a prejudice against someone, perhaps a member of the church, because of some faithful dealing with his soul. He dwells on this, and will never be converted until he gives it up. Whatever it may be, you should search it out, and tell him the truth, plainly and faithfully.

(f) He may feel ill will towards someone, or be angry, and cherish strong feelings of resentment, which prevent him from obtaining mercy from God. "And whenever you stand praying, forgive, if you have anything against anyone, so that your Father also who is in heaven may forgive you your trespasses" (Mark 11:25).

(g) Perhaps he has some errors in doctrine, or some wrong notions about what is to be done, or the way of doing it, which may be keeping him out of the kingdom. Perhaps he is waiting for God to do something to him before he submits — in fact, is waiting for God to do for him what God has required the sinner to do himself.

He may be waiting for more conviction. People often do not know what conviction is, and think they are not under conviction when in

---

[1] This story is the story of Benjamin Wright, whom Finney worked under as a law clerk. Finney himself had been converted in this grove and Wright knew about it. As described in the story, Wright eventually went there and gave his heart to God.

[2] The anxious seat was a front pew that was left open after preaching for those interested in becoming Christians. People would come to the seat and receive individual instruction and prayer.

fact they are under powerful conviction. They often think nothing is conviction unless they have great fears of hell. But the fact is, individuals often have strong convictions with very little fear of hell. Show them what is the truth, and let them see that they have no need to wait.

Perhaps he may be waiting for certain feelings, which he has heard somebody else had before obtaining mercy. This is very common in revivals where one of the first converts has told of remarkable experiences. Others who are awakened are very likely to think they must wait for such feelings. I knew a young man similarly awakened. His companion had been converted in a remarkable way, and he was waiting for just such feelings. He said he was "using the means, and praying for them," but he finally found that he was a Christian, although he had not gone through the course of feeling that he expected.

Sinners often lay out a plan of what they expect to feel, and how they expect to be converted. They in fact lay out the work for God, determined that they will go in that path or not at all. Tell them this is all wrong — they must not lay out any such path beforehand, but let God lead them as he thinks best. God always leads the blind by a way they do not know. There never was a sinner brought into the kingdom through such a course of feeling as he expected. Very often they are amazed to find that they are in the kingdom, and have not had the experiences they expected.

It is very common for persons to be waiting to be made subjects of prayer, or for some other particular means to be used, or to see if they cannot make themselves better. They are so wicked, they say, that they cannot come to Christ. They want to try, by humiliation, and suffering, and prayer, to enable themselves to come. You will have to hunt them out of all these refuges. It is astonishing into how many corners they will often run before they will go to Christ. I have known persons almost deranged for the lack of a little correct instruction.

Sometimes such people think their sins are too great to be forgiven, or that they have grieved the Spirit of God away, when that Spirit is all the while convicting them. They pretend that their sins are greater than Christ's mercy, thus actually insulting the Lord Jesus.

Sometimes sinners get the idea that God has given up on them, and that now they cannot be saved. It is often very difficult to beat persons off from this ground. Many of the most distressing cases I have met with have been of this character.

In a place where I was working during a revival, one day before the meeting commenced, I heard a low, moaning, distressing, unearthly noise. I looked and saw several women gathered around the person who made it. They said she was a woman in despair. She had been a long time in that state. Her husband was a drunkard. He had brought her to the meeting place, and had gone himself to the tavern. I conversed with her, saw her state, and realized that it was very difficult to reach someone in her situation. As I was going to begin the meeting she said she must go out, for she could not bear to hear praying or singing. I told her she must not go, and asked the ladies to detain her, if necessary, by force. I felt that, if the devil had hold of her, God was stronger than the devil and could deliver her. The meeting began, and she made some noise at first. But presently she looked up. The subject was chosen with special reference to her situation, and as it proceeded her attention was gained, her eyes were fixed — I never shall forget how she looked — her eyes and mouth open, her head up, and how she almost rose from her seat as the truth poured in upon her mind. Finally, as the truth knocked away every foundation on which her despair had rested, she shrieked out, put her head down, and sat perfectly still until the meeting was over. I went to her, and found her perfectly calm and happy in God. I saw her a long time afterwards, and she still remained in that state of rest. Thus Providence led her where she never expected to be, and compelled her to hear instruction adapted to her case. You may often do incalculable good by finding out precisely where the difficulty lies, and then bringing the truth to bear on that point.

Sometimes persons will strenuously maintain that they have committed the unpardonable sin. When they get that idea into their minds, they will turn everything you say against themselves. In some such cases, it is a good way to take them on their own ground, and reason with them in this way, "Suppose you have committed the unpardonable sin, what then? It is reasonable that you should submit to God, and be sorry for your sins, and break off from them, and do all the good you can, even if God will not forgive you. Even if you go to hell, you should do this." Press this thought until you find they understand and consent to it.

It is common for persons in such cases to keep their eyes on themselves. They will keep to themselves, looking at their own darkness, instead of looking away to Christ. Now, if you can take their minds off from themselves, and get them to think of Christ, you may draw them away from brooding over their own present feelings, and get them to lay hold of the hope set before them in the gospel.

2. Be careful, in talking with convicted sinners, not to make any com-

romise with them on any point where they have a difficulty. If you do, 1ey will be sure to take advantage of it, and thus get a false hope. Con-icted sinners often get into a difficulty, in regard to giving up some recious sin, or yielding some point where conscience and the Holy pirit are at war with them. And if they come across an individual /ho will yield the point, they feel better, and are happy, and think they re converted. The young man who came to Christ was of this char-cter. He had one difficulty, and Jesus Christ knew just what it was. Ie knew that he loved his money. Instead of compromising the matter nd thus trying to comfort him, he just put his finger on the very place nd told him, "Go, sell what you have and give it to the poor, then ome and follow me" (Matthew 19:21*). What was the effect? Why, the oung man "went away sorrowful." Very likely, if Christ had told him o do anything else, he would have felt relieved and felt a hope, would ιave professed himself a disciple, joined the church, and gone to hell.

'eople are often amazingly anxious to make a compromise. They will sk such questions like this. Do you think a person may be a Christian, nd yet do such-and-such things? Or, if he may be a Christian and not lo such-and-such things? Now, do not yield an inch to any such ques-ions. The questions themselves may often show you the very point hat is laboring in their minds. They will show you that it is pride, r love of the world, or something like that, which is preventing them rom becoming Christians.

3e careful to make thorough work on this point — the love of the vorld. I believe there have been more false hopes built on wrong in-tructions here, than in any other way. I once heard a Doctor of Divinity rying to persuade his hearers to give up the world. But he told them, 'If you will only give it up, God will give it right back to you. He is villing that you should enjoy the world." Miserable! God never gives ιack the world to a Christian, in the same sense that he requires a con-victed sinner to give it up. He requires us to give up the ownership of everything to him, so that we shall never again for a moment consider t as our own. One man said, the other day, that he had promised he 1ever would give any of his property to educate young men for the ninistry. So, when he is asked to, he just answers, "I have said I never vill give to any such object, and I never will." Did Jesus Christ ever ell you to act so with his money? Has he laid down any such rule? Remember, it is his money you are talking about, and if he wants it o educate ministers, you keep it at your peril. Such a man has yet to earn the first principle of religion, that he is not his own, and that the noney which he "possesses" is Jesus Christ's.

Here is the great reason why the church is so full of false hopes. People have been left to suppose they could be Christians while holding on to their money. And this has served as an obstruction to every enterprise. It is an undoubted fact, that the church has enough funds to immediately supply the world with Bibles, and tracts, and missionaries. But the truth is, that professing Christians do not believe that "the earth is the LORD's, and the fullness thereof."[3] Everyone supposes he has right to decide how to spend his own money. And they have no idea that Jesus Christ should dictate to them on this subject.

Be sure to deal thoroughly on this point. The church is now filled with hypocrites, because people were never made to see that unless they entirely consecrate everything to Christ — all their time, all their talents, all their influence — they would never go to heaven. Many think they can be Christians, and yet dream along through life, and use all their time and property for themselves, only giving a little now and then, just for the appearance, and when they can do it with perfect convenience. But it is a sad mistake, and they will find it so, if they do not use their energies for God. And when they die, instead of finding heaven at the end of the path they are pursuing, they will find hell.

In dealing with a convicted sinner, be sure to drive him away from every refuge, and not leave him an inch of ground to stand on so long as he resists God. This need not take a long time to do. When the Spirit of God is at work striving with a sinner, it is easy to drive him from his refuges. You will find the truth to be like a hammer, crushing wherever it strikes. Make clean work with it, so that he shall give up all for God.

Make the sinner see clearly the nature and extent of the divine law, and press the main question of entire submission to God. Bear down on that point as soon as you have made him clearly understand what you aim at, and do not turn off on anything else.

Be careful, in illustrating the subject, not to mislead the mind by leaving the impression that a selfish submission will do. Do not teach a selfish acceptance of the atonement, or a selfish surrender to Christ and receiving him, as if a person were making a good bargain by giving up his sins and receiving salvation in exchange. This is mere barter and not submission to God. Leave no ground in your explanations or illustrations for such a view of the matter. A person's selfish heart will eagerly seize such a view of Christianity, if it is presented, and very likely accept it and thus get a false hope.

REMARKS

---

[3] Psalm 24:1

1. Make it an object of constant study, and of daily reflection and prayer, to learn how to deal with sinners so as to promote their conversion. It is the great business on earth of every Christian, to save souls. People often complain that they do not know how to accomplish this matter. Why, the reason is obvious — they have never studied it. They have never taken the proper effort to qualify themselves for the work. If people paid the same attention to their worldly business as they do to saving souls, how do you think they would succeed? Now, if you are thus neglecting the main business of life, what are you living for? If you do not make it a matter of study, how you may most successfully act in building up the kingdom of Christ, you are playing a very wicked and absurd role as a Christian.

2. Many professing Christians do more harm than good, when they attempt to talk to impenitent sinners. They have so little knowledge and skill, that their remarks divert attention rather than increase it.

3. Be careful to find the point where the Spirit of God is pressing a sinner, and press the same point in all your remarks. If you divert his attention from that, you will be in great danger of destroying his convictions. Put effort to learn the state of his mind, what he is thinking of, how he feels, and what he feels most deeply upon, and then press that chief point thoroughly. Do not divert his mind by talking about anything else. Do not fear to press that point for fear of driving him to distraction. Some people hesitate to press a point to which the mind is tremblingly alive, for fear they should injure the mind, even though the Spirit of God is clearly debating that very point with the sinner. This is an attempt to be wiser than God. You should clear up the point, throw the light of truth all around it, and bring the soul to yield, and then the mind will be at rest.

4. Great evils have arisen, and many false hopes have been created, by not recognizing an awakened sinner from a convicted sinner. Because of the lack of this recognition, persons who are only awakened are immediately pressed to submit — "you must repent," "submit to God" — when they are in fact neither convinced of their guilt, nor instructed to even know what submission means. This is one way in which revivals have been greatly injured — by indiscriminate exhortations to repent, unaccompanied by proper instruction.

5. Anxious sinners are to be regarded as being in a very solemn and critical state. They have, in fact, come to a turning point. It is a time when their destiny is likely to be settled forever. Christians should feel deeply for them. In many respects their circumstances are more solemn than those of the Judgment. Here their destiny is settled. The Judg-

ment Day reveals it. And the particular time when it is done is when the Spirit is striving with them. Christians should remember their awesome responsibility at such times. The physician, if he knows anything of his duty, sometimes feels himself under a very solemn responsibility. His patient is in a critical state, where a little error will destroy life, and hangs quivering between life and death. If such responsibility should be felt in relation to the body, what awesome responsibility should be felt in relation to the soul, when it is seen to hang trembling on a point, and its destiny is now to be decided. One false impression, one indiscreet remark, one sentence misunderstood, a slight diversion of mind, may wear him the wrong way and his soul will be lost. Never was an angel employed in a more solemn work, than that of dealing with sinners who are under conviction. How solemnly and carefully then should Christians walk, how wisely and skillfully work, if they do not wish to be the reason for the loss of a soul!

Finally, if there is a sinner in this house, let me say to him, "Abandon all your excuses. You have been told tonight that they are all in vain. This very hour may seal your eternal destiny. Will you submit to God tonight — NOW?"

Chapter 11

FALSE COMFORTS FOR SINNERS

"How then will you comfort me with empty nothings? There is nothing left of your answers but falsehood." (Job 21:34)

Job's three friends insisted that his sufferings were a punishment for his sins, and were conclusive evidence that he was a hypocrite, and not a good man as he professed to be. A lengthy argument followed, in which Job referred to past experience, to prove that people are not dealt with in this way according to their character. His friends maintained the opposite, and suggested that this world is also a place of rewards and punishments, in which people receive good or evil according to their deeds. In this chapter, Job urges, by appealing to common sense and experience, that this cannot be true because the wicked are often prosperous in this world. Hence he infers that their judgment and punishment must be reserved for a future state. Since the friends who came to comfort him were in error on this fundamental point and could not understand his situation, they could not afford him any comfort but instead aggravated his grief. Job insisted that he would still look to a future state for consolation. In the bitterness of his soul, he rebuked them by exclaiming, "How then will you comfort me with empty nothings? There is nothing left of your answers but falsehood."

My present purpose is to make some remarks upon the various methods used in comforting anxious sinners. I intend:

I. To note briefly the necessity and goal of instructing anxious sinners.

II. To show that anxious sinners are always seeking comfort — indeed it is their supreme goal.

III. To notice some of the false comforts often given.

IV. Errors made in praying for sinners.

I. INSTRUCTING ANXIOUS SINNERS

The very idea of anxiety implies the sinner has had some instruction. A sinner will not be anxious at all about his future state, unless he has enough light to know that he is a sinner, and that he is in danger of punishment and needs forgiveness. But people are to be converted neither by physical force nor by a change in their constitution by creative power, but by the truth made effective by the Holy Spirit. Conversion is yielding to the truth. Therefore, the more that truth can be brought to bear on the mind, other things being equal, the more probable it is that the individual will be converted. Unless the truth is brought to bear upon him, it is certain he will not be converted. If it is brought to bear, it is not absolutely certain that it will be effective, but the probability is in proportion to the extent to which the truth is brought to bear.

The great goal in dealing with an anxious sinner is to clear up all his difficulties and ignorance, do away with all his errors, sap the foundation of his self-righteous hopes, and sweep away every vestige of comfort that he can find in himself. There is often much difficulty in all this, and much instruction is required. Sinners often cling with a death-grasp to their false dependencies. The last place to which a sinner ever takes himself for relief is to Jesus Christ. Sinners would rather be saved in any other way in the world. They would rather make any sacrifice, go to any expense, or endure any suffering, than just throw themselves as guilty and lost rebels upon Christ alone for salvation. This is the very last way in which they are ever willing to be saved. It cuts up all their self-righteousness, and annihilates their pride and self-satisfaction so completely that they are exceedingly unwilling to adopt it. But this is the only way in which a sinner can find relief.

Now, the goal of instructing an anxious sinner should be to bring his mind by the shortest route to the practical conclusion that there is no other way in which he can be relieved and saved, but to renounce himself, and rest in Christ alone. To do this with effect requires great skill. It requires a thorough knowledge of the human heart, a clear understanding of the plan of salvation, and a precise idea of what a sinner must do in order to be saved. The ability to give such instruction effectively is one of the most rare qualifications in the ministry. It is distressing to see how few ministers and how few professing Christians there are who have a clear idea of what needs to be done. Only a few an go to an anxious sinner and tell him exactly what he has to do, and ow to do it, and can show him clearly that there is no possible way or him to be saved, unless he does that very thing which they tell him r else he will certainly be lost.

I. ANXIOUS SINNERS ARE ALWAYS SEEKING COMFORT

inners often imagine they are seeking Jesus Christ and seeking reli-ion, but this is a mistake. No person ever sought religion, and yet emained irreligious. What is religion? It is obeying God. Seeking re-gion is seeking to obey God. The soul that hungers and thirsts after ighteousness is the soul of a Christian. To say that a person can seek o obey God, and yet not obey him, is absurd. If he is seeking religion, ie is not an impenitent sinner. To seek religion implies a willingness to bey God, and a willingness to obey God is religion. It is a contradic-ion to say that an impenitent sinner is seeking religion. It is the same s to say that he seeks and actually longs to obey God, and God will ιot let him, or that he longs to embrace Jesus Christ, and Jesus Christ vill not let him come. The fact is, the anxious sinner is seeking a hope, ie is seeking pardon, and comfort, and deliverance from hell. He is nxiously looking for someone to comfort him and make him feel bet-er, without being obliged to conform to such humiliating conditions s those of the gospel. And his anxiety and distress continue, only be-ause he will not yield to these terms. Unfortunately, anxious sinners ind comforters enough to their liking. They are miserable comforters ιecause, "There is nothing left of their answers but falsehood." No loubt, millions and millions are now in hell, because there were those round them who gave them false comfort, who had so much false pity ιr were themselves in so much ignorance, that they would not let sin-iers remain in anxiety until they had submitted their hearts to God, ιut administered falsehood.

II. WAYS IN WHICH FALSE COMFORT IS GIVEN

There is an endless variety of ways in which false comfort is given to ιnxious sinners. The more I observe the ways in which even good ιeople deal with anxious sinners, the more I feel grieved at the endless alsehoods with which they attempt to comfort their anxious friends, ιnd thus actually deceive them out of their salvation. It often reminds ne of the manner in which people act when any one is ill. If any one ιf you is ill with almost any disease in the world, you will find that ιvery person you meet with has a remedy for that disorder, a certain :ure, some panacea. You will find such a world of quackery all around ιou that if you are not careful and shut it all out, you will certainly .ose your life. A person must exercise his own judgment because he

will find as many remedies as he has friends, and each one believes in
his own medicine, and perhaps will feel hurt if it is not taken. And no
doubt this miserable system of quackery kills a great many people.

This is even more true concerning diseases of the mind than diseases
of the body. People have their cures and their panaceas to comfort
distressed souls. Whenever they begin to talk with an anxious sinner
they will bring in their false comforts — so much that if he is not careful to heed the Word of God, he will certainly be deceived to his own
destruction. I propose to mention a few of the falsehoods that are often brought forward in attempting to comfort anxious sinners. Time
would fail me to name them all.

The direct goal of many people is to comfort sinners. They are often
so intent on this that when they see their friends distressed, they pity
them, and they feel very compassionate, "Oh, oh, I cannot bear to see
them so distressed, I must comfort them somehow." And so they try
one way, and another, and all to comfort them! Now, God desires they
should be comforted. He is benevolent, and has kind feelings, and
his heart pities them when he sees them so distressed. But he sees
that there is only one way to give a sinner real comfort. He has more
benevolence and compassion than all people, and wishes to comfort
them. But he has fixed the terms, as unyielding as his throne, on which
he will give a sinner relief. He will not change. He knows that nothing
else will do the sinner good, for nothing can make him happy, until he
repents of his sins and forsakes them, and turns to God. And therefore
God will not yield. Our goal should be the same as that of God. We
should feel compassion and benevolence just as he does, and be as
ready to give comfort, but we should also be sure that it is the right
kind.

Our prime goal should be to induce the sinner to obey God. The sinner's comfort should be, both for us and for him, only a secondary
goal. When we are more eager to relieve his distress than to have him
stop abusing and dishonoring God, we are not likely to do him any
real good with our instructions. This is clearly overlooked by many,
who seem to have no higher motives than sympathy or compassion
for the sinner. If in preaching the gospel or instructing the anxious,
we are not motivated by a high regard for the honor of God, and rise
no higher than to desire to relieve the distressed, this is going no farther than natural sympathy or compassion would carry us. Overlook-
ing this principle has often misled professing Christians. When they
have heard others correctly dealing with anxious sinners, they have
accused them of cruelty. I have often had professing Christians bring

anxious sinners to me, and beg me to comfort them. Then, when I have probed the conscience of the sinner, they have shuddered, and sometimes taken his side. It is sometimes impossible to deal effectively with anxious young people, in the presence of their parents, because the parents have so much more compassion for their children than regard for the honor of God. This is a position that is all wrong. With such views and feelings you had better hold your tongue than say anything to the anxious.

1. One of the ways in which people give false comfort to distressed sinners is by asking them, "What have you done? You are not so bad!" This is as if they had never done anything wicked, and had in reality no occasion to feel distressed at all. A fashionable lady was spiritually awakened, and she was going to see a minister to talk with him when she was met by a friend, who sent her back, and drove off her anxiety by saying, "What have you done to make you feel this way? I am sure you have never committed any sin that you should feel like this!"

I have often met with cases like this. A mother will tell her anxious son what an obedient child he has always been, how good and how kind, and she begs him "not to carry on so." So a husband will tell his wife, or a wife her husband, "How good you are!" and say, "Why, you are not so bad. You have been to hear that frightful minister, who frightens people, and you have got agitated. Be comforted, for I am sure you have not been bad enough to justify such distress." The truth is that they have been a great deal worse than they think they have. No sinner ever has an idea of his sins greater than they really are. No sinner ever has an adequate idea of how great a sinner he is. It is unlikely that any person could live under a full sight of his sins. God has mercifully spared all his creatures on earth that worst of sights, a naked human heart. The sinner's guilt is much more deep and damning than he thinks, and his danger is much greater than he thinks it is. If he should see his sins as they are, he would probably not live one moment. True, a sinner may have false notions on the subject, which may create distress, but which have no foundation. He may think he has committed the unpardonable sin, or that he has grieved away the Spirit, or sinned away his day of grace. But to tell the most moral and naturally amiable person in the world that he is good enough, or that he is not as bad as he thinks he is, is not giving him rational comfort, but is deceiving him and ruining his soul. Let those who do it, beware.

2. Others tell awakened sinners that "conversion is a progressive work," and in this way ease their anxiety. When a person is distressed, because he sees himself to be such a sinner and that unless he turns to God he

will be lost, it is a great relief to have some friend hold out the idea that he can get better by degrees, and that he is now "moving on," little by little. They tell him, "You cannot expect to move along all at once. do not believe in these sudden conversions, you must wait and let it work. You have begun well, and eventually you will get comfort." All this is false as the bottomless pit. The truth is, regeneration, or conversion, is not a progressive work. What is regeneration? What is it but the beginning of obedience to God? And is the beginning of anything progressive? It is the first act of genuine obedience to God — the first voluntary action of the mind that God approves of, or that can be regarded as obedience to God. That is conversion. When people talk about conversion as a progressive work, it is absurd. They show that they know just as much about regeneration or conversion as Nicodemus did. They know nothing about it as they should know, and are no more fit to instruct anxious sinners than Nicodemus was.

3. Another way in which anxious sinners are deceived with false comfort is by being advised to "dismiss the subject for the present." People who are supposed to be wise and good have assumed to be so much wiser than God, that when God is dealing with a sinner by his Spirit and is trying to bring him to an immediate decision, they think God is crowding too hard, and that it is necessary for them to interfere. They will advise the person to take a ride, or to go into company, or engage in business or do something that will relieve his mind a little, at least for the present. They might just as well say to God in plain words, "O God, you are too difficult, you go too fast, you will make him crazy, or kill him. He cannot stand it, poor creature. If he is so pressed he will die." Just so they take sides against God, and practically tell the sinner himself, "God will make you crazy if you do not dismiss the subject, and resist the Spirit, and drive him away from your mind."

Such advice, if it is truly conviction of sin that distresses the sinner, is in no case either safe or lawful. The strivings of the Spirit, to bring the sinner to Christ, will never hurt him nor drive him crazy. He may make himself deranged by resisting. But it is blasphemous to think that the blessed, wise, and benevolent Spirit of God would ever act with so little care to derange and destroy the soul that he came to sanctify and save. The proper course to take with a sinner, when the striving of the Spirit distresses him, is to instruct him, clear up his views, correct his mistakes, and make the way of salvation so plain that he may see it right before him. Remember, if an awakened sinner should voluntarily dismiss the subject once, he will probably never take it up again.

4. Sometimes an awakened sinner is comforted by being told, "Chris-

tianity does not consist in feeling bad." I once heard of a Doctor of Divinity advise this to an anxious sinner who was suffering under the arrows of the Almighty. He said, "Christianity is cheerful, Christianity is not gloomy. Do not be distressed, but dismiss your fears. Be comforted, you should not feel so bad," and similar miserable comforts. In fact, the man had infinite reason to be distressed, for he was resisting the Holy Spirit, and was in danger of grieving him away forever.

It is true that Christianity does not consist in "feeling bad." But the sinner has reason to be distressed, because he is not a Christian. If he had religion, he would not feel so. Were he a Christian, he would rejoice. But to tell an impenitent sinner to be cheerful! Why, you might as well preach this doctrine in hell, and tell them there, "Cheer up here, cheer up. Do not feel so bad!"

The sinner is on the very verge of hell, he is in rebellion against God, and his danger is infinitely greater than he imagines. Oh, what a doctrine of devils it is to tell a rebel against heaven not to be distressed! What is all his distress but rebellion itself? He is not comforted, because he refuses to be comforted. God is ready to comfort him. You do not need to think to be more compassionate than God. He will fill the sinner with comfort in an instant on submission. There stands the sinner, struggling against God, the Holy Spirit, and conscience, until he is distressed almost to death, but still he will not yield. Now someone comes in saying, "Oh, I hate to see you feel so bad, do not be so distressed. Cheer up, cheer up. Religion does not consist in being gloomy. Be comforted." How terrible!

5. Whatever makes the subject of religion mysterious will give a sinner false comfort. When a sinner is anxious on the subject of Christianity, if you cloud it in mystery, he will very likely feel relieved. The sinner's distress arises from the pressure of present obligation. Enlighten him on this point and clear it up, and if he will not yield, it will only increase his distress. But tell him that regeneration is all a mystery, something he cannot understand, and by leaving him in a fog, you relieve his anxiety. It is his clear view of the nature and duty of repentance that produces his distress. It is the light that brings agony to his mind, while he refuses to obey. It is that which makes up the pains of hell. And this light will almost make hell in the sinner's heart, if only made clear enough. Only cover up this light, and his anxiety will immediately become far less acute. But if you take up a clear light, and shine it broadly upon his soul, then if he will not yield, you kindle up the tortures of hell in his heart.

6. Whatever relieves the sinner from a sense of blame will give him

false comfort. The more a person feels himself to blame, the deeper is his distress. So anything that lessens his sense of blame naturally lessens his distress — but it is a comfort full of death. If anything will help him reduce the blame and put it on God, it will give him comfort. But it is a relief that will destroy his soul.

7. To tell him of his inability is false comfort. Suppose you say to an anxious sinner, "What can you do? You are a poor feeble creature, you can do nothing." You will thereby make him feel a kind of gloom, but it is not that keen agony of remorse with which God wrings the soul when he is working to bring the sinner to repentance.

If you tell him he is unable to comply with the gospel, he naturally is relieved. He says to himself, "Yes, I am unable, I am a poor, feeble creature, I cannot do this, and certainly God cannot send me to hell for not doing what I cannot do." Why, if I believed that a sinner was unable, I would tell him plainly, "Do not be afraid, you are not to blame for not complying with the call of the gospel. For you are unable, and God will not send you to hell for not doing what you have no strength to do — 'Shall not the Judge of all the earth do right?' " I know it is not common for those who talk about the sinner being "unable," to be consistent and carry out their theory. But the sinner infers all this, and so he feels relieved. It is false and all the comfort from it is only storing up wrath for the Day of Wrath.

8. Whatever makes the impression on a sinner's mind that he is to be passive in religion will give him false comfort. Give him the idea that he has nothing to do but to wait for God's time, tell him that conversion is the work of God, and he should leave it to him, and that he must be careful not to try to take the work out of God's hand — the sinner will infer as before, that he is not to blame and will feel relieved. If he has only to stand still, and let God do the work, just as a man holds still to have his arm amputated, he feels relieved. But this instruction is all wrong. If the sinner is thus to stand still and let God do it, he instantly infers that he is not to blame for not doing it himself. The inference is not only natural but also legitimate.

It is true that there is a sense in which conversion is the work of God. But it is false as it is often represented. It is also true that there is a sense in which conversion is the sinner's own act. It is ridiculous, therefore, to say that a sinner is passive in regeneration, or passive in being converted, because conversion is his own act. What is to be done is that which cannot be done for him. It is something that he must do, or it will never be done.

Telling a sinner to wait God's time. Some years ago, in Philadelphia, met a woman who was anxious about her soul, and had been a long me in that state. I conversed with her and tried to learn her state. She ld me many things, and finally said she knew she should be willing to ait on God as long as he had waited upon her. She said that God had aited on her a great many years before she would give any attention) his call, and now she believed it was her duty to wait God's time) show mercy to her and convert her soul. And she said this was the istruction she had received. She must be patient, she thought, wait od's time, and, eventually he would give her relief. Oh, amazing lly!

[ere is the sinner in rebellion. God comes with pardon in one hand and sword in the other, and tells the sinner to repent and receive pardon, r refuse and perish. And now here comes a minister of the gospel and lls the sinner to "wait God's time." He virtually says that God is not ady to have him repent now, and is not ready to pardon him now, nd thus in fact throws off the blame of his impenitence upon God. istead of pointing out the sinner's guilt, in not submitting at once to od, he points out God's "insincerity" — in making an offer when in ict, he was not ready to grant the blessing!

have often thought such teachers needed the rebuke of Elijah, when e met the priests of Baal. "Cry aloud, for he is a god. Either he is ausing, or he is relieving himself, or he is on a journey, or perhaps he s asleep and must be awakened" (1 Kings 18:27). The minister who uggests that God is not ready, and tells the sinner to wait God's time, night almost as well tell him that God is asleep, or gone on a journey, nd cannot attend to him at present. Miserable comforters, indeed! t is little less than outrageous blasphemy of God. How many have one to the judgment, red all over with the blood of souls that they ave deceived and destroyed — by telling them God was not ready o save them, and that they must wait God's time. No doubt such a loctrine gives present relief to an anxious sinner. It authorizes him to ay, "God is not ready, I must wait God's time, and thus I can live in sin while longer, until he is ready to attend to me, and then I will become Christian."

0. It is false comfort to tell an anxious sinner to do anything for relief nd not submit his heart to God. An anxious sinner is often willing to lo anything else but the very thing that God requires him to do. He is villing to go to the ends of the earth, or to pay his money, or to endure uffering, or do anything but make full and instantaneous submission o God. Now, if you will compromise the matter with him, and tell

him of something else that he may do, and yet evade that point, h
will be very much comforted. He likes that instruction. He says, "Ol
yes, I will do that. I like that minister — he is not as severe as other:
He seems to understand my particular case and knows how to mak
allowances."

It often reminds me of the conduct of a patient who is very sick, bu
has a great dislike for a certain physician and a particular medicine
but that is the very physician who alone understands treatment for hi
disease. Now, the patient is willing to do anything else and call in an
other physician. He is anxious and in distress, asking all his friend
what he should do. He will take all the quack medicines in the cour
try before he will submit to the only course that can bring him relie
Eventually, after he has tried everything without receiving any benefi
if he survives the experiment, he gives up this unreasonable opposi
tion, calls in the physician, takes the proper medicine, and is cured. I
is the same with sinners. They will eagerly do anything, if you wi
only let them off from this intolerable pressure of present obligation t
submit to God.

I will mention a few of the things that distract sinners from the poin
of immediate submission.

(a) Telling a sinner he must use the means by attending meetings an
praying. Tell an anxious sinner, "You must use the means," and he i
relieved. "Oh, yes, I will do that, if that is all. I thought that God re
quired me to repent and submit to him now. But if 'using the means
will suffice, I will do that with all my heart." He was distressed before
because he was cornered, and did not know which way to turn. Con
science had troubled him, like a wall of fire, and urged him to repen
NOW. But this relieves him at once. He feels better, and is very thank
ful that he has found such a good adviser in his distress! But he ma
"use the means," as he says, until the Day of Judgment, and not be a
particle the better for it, but only hasten his way to death. What is th
sinner's use of means, but rebellion against God? God uses means —
the church uses means, to convert and save sinners, to impress them
and bring them to submission. But what has the sinner to do with sucl
means? It is just telling him, "You need not submit to God now, but jus
use the means awhile, and see if you cannot melt God's heart down to
you, so that he will yield this point of unconditional submission." It i
a mere petty objection to evade the duty of immediate submission to
God. It is true that sinners, motivated by a regard to their own hap
piness, often give attention to the subject of religion, attend meetings
pray, read, and many such things. But in all this they have no regar

to the honor of God, nor do they so much as intend to obey him. Their goal is not obedience, for if it were, they would not be impenitent sinners. They are not, therefore, using means to be Christians, but to obtain pardon, and a hope. It is absurd to say that an impenitent sinner is using means to repent, for this is the same as to say he is willing to repent, or, in other words, that he does repent, and so is not an impenitent sinner. So to say that an unconverted sinner uses means with the intent to become a Christian is a contradiction. It is saying that he is willing to be a Christian, which is the same as to say he is a Christian already.

b) Telling a sinner to pray for a new heart. I once heard a celebrated Sunday-school teacher do this. He was almost the father of Sunday schools in America. He called a little girl up to him, and began to talk to her. "My little girl, are you a Christian?" "No, sir." "Well, you cannot be a Christian yourself, can you?" "No, sir." "No, you cannot be a Christian yourself, you cannot change your heart yourself, but you must pray for a new heart, that is all you can do. Pray to God, God will give you a new heart." He was an aged and venerable man, but I almost felt inclined to rebuke him in the name of the Lord. I could not bear to hear him deceive that child, practically telling her she could not be a Christian. Does God say, "Pray for a new heart"? Never. He says, "Make yourselves a new heart" (Ezekiel 18:31). The sinner is not to be told to pray to God to do his duty for him, but to go and do it himself. I know the Psalmist prayed, "Create in me a clean heart, and renew a right spirit within me" (Psalm 51:10). He had faith, and prayed in faith. But that is a very different thing from telling an obstinate rebel to pray for a new heart. An anxious sinner will be delighted with such instruction, saying, "I knew I needed a new heart, and that I should repent, but I thought I must do it myself. I am very willing to ask God to do it. I hated to do it myself, but have no objection that God should do it, if he will, and I will pray for it, if that is all that is required."

(c) Telling the sinner to persevere. And suppose he does persevere? He is as certain to be lost as if he had been in hell ever since the foundation of the world. His anxiety comes only from his resistance. If he would submit, it would cease. Will you tell him to persevere in the very thing that causes his distress? Suppose my child should, in a fit of emotion, throw a book or something on the floor. I tell him, "Pick it up," but instead of minding what I say, he runs off and plays. "Pick it up!" He sees I am sincere, and begins to look serious. "Pick it up, or I shall get a rod." And I put up my arm to get the rod. He stands still. "Pick it up, or you must be whipped." He comes slowly along to the place, and begins to weep. "Pick it up, my child, or you will certainly be punished."

Now he is in distress, and sobs and sighs as if his chest would burst. But he still remains as stubborn as if he knew I could not punish him. Now I begin to press him with reasons to submit and obey, but there he stands in agony and eventually bursts out, "Oh, father, I do feel so bad, I think I am getting better." And now, suppose a neighbor comes in and sees the child standing there, in all his agony and stubbornness. The neighbor asks him what he is standing there for, and what he is doing. "Oh, I am using means to pick up that book." If this neighbor should tell the child, "Persevere, persevere, my boy, you will get it eventually," what should I do? Why, I would ask him to leave the house. What does he mean by encouraging my child in rebellion?

Now, God calls the sinner to repent, he threatens him, he draws the glittering sword, he persuades him, he gives reasons, and the sinner is distressed to agony, for he sees himself driven to the dreadful alternative of giving up his sins or going to hell. He should instantly lay down his weapons, and break his heart at once. But he resists, and struggles against conviction, and that creates his distress. Now, will you tell him to persevere? Persevere in what? In struggling against God! That is just the direction the devil would give. All the devil wants is to see him persevere just in the way he is going on, and his destruction is sure.

(d) Telling a sinner to press forward. That is, to say to him, "You are on a good path, only press forward, and you will get to heaven." This is on the supposition that his face is toward heaven, when in fact his face is toward hell, and he is pressing forward, and never more rapidly than now, while he is resisting the Holy Spirit. Often have I heard this direction given, when the sinner was in as bad a way as he could be. What you should tell him is, "STOP, sinner, stop, do not take another step that way, it leads to hell." God tells him to stop, and because he does not wish to stop, he is distressed. Now, why should you attempt to comfort him in this way?

(e) Telling a sinner that he must "try" to repent and give his heart to God. "Oh, yes," says the sinner, "I am willing to try, I have often tried to do it, and I will try again." Does God tell you to "try" to repent? The whole world would be willing to "try" to repent, in their way. Giving this direction implies that it is very difficult to repent, and perhaps impossible, and that the best thing a sinner can do is to try to see whether he can do it or not. What is this, but substituting your own commandment in the place of God's? God requires nothing short of repentance and a holy heart. Anything short of that is comforting the sinner in vain. "There is nothing left of your answers but falsehood."

f) Telling him to pray for repentance. "Oh, yes, I will pray for repentance, if that is all. I was distressed because I thought God required me to repent, but I can wait." And so he feels relieved, and is quite comfortable.

g) Telling a sinner to pray for conviction, or pray for the Holy Spirit to show him his sins, or to work to get more light on the subject of his guilt, in order to increase his conviction. All this is just what the sinner wants, because it lets him off from the pressure of present obligation. He wants just a little more time. Anything that will defer that present pressure of obligation to repent immediately is a relief. What does he want more conviction for? Does God give any such direction to an impenitent sinner? God takes it for granted that he has conviction enough already. Do you say he cannot realize all his sins? If he can realize only one of them, let him repent of that one, and he is a Christian. Suppose he could see them all, what reason is there to think he would repent of them all, any more than he would repent of that one that he does see? All this is comforting the sinner by telling him to do that which he can do, and yet not submit his heart to God.

11. Another way in which false comfort is given to anxious sinners is, to tell them God is trying their faith by keeping them in the furnace, and they must wait patiently upon the Lord. As if God were at fault, or stood in the way of a sinner becoming a Christian. Or as if an impenitent sinner had faith! What an abomination! Suppose somebody should tell my child, while he was standing by the book that I have described, "Wait patiently, my boy, your father is trying your faith." No. The sinner is trying the patience of God. God is not setting himself to torture a sinner, and teach him a lesson of patience. But he is waiting upon him, and working to bring him at once into such a state of mind as will make it consistent to fill his soul with the peace of heaven. Shall the sinner be encouraged to resist? BE CAREFUL! God has said his Spirit will not always strive.

12. Another false comfort is saying to the sinner, "Do your duty, and leave your conversion with God." I once heard an elder of a church say to an anxious sinner, "Do your duty, and leave your conversion to God. He will do it in his own time and way." That was just the same as telling him, that it was not his duty to be converted NOW. He did not say, "Do your duty, and leave your salvation with God." That would have been proper enough, for it would have been simply telling him to submit to God, and would have included conversion as the first duty of all. But he told him to leave his conversion to God. And this elder that gave such advice was also a man of liberal education. How absurd! As

if the sinner could do his duty and not be converted! God has required him, "Make yourselves a new heart" (Ezekiel 18:31). Beware how you comfort him with an answer of falsehood.

13. Sometimes professing Christians will try to comfort a sinner by telling him, "Do not be discouraged. I was like you for a long time before I found comfort." They will tell him, "I was under conviction so many weeks — or perhaps so many months, or sometimes years — and have gone through all this, and know just how you feel. Your experience is precisely the same as mine. After a long time I found relief, and I do not doubt you will find it eventually. Do not despair, God will comfort you soon." Tell a sinner to take courage in his rebellion! Oh, horrible! Such professors should be ashamed. Suppose you were under conviction so many weeks, and afterwards found relief, it is the very last thing you should tell an anxious sinner. What is it but encouraging him to hold out, when his business is to submit? Did you hold out so many weeks while the Spirit was striving with you? You only deserved so much more to be lost, for your obstinacy and dullness.

Sinner! This is not a sign that God will spare you so long, or that his Spirit will remain with you to be resisted. And remember, if the Spirit is taken away, you will be sent to hell.

14. Another false comfort is to say, "I have faith to believe you will be converted." You have faith to believe? The very intention and goal of the Spirit of God is to tear away from the sinner his last vestige of a hope while remaining in sin — to annihilate every rock and twig he may cling to. The goal of your instruction should be the same. You should fall in with the plan of God. It is only in this way that you can ever do any good — by urging him to submit at once, and leave his soul in the hands of God. By telling him, "I have faith to believe you will be converted," it upholds him in a false expectation. Instead of tearing him away from his false hopes, and throwing him upon Christ, you just turn him aside to depend upon your faith, and to find comfort because you have faith for him. This is all false comfort that brings death.

15. Sometimes professing Christians try to comfort an anxious sinner by telling him, "I will pray for you." This is false comfort, for it leads the sinner to trust in those prayers, instead of trusting in Christ. The sinner says, "He is a good person, and God hears the prayers of good people. No doubt his prayers will prevail. I shall be converted in some time. I do not think I will be lost." And his anxiety and agony is all gone. A woman said to a minister, "I have no hope now, but I have faith in your prayers." This is the kind of faith that the devil wants

ιem to have — faith in prayers instead of faith in Christ.

΄. It is an equally false comfort to say, "I rejoice to see you in this way, ιd I hope you will be faithful, and hold out." What is this but rejoicing ᴵ see him in rebellion against God? For that is precisely the ground on ʰich he stands. He is resisting conviction, resisting conscience, and ᴇsisting the Holy Spirit, and yet you rejoice to see him in this way, and ope he will be faithful, and hold out! There is indeed a sense in which may be said that his situation is more hopeful than when he was in ᵤllness. For God has convinced him and may succeed in turning and ᵤbduing him. But that is not the sense in which the sinner himself ʳill understand it. He will suppose that you think of him in a hopeful ιanner, because he is doing better than before. In fact, his guilt and anger are greater than they ever were before. Instead of rejoicing, ου should be distressed and in agony, to see him resisting the Holy pirit. Every moment he does this, he is in danger of being left by God, nd given up to hardness of heart and to despair.

΄. Another false comfort is to tell the sinner he has not repented nough. The truth is, he has not really repented at all. As soon as ιe sinner repents, God always comforts him. This false comfort im-·lies that his feelings are right as far as they go. To tell him that he has ny repentance is to tell him a lie, and cheat him out of his soul.

,8. People sometimes comfort a sinner by telling him, "If you are lected, you will be brought in." I once heard of a case where a person ᵥith great distress of mind was sent to talk with a neighboring minis-ᴇr. They talked for a long time. As the person went away, the minister aid to him, "I would like to send a message with you to your father." ᴵis father was a pious man. The minister wrote the letter, and forgot ᴵ seal it. As the sinner was going home, he saw that the letter was ᴵot sealed, and he thought to himself that the minister had probably ᵥritten about him. His curiosity eventually led him to open and read ᴵ. And there he found it written to this effect, "Dear Sir, I found your on under conviction, and in great distress, and it seems difficult to say ᴵnything to give him relief. But, if he is one of the elect, he is sure to ᴵe brought in." He had wanted to say something to comfort the father. ᴵut note, that letter had nearly ruined the son's soul. He settled down ᴵn the doctrine of Election, saying, "If I am elected, I shall be brought ᴵ," and his conviction was gone. Years afterwards he was awakened ιnd converted, but only after a great struggle, and never until that false ᴵmpression had been obliterated from his mind and he had been made ᴵ see if he did not repent he would be lost.

΄9. It is very common for some people to tell an awakened sinner, "You

are doing well. I am glad to see you like this, and feel encouraged abou
you." It sometimes seems as if the church were in league with the dev
to help sinners to resist the Holy Spirit. The thing that the Holy Spir:
wants to make the sinner feel is, that all his ways are wrong, and tha
they lead to hell. And everybody is conspiring to make the opposit
impression! The Spirit is trying to discourage him, and they are tryin
to encourage him — the Spirit to distress him by showing him that h
is all wrong, and they to comfort him by saying he is doing well. Has i
come to this, that the worst counteraction to the truth and the greate:
obstacle to the Spirit spring from the church? Sinner, do not believ
them! You are not in a hopeful way. You are not doing well, but badl
— as badly as possible, while resisting the Holy Spirit.

20. Another fatal way in which false comfort is given to sinners is b
applying to them certain Scripture promises which were intended onl
for saints. This is a grand device of the devil. It is much practiced b
the Universalists. But Christians often do it also. For example:

(a) "Blessed are those who mourn, for they shall be comforted" (Matthe
5:4). This passage has often been applied to anxious sinners who wer
in distress because they would not submit to God. "Blessed are thos
who mourn." That is true, where they mourn with godly sorrow. Bu
what is this sinner mourning about? He is mourning because God'
law is holy, and the terms of salvation so fixed that he cannot brin:
them down to his mind. Will you tell such a rebel, "Blessed are thos
who mourn"? You might just as well apply it to those that are in hel
There is mourning there too. The sinner is mourning because there i
no other way of salvation, because God is so holy that he requires him
to give up all his sins, and he feels that the time has come, that he mus
either give them up or be lost. Shall we tell him he shall be comforted
Shall we tell the devil, "You mourn now, but the Bible says you ar
blessed if you mourn. You shall eventually be comforted!"

(b) "Seek, and you will find" (Matthew 7:7). This is said to sinners ir
such a way as to imply that the anxious sinner is seeking religion. Thi
promise was made in reference to Christians, who ask in faith and seel
to do the will of God. It is not applicable to those who are seeking
hope or comfort, but only to holy seeking. To apply it to an impeniten
sinner is only to deceive him, for his seeking is not of this character. Tc
tell him, "You are seeking, are you? Well, seek, and you will find," is tc
cherish a fatal delusion. If the sinner had a desire to do his duty, if he
were seeking to do the will of God, and give up his sins, he would be a
Christian. But to comfort an impenitent sinner with such a promise —
you might just as well comfort Satan!

(c) "Let us not grow weary of doing good, for in due season we will reap, if we do not give up" (Galatians 6:9). To apply this for a sinner's comfort is absurd. As if he were doing something to please God! He has never done what is good, and never has done more badly than now. Suppose my neighbor, who came in while I was trying to subdue my child, should say to the child, "In due season you will reap, if you do not give up," what should I say? "Reap? Yes, you shall reap. If you do not give up your obstinacy, you shall reap indeed, for I will apply the rod." So the struggling sinner shall reap the damnation of hell, if he does not give up his sins.

21. Some professing Christians, when they talk with awakened sinners, are very fond of saying, "I will tell you my experience." This is a dangerous snare, and often gives the devil a handle to lead the sinner to hell, by getting him to copy your experience. If you tell it to the sinner, and he thinks it is a Christian experience, he will almost inevitably be trying to imitate it so that instead of following the gospel, or the leadings of the Spirit in his own soul, he is following your example. This is absurd as well as dangerous. No two were ever moved in the same way. People's experiences are as different as are their faces. Such a course is likely to mislead him. The intention is often to encourage him at the very point where he should not be encouraged, before he has submitted to God. And it will impede the work of God in his soul.

22. Many times people will tell an awakened sinner that God has begun a good work in him, and will carry it on. I have known parents talk like this with their children. As soon as they have seen their children awakened, they give up all anxiety about them and settle down at ease, thinking that since now God had begun a work in their children he would carry it on. It would be just as rational for a farmer to say about his grain, as soon as it comes up out of the ground, "Well, God has begun a good work in my field, and he will carry it on." What would be thought of a farmer who should neglect to put up his fence, because God has begun the work of giving him a crop of grain? If you tell a sinner so, and he believes you, it will certainly be his destruction, for it will prevent his doing that which is absolutely indispensable to his being saved. If as soon as the sinner is awakened he is taught that God has begun a good work and he will surely carry it on, the sinner sees that there is no further occasion to be anxious, for he has nothing more to do. And so he will be relieved from that intolerable pressure of present obligation to repent and submit to God. And if he is relieved from his sense of obligation to do it, he will never do it.

23. Some will tell the sinner, "Well, you have broken off your sins."

"Oh, yes," says the sinner, when it is all false. He has never forsaken his sins for a moment, he has only exchanged one form of sin for another — only placed himself in a new attitude of resistance. And to tell him that he has broken them off is to give him false comfort.

24. Sometimes this direction is given for the purpose of relieving the agony of an anxious sinner, "Do what you can, and God will do the rest." Or, "Do what you can, and God will help you." This is the same as telling a sinner, "You cannot do what God requires you to do, but if you do what you can, God will help you with the rest." Now, sinners often get the idea that they have done all they can, when, in fact, they have done nothing at all, except that they have resisted God with all their might. I have often heard them say, "I have done all I can, and I get no relief, what can I do more?" You can see how comforting it must be to have a professing Christian say, "If you will do what you can, God will help you." It relieves all his keen distress at once. He may be uneasy and unhappy, but his agony is gone.

25. Again, they say, "You should be thankful for what you have, and hope for more." If the sinner is convicted, they tell him he should be thankful for conviction, and hope for conversion. Indeed, he has reason to be thankful: thankful that he is out of hell, and thankful that God is waiting on him. But it is ridiculous to tell him that he should be thankful in regard to the state of his mind, when he is all the while resisting his Maker with all his might.

IV. ERRORS MADE IN PRAYING FOR SINNERS

I will here mention a few errors that are made in praying for sinners, by which an unfortunate impression is made on their minds, resulting in false comfort in their distress.

1. People sometimes pray for sinners as if they deserved TO BE PITIED more than BLAMED. They pray for them as "mourners." "Lord, help these pensive mourners!" As if they were just mourners, like one that had lost a friend or met with some other calamity, which they could not help, and so were to be pitied greatly, sitting there, sad, pensive, and sighing. The Bible never talks like this. It pities sinners, but it pities them as mad and guilty rebels, deserving to go to hell, not as poor pensive mourners, who want relief, but can do nothing but sit and mourn.

2. Praying for them as "poor sinners." Does the Bible ever use such language as this? The Bible never speaks of them as "poor sinners," as if they deserved to be pitied more than blamed. Christ pities sinners in his heart. He feels in his heart great compassion for them, when he

sees them going on, stubborn in gratifying their own lusts, at the peril of his eternal wrath. But he never projects an impression as if the sinner were just a "poor creature" to be pitied, as if he could not help his position. The idea that he is poor, rather than wicked — unfortunate, rather than guilty — relieves the sinner greatly. I have seen the sinner writhe with agony under the truth in a meeting until somebody began to pray for him as a "poor" creature. And then he would gush out into tears, weep profusely, and think he was greatly benefited by such a prayer, saying, "Oh, what a good prayer that was!" If you go now and talk with that sinner, you will probably find that he is still pitying himself as a poor unfortunate creature — perhaps even weeping over his unhappy condition. But his conviction of sin and his deep impressions of awful guilt are all gone.

3. Praying that God would "help the sinner to repent." "O Lord, enable this poor sinner to repent now." This conveys the idea to the sinner's mind, that he is now trying with all his might to repent, and that he cannot do it, and therefore Christians are calling on God to help him and enable him to do it. Most professing Christians pray for sinners, not that God would make them willing to repent, but that he would enable them, or make them able. No wonder their prayers are not heard. They relieve the sinner of his sense of responsibility and that relieves his distress. But it is an insult to God, as if God had commanded a sinner to do what he could not do.

4. People sometimes pray, "Lord, these sinners are seeking you in sorrow." This prayer represents sinners as seeking Jesus, but he hides himself from them, and they look all around, and hunt, and try to find him, and wonder where he is. It is a LIE! No sinner ever sought Jesus with all his heart three days, or three minutes, and could not find him. Jesus "stands at the door, and knocks" (Revelation 3:20). He is right before the sinner, pleading with him, and facing him with all his false pretenses. Seeking Jesus! The sinner may cry, "Oh, how I am in sorrow and seeking Jesus," but it is not true. Jesus is seeking him.[1] And yet how many oppressed consciences are relieved and comforted by hearing one of these prayers.

5. "Lord, have mercy on these sinners, who are seeking to know your love." This is a favorite expression with many, as if sinners were seeking to know the love of Christ, and could not. Not true. They are not

---

[1] This point is especially powerful given today's practice of calling nonbelievers who are reading the Bible or going to Christian meetings by the title of *seekers*. Finney would clearly object to this practice. With respect to God and the unbeliever, it is only God who should be called "seeker."

seeking the love of Christ, but seeking to get to heaven without Jesus Christ. As if they were seeking it, and he was so hard-hearted that he would not let them have it!

6. "Lord, have mercy on these penitent souls." This prayer calls anxious sinners "penitent souls"! If they are truly penitent, they are Christians. To make the impression on an unconverted sinner that he is penitent is to make him believe a lie. But it is very comforting to the sinner, and he likes to take it up, and pray it over again, "O Lord, I am a poor penitent soul, I am very penitent, I am so distressed. Lord, have mercy on a poor penitent." Dreadful delusion, to lead an impenitent sinner to pray as a penitent!

7. Sometimes people pray for anxious sinners as "humble souls." "O Lord, these sinners have humbled themselves." But it is not true — they have not humbled themselves. If they had, the Lord would have raised them up and comforted them, as he has promised. There is a hymn of this character that has done much mischief. It begins:

> Come, humble sinner, in whose breast
> A thousand thoughts revolve.

A minister once gave this hymn to an awakened sinner for his case. He began to read, "Come, humble sinner." He stopped, "Humble sinner? That is not applicable to me, I am not a humble sinner." Ah, how well was it for him that the Holy Spirit had taught him better than the hymn! If the hymn had said, "Come, anxious sinner," or "guilty sinner," or "trembling sinner," it would have been well enough, but to call him a "humble" sinner would not do. There are vast numbers of hymns of the same character. It is very common to find sinners quoting the false sentiments of some hymn, to excuse themselves in rebellion against God.

8. People pray that sinners "may have more conviction." Or, they pray that sinners may "go home solemn and tender, and take the subject into consideration," instead of praying that they may repent now. Or, they pray as if they supposed the sinner to be willing to do what is required. All such prayers are the kind of prayers that the devil wants and he does not care how many like these are offered.

REMARKS

1. Many people who deal in this way with anxious sinners do so from false pity. They feel so much sympathy and compassion that they cannot bear to tell sinners the truth that is necessary to save them. A sur-

eon might as well, when he sees that a person's arm must be ampu-
ated or death must result, indulge this feeling of false pity, and just
ut on a cast and give him a painkiller. There is no benevolence in that.
rue benevolence would lead the surgeon to be cool and calm, and,
vith a keen knife, cut the limb off, and save the life. It is false tender-
ess to do anything short of that. I once saw a woman under distress of
nind, who for months had been nearly driven to despair. Her friends
ad tried all the false comforts without effect, and they brought her
> see a minister. She was emaciated, and worn out with agony. The
ninister set his eye upon her, and poured in the truth upon her mind,
nd rebuked her in a most pointed manner. The woman with her inter-
ered. She thought it was cruel, and said, "Oh, do comfort her, she is so
listressed. Do not trouble her any more, she cannot bear it." Then the
ninister turned, and rebuked her, and sent her away, and then poured
n the truth upon the anxious sinner like fire, so that in five minutes she
vas converted, and went home full of joy. The plain truth swept all her
alse notions away, and in a few moments she was joyful in God.

. The treatment of anxious sinners that gives such false comforts is
ctually cruelty. It is cruel as the grave, as cruel as hell, for it is cal-
ulated to send the sinner down to the burning abyss. Christians feel
ompassion for the anxious, and so they should. But the last thing they
hould do is to flinch just at the point where it comes to a crisis. They
hould feel compassion, but they should show it just as the surgeon
loes, when he deliberately goes to work, in the right and best way,
nd cuts off the person's arm, and thus cures him and saves his life.
ust so Christians should let the sinner see their compassion and ten-
lerness, but they should take God's part, fully and decidedly. They
hould expose to the sinner his guilt and danger, lead him right up to
he cross, and insist on instant submission. They must have firmness
nough to do this work thoroughly. If they see the sinner distressed
nd in agony, they must still press him right on, and not give way in
he least until he yields.

To do this often requires nerve. I have often been placed in circum-
tances where I have realized this. I have found myself surrounded
with anxious sinners, in such distress as to make every nerve tremble:
ome overcome with emotion and lying on the floor; some applying
amphor to prevent their fainting; others shrieking out as if they were
ust going to hell. Now, suppose any one should give false comfort in
uch a case as this? Suppose he had not enough nerve to bring them
ight up to the point of instant and absolute submission? How unfit
vould such a person be, to be trusted in such a case!

3. Sometimes sinners become deranged through despair and anguis of mind. Whenever this is the case, it is almost always because thos who deal with them try to encourage them with false comfort, an thus lead them to such a conflict with the Holy Spirit. They try to hol them up, while God is trying to break them down. And eventually th sinner's mind gets confused with these opposing influences, and h either goes deranged, or is driven to despair.

4. If you are going to deal with sinners, remember that you are soon t meet them in Judgment. Therefore be sure to treat them in such a wa that if they are lost, it will be their own fault. Do not try to comfor them with false notions now, and have them reproach you with it ther Better to suppress your false sympathy, and let the naked truth "pierc even to the division of soul and of spirit, and of joints and of marrow (Hebrews 4:12), than to soothe them with false comfort, and deceiv them away from God!

5. Sinner, if you talk with any Christians, and they tell you to do any thing, first ask, "If I do that, shall I be saved?" You may be anxious and not be saved. You may pray, and not be saved. You may read you Bible, and not be saved. You may use means in your own way, and not be saved. Whatever they tell you to do, if you can do it and no be saved, do not listen to such instructions. They will give you fals comfort, and divert your attention from the main thing to be done, and deceive you down to hell. Do not follow any such directions, lest yo should die while doing so.

6. Finally, let a Christian never tell a sinner anything, or give him any direction, that will lead him to stop short of, or that does not include submission to God. To let him stop at any point short of this is in finitely dangerous. Suppose you are at an anxious meeting, or a praye meeting, and you tell a sinner to pray, or to read, or to do anything that comes short of saving repentance, and he should fall and breal his neck that night, of whom would his blood be required? A youth ir New England once met a minister in the street, and asked him "wha he should do to be saved?" The minister told him to go home, and go into his room, and kneel down and give his heart to God. "Sir," said the boy, "I feel so bad, I am afraid I shall not live to get home." The minister saw his error, felt the rebuke thus unconsciously given by a youth, and then told him, "Well, then, give your heart to God here and then go home to your room and tell him of it."

It is enough to make one's heart bleed to see so many miserable com-forters for anxious sinners. "There is nothing left of their answers bu falsehood." What a vast amount of spiritual quackery there is in the world, and how many liars there are, "worthless physicians" (Job 13:4) who know no better than to comfort sinners with false hopes, and delude them with their "irreverent, silly myths" (1 Timothy 4:7) and nonsense. How many give way to false tenderness and sympathy, until they have not firmness enough to see the sword of the Spirit applied, cutting to the soul, and laying open the sinner's naked heart. Alas, so many are going into the ministry who do not have enough skill to stand by and watch the Spirit of God to do his work, breaking up the old foundations, crushing all the rotten hopes of a sinner, and breaking him down at the feet of Jesus.

Chapter 12

INSTRUCTIONS TO SINNERS

"What must I do to be saved?" (Acts 16:30)

These are the words of the jailer at Philippi, the question that he asked Paul and Silas, who were then under his care as prisoners. In my last lecture, I dwelt at some length on the false instructions given to sinners under conviction, and the false comforts often given, and the erroneous instructions that such persons receive. It is my intent now to describe the instructions that should be given to anxious sinners for their speedy and effective conversion. In other words, I will explain to you, what answer should be given to those who make the inquiry, "What must I do to be saved?" I propose:

I. To show what is not a proper instruction to be given to sinners, when they ask the question in the text.

II. To show what is a proper answer to the question.

III. To specify several errors into which anxious sinners are likely to fall.

I. WHAT ARE NOT PROPER INSTRUCTIONS

No more important question was ever asked than this, "What must I do to be saved?" People are likely enough to ask, "What shall I eat, and what shall I drink?" and the question may be answered in various ways, with little danger. But when a sinner sincerely asks, "What must I do to be saved?" it is of infinite importance that he should receive the right answer.

1. No instruction should be given to a sinner that will leave him still "in the gall of bitterness and in the bond of iniquity" (Acts 8:23). No answer is right to give if by agreeing with it he would not go to heaven if he should die the next moment.

2. No instruction should be given that does not include a change of heart and full obedience to Christ. In other words, nothing is proper which does not imply actually becoming a Christian. Any other instruction that falls short of this is of no use. It will not bring him any nearer to the kingdom and it will do no good, but will lead him to defer the very thing that he must do in order to be saved. The sinner should be told plainly what he must do to not be lost. He should be told nothing that does not include a right state of heart. Whatever you may do, sinner, which does not include a right heart is sin. Whether you read the Bible or not, you are in sin, so long as you remain in rebellion. Whether you go to religious services or stay away, whether you pray or not, it is nothing but rebellion, every moment. It is surprising that a sinner should suppose himself to be doing service to God when he prays, and reads his Bible. Suppose a rebel against the government reads the law-book while he continues in rebellion, and has no intention to obey. If he asks for pardon while he holds on to his weapons of resistance and warfare, would you think him doing his country a service? No. You would say that all his reading and praying were only an insult to the majesty both of the lawgiver and the law. So you, sinner, while you remain in impenitence, are insulting God and being defiant, whether you read his Word, and pray, or leave it alone. No matter what place or what attitude your body is in, on your knees or in the house of God — so long as your heart is not right, so long as you resist the Holy Spirit, and reject Christ, you are a rebel against your Maker.

II. WHAT IS A PROPER ANSWER

Generally, you may give the sinner any instruction, or tell him to do anything, that includes a right heart. If you make him understand, and he follows the instructions, he will be saved. The Spirit of God, in striving with sinners, suits his strivings to the state of mind in which he finds them. His great object in striving with them is to dislodge them from their hiding places, and bring them to immediately submit to God. These objections, difficulties, and states of mind, are as various as the circumstances of mankind — as many as there are individuals. The characters of individuals afford an endless diversity. What is to be done with each one, and how he is to be converted, depends on his particular errors. It is necessary to ascertain his errors, to find out what he understands, and what he needs to be taught more perfectly — to e what points the Spirit of God is pressing upon his conscience, and press the same things, and thus bring him to Christ.

he most common instructions are the following:

It is generally a safe and suitable instruction to tell a sinner to re-ent. I say, generally. For sometimes the Spirit of God seems not so uch to direct the sinner's attention to his own sins as to some other hing. In the days of the apostles, the minds of the people seem to have een agitated mainly on the question of whether Jesus was the true lessiah. And so the apostles directed much of their instruction to this oint, to prove that he was the Christ. And whenever anxious sinners sked them what they must do, they most commonly exhorted them "believe on the Lord Jesus Christ." They emphasized this point, be-ause this was where the Spirit of God was striving, and this was the ubject that especially agitated the minds of the people. Consequently, is would probably be the first thing a person would do on submit-ng to God. It was the grand point at issue between God and the Jew nd Gentile of those days, whether Jesus Christ was the Son of God. It vas the point in dispute. To bring the sinner to yield this controversial uestion was the most effective way to humble him.

t other times, it will be found that the Spirit of God is dealing with inners mainly about their own sins. Sometimes he deals with them in egard to a particular duty, like prayer — perhaps family prayer. The inner will be found to be contesting that point with God, whether it is ight for him to pray, or whether he should pray in his family. I have nown striking cases of this kind, where the individual was struggling n this point, and as soon as he fell on his knees to pray, he yielded is heart, showing that this was the very point which the Spirit of God vas contesting, and the hinge on which his controversy with God all urned. That was conversion.

he instruction to repent is always proper, but will not always be effec-ive, for there may be some other thing that the sinner needs to be told lso. And where it is the pertinent instruction, sinners need not only o be told to repent, but to have it explained to them what repentance s. Since there has been so much mysticism, false philosophy, and false heology thrown around the subject, it has become necessary to tell sin-ers not only what you mean by repentance, but also to tell them what ou do not mean. Words that used to be plain and easily understood ave now become so perverted that they need to be explained to sin-ers or they will often convey a wrong impression to their minds. This s the case with the word "repentance." Many suppose that remorse, or a sense of guilt, is repentance. Then, hell is full of repentance, for it is full of remorse, unspeakable and eternal. Others feel regret tha they have done such a thing, and they call that repenting. But the only regret that they have sinned, because of the consequences, an not because they detest sin. This is not repentance. Others suppos that convictions of sin and strong fears of hell are repentance. Other consider the protests of conscience as repentance. They say, "I never d anything wrong without repenting and feeling sorry I did it." Sinner must be shown that all these things are not repentance. They are no only consistent with the utmost wickedness, but the devil might hav them all and yet remain a devil. Repentance is a change of mind re garding God and towards sin. It is not only a change of views, but als a change of the ultimate preference or choice of the soul. It is a volun tary change, and by consequence involves a change of feeling and action toward God and toward sin. It is what is naturally understoo by a change of mind on any subject of interest and importance. W hear that a person has changed his mind in politics. Everyone under stands that he has undergone a change in his views, his feelings, an his conduct. This is repentance, on that subject: it is a change of mind but not toward God. Evangelical repentance is a change of willing, feeling, and of life, with respect to God.

Repentance always implies abhorrence of sin. It of course involves th love of God and the forsaking of sin. The sinner who truly repents doe not feel as impenitent sinners think they should feel at giving up thei sins, if they should become religious. Impenitent sinners look upo religion in this way: if they become pious, they should be obliged t stay away from balls and parties, and obliged to give up theaters, o gambling, or other things that they now take delight in. And they d not see how they could ever enjoy themselves, if they should break of from all those things. But this is very far from being a correct view of the matter. Christianity does not make them unhappy, by shuttin them out from things in which they delight, because the first step i religion is to repent, to change their mind in regard to all these things They do not seem to realize, that the person who has repented ha no inclination for these things. He has given them up and turned hi mind away from them. Sinners feel as if they should want to go to suc places, and want to mingle in such scenes, just as much as they do now and that it will be such a continual sacrifice as to make them unhappy This is a great mistake.

I know there are some professing Christians who would be very glad t go back to their former practices, were it not that they feel constrained for fear of losing their character, or the like. But, mark my words: i they feel this way, it is because they have no religion. They do not hate sin. If they desire their former ways, they have no religion. They have never repented, for repentance always consists in a change of views and feelings. If they were really converted, instead of choosing such things, they would turn away from them with loathing. Instead of lusting after the flesh-pots of Egypt, and desiring to go into their former circles, parties, balls, and the like, they would find their highest pleasure in obeying God.

2. Sinners should be told to believe the gospel. Here, they also need to have it explained to them, and to be told what faith is and what it is not. Nothing is more common than for a sinner, when told to believe the gospel, to say, "I do believe it." The fact is that he has been brought up to admit the fact that the gospel is true, but he does not believe it. He knows nothing about the evidence of it, and all his faith is a mere admission without evidence. He holds it to be true, in a kind of loose, indefinite sense, so that he is always ready to say, "I do believe the Bible." It is strange that they do not see that they are deceived in thinking that they believe, for they must see that they have never acted upon these truths, as they do upon those things that they do believe. Yet it is often quite difficult to convince them that they do not believe.

But the fact is, that the apathetic sinner does not believe the gospel at all. The idea that the apathetic sinner is an intellectual believer is absurd. The devil is an intellectual believer, and that is what makes him tremble. What makes a sinner anxious is, that he begins to be an intellectual believer, and that makes him feel. No being in heaven, earth, or hell, can intellectually believe the truths of the gospel, and not feel on the subject. The anxious sinner has faith of the same kind with devils, though not as much, and therefore he does not feel as much. The person who does not feel or act at all on the subject of Christianity is an infidel, no matter what he says. He who feels nothing, and does nothing, believes nothing. This is a logical fact.

Faith does not consist in an intellectual conviction that Christ died for you in particular, or in a belief that you are a Christian, or that you ever shall be, or that your sins are forgiven. But faith is that trust or confidence in God, and in Christ, which commits the whole soul to him in all his relations to us. It is a voluntary trust in his person, his veracity, and his word. This was the faith of Abraham. He had that confidence in what God said, which led him to act as accepting its truth. This is the way the apostle illustrates it in the eleventh chapter of Hebrews. "Faith is the assurance of things hoped for, the conviction of things not seen" (Hebrews 11:1).

Take the case of Noah, who was warned by God of things not yet seen.

He was assured that God was going to drown the world, and he believed it, and acted accordingly. He prepared an ark to save his family, and by so doing, he condemned the world that would not believe. His actions gave evidence that he was sincere. Read the whole chapter, and you will find many examples of the same kind. The whole intent of the chapter is to illustrate the nature of faith, and to show that it always results in action. The sinner should have it explained to him and be made to see that the faith which the gospel requires is just that confidence in Christ which leads him to act on what he says as being a sure fact. This is believing in Christ.

3. Another instruction, proper to be given to the sinner is that he should give his heart to God. God says, "My son, give me your heart" (Proverbs 23:26). But here also there needs to be explanation, to make him understand what it is. It is amazing that there should be any confusion here. It is the language of common life, and everyone understands just what it means when we use it regarding anything else. But when it comes to religion, they seem to be all in the dark. Ask a sinner, no matter what his age or education, what it means to give the heart to God, and he is at a loss for an answer. Ask a woman what it is to give her heart to her husband, or a man what it is to give his heart to his wife. They understand it. But then they are totally blind as to giving their hearts to God. I suppose I have asked more than a thousand anxious sinners this question. When I have told them that they must give their hearts to God, they have always said that they were willing to do it, and sometimes, that they were anxious to do it, and they have even seemed to be in an agony of desire about it. Then I have asked them what they understood to be meant by giving their hearts to God, since they were so willing to do it. And very seldom have I received a correct or rational answer from a sinner of any age. I have sometimes heard the strangest answers that could be imagined.

Now, to give your heart to God is the same thing as to give your heart to anybody else — the same as for a woman to give her heart to her husband. Ask that woman if she understands this. "Oh, yes, that is clear enough. It is to place my affections with him, and strive to please him in everything." Very well, place your affections on God, and strive to please him in everything. But when they come to the subject of religion, people suppose there is some mystery about it. Some talk as if they suppose it means taking out this bundle of muscles, or fleshy organ, in their chest, and giving it to God. Sinner, what God asks of you is that you should love him supremely.

4. "Submit to God," is also a proper instruction to anxious sinners.

And oh, how confused sinners are here, too! Scarcely a sinner can be found who will not tell you that he is willing to submit to God. But they do not understand. They need to be told what true submission is. True submission is yielding obedience to God. Suppose a rebel, in arms against the government, is called on to submit, what would he understand by it? Why, that he should yield the point, and lay down his arms, and obey the laws. That is just what it means for a sinner to submit to God. He must cease his strife and conflict against his Maker, and take the attitude of a willing and obedient child, willing to be and do whatever God requires.

5. Another proper instruction to be given to sinners is to confess and forsake their sins. They must confess to God their sins against God, and confess to people their sins against people — and forsake them all. A person does not forsake his sins until he has made all the reparation in his power. If he has stolen money or defrauded his neighbor out of property, he does not forsake his sins by merely resolving not to steal any more, nor to cheat again. He must make reparation to the extent of his power. So, if he has slandered any one, he does not forsake his sin by merely saying he will not do so again — he must make reparation. So, in like manner, if he has robbed God, as all sinners have, he must make reparation as far as he has power.

Suppose a person has made money in rebellion against God, and has withheld from him his time, talents, and service, and refused to give himself for the salvation of the world. This person has robbed God. Now, if he should die, feeling this money to be his own, and should he leave it to his heirs without consulting the will of God — why, he is just as certain to go to hell as a highway robber. With all his whining and pious talk, he has never confessed his sin to God, nor forsaken his sin, for he has neither felt nor acknowledged himself to be the steward of God. If he refuses to hold the property in his possession as the steward of God, if he treats it as his own, and as such gives it to his children, he says in effect to God, "That property is not yours, it is mine, and I will give it to my children." He has continued to persevere in his sin, for he does not relinquish the ownership of that of which he has robbed God.

6. Another proper instruction to be given to sinners is, "Choose this day whom you will serve" (Joshua 24:15). In Old Testament times, this, or something equivalent to it, was the most common instruction given. It was not common to call on people to believe in Christ until the days of John the Baptist. He baptized those who came to him with the baptism of repentance, and directed them to believe on him who should come after him. Under Joshua, the text was something that the

people all understood more easily than they would a call to believe on the distant Messiah. It was, "Choose this day whom you will serve." On another occasion, Moses said to them, "I call heaven and earth to witness against you today, that I have set before you life and death, blessing and curse. Therefore choose life, that you and your offspring may live" (Deuteronomy 30:19). The instruction was accommodated to the people's knowledge. And it is as good now as it was then. What are sinners called upon to choose? Whether they will serve God or the world, whether they will follow holiness or sin. Let them be made to understand what is meant by choosing, and what is to be chosen, and then if it is done from the heart, they will be saved.

Any of these instructions, if complied with, will constitute true conversion. The particular exercises may vary in different cases. Sometimes the first exercise in conversion is submission to God, sometimes repentance, sometimes faith, sometimes the choice of God and his service — in short, whatever their thoughts are taken up with at the time. If their thoughts are directed to Christ at the moment, the first exercise will be faith. If to sin, the first exercise will be repentance. If to their future course of life, it is choosing the service of God. If to the divine government, it is submission. It is important to find out just where the Holy Spirit is pressing the sinner at the time, and then take care to push that point. If it is in regard to Christ, press that. If it is in regard to his future course of life, push him right up to an immediate choice of obedience to God.

It is a great error to suppose that any one particular exercise is always foremost in conversion, or that every sinner must have faith first, or submission first. There is a great variety in people's exercises. Whatever point is taken hold of between God and the sinner, when the sinner yields that, he is converted. Whatever the particular exercise may be, if it includes obedience of heart to God on any point, it is true conversion. When he yields one point to God's authority, he is ready to yield all. When he changes his mind, and obeys in one thing, because it is God's will, he will obey in other things, so far as he sees it to be God's will. Where there is right choice, whenever the mind is directed to any one point of duty, he is ready to follow. It matters very little which of these instructions is given, if it is only made clear, and if it is to the point, to serve as a test of obedience to God. If it is to the point that the Spirit of God is debating with the sinner's mind, so as to join the Spirit's work, and not to divert the sinner's attention from the very point in controversy, let it be made perfectly clear, and then pressed until the sinner yields, and he will be saved.

II. ERRORS INTO WHICH ANXIOUS SINNERS ARE LIKELY TO ALL

. The first error is in supposing that they must make themselves better, r prepare themselves, so as in some way to recommend themselves to he mercy of God. It is remarkable that sinners will not understand hat all they have to do is to accept salvation from God. But they all, ducated or uneducated, at first try a legalistic course to get relief. This ; one main reason why they will not become Christians at once. They magine that they must be, in some way or other, prepared to come. hey are not willing to come just as they are, in their rags and poverty. hey must have something more on, before they can approach God. hey should be shown, at once, that it is impossible to be any better ntil they do what God requires. Every pulse that beats, every breath hey draw, they are growing worse, because they are standing out in ebellion against God, so long as they do not do the very thing which ;od requires of them as the first thing to be done.

. Another error is, in supposing that they must suffer a considerable ime under conviction, as a kind of punishment, before they are prop-rly ready to come to Christ. So they will pray for conviction, and hey think that if they are ground down to the earth with distress for ong enough, then God will pity them, and be more ready to help them vhen he sees them so very miserable! They should be made to un-lerstand clearly that they are thus unhappy and miserable, merely be-·ause they refuse to accept the relief that God offers.

. Sometimes sinners imagine they must wait for different feelings be-ore they submit to God. They say, "I do not think I feel right yet to iccept Christ. I do not think I am prepared to be converted yet." They :hould be made to see that what God requires of them is to will right. If hey obey and submit with the will, the feelings will adjust themselves n due time. It is not a question of feeling, but of willing and acting.

The feelings are involuntary, and have no moral character except what hey derive from the action of the will, with which action they sympa-hize. Before the will is right, the feelings will of course not be right. The sinner should come to Christ by accepting him at once. He must do his, not in obedience to his feelings, but in obedience to his conscience. Obey, submit, trust. Give up all instantly, and your feelings will come ight. Do not wait for better feelings, but commit your whole being o God at once, and this will soon result in the feelings for which you ire waiting. What God requires of you is the present act of your mind, n turning from sin to holiness, and from the service of Satan to the ervice of the living God.

4. Another error of sinners is to suppose that they must wait until their hearts are changed. "What?" they say, "am I to believe in Christ before my heart is changed? Do you mean that I am to repent before my heart is changed?" Now, the simple answer to all this is that the change of heart is the very thing in question. God requires the sinner to love him: that is to change his hearts. God requires the sinner to believe the gospel. That is to change his heart. God requires him to repent. That is to change his heart. God does not tell him to wait until his heart is changed, and then repent and believe, and love God. The very word itself, repent, signifies a change of mind or heart. To do either of these things is to change your heart, and to "make yourselves a new heart" (Ezekiel 18:31), just as God requires.

5. Sinners often get the idea that they are perfectly willing to do what God requires. Tell them to do this thing, or that, to repent, or believe or give God their hearts, and they say, "Oh, yes, I am perfectly willing to do that. I wish I could do it, I would give anything if I could do it." They should understand that being truly willing is doing it, but there is a difference between willing and desiring. People often desire to be Christians, when they are wholly unwilling to be so. When we see anything that appears to be a good, we are so constituted that we desire it. We necessarily desire it when it is before our minds. We cannot help desiring it in proportion as its goodness is presented to our minds. But yet we may not be willing to have it, under all the circumstances. A man may desire on many accounts to go to Philadelphia, while, for still more weighty reasons, he chooses not to go there. So the sinner may desire to be a Christian. He may see that if he were a Christian he would be happier, and that he should go to heaven when he dies — but yet he is not willing to be a Christian. Willing to obey Christ is to be a Christian. When an individual actually chooses to obey God, he is a Christian. But all such desires that do not terminate in actual choice are nothing.

6. The sinner will sometimes say that he offers to give God his heart but he hints that God is unwilling. But this is absurd. What does God ask? Why, that you should love him. Now for you to say that you are willing to give God your heart, but that God is unwilling, is the same as saying that you are willing to love God, but God is not willing to be loved by you, and will not tolerate you to love him. It is important to clear up all these points in the sinner's mind, that he may have no dark and mysterious corner to rest in, where the truth will not reach him.

7. Sinners sometimes get the idea that they repent when they are only convicted. Whenever the sinner is found resting in any LIE let the truth

sweep it away, however much it may cause pain and distress. If he has any error of this kind, you must tear it away from him.

8. Sinners are often wholly taken up with looking at themselves, to see if they cannot find something there, some kind of feeling or other that will recommend them to God. Evidently for lack of proper instruction, David Brainerd[1] was taken up with his state of mind for a long time, looking for some feelings that would recommend him to God. Sometimes he imagined that he had such feelings, and would tell God in prayer that now he felt as he should, in order to receive his mercy. Then he would see that he had been all wrong. Thus the poor man, for lack of correct instruction, was driven almost to despair. It is easy to see that his comfort and usefulness were much impaired by the false beliefs he had adopted on this point. You must turn the sinner away from himself.

REMARKS

1. The work of ministers is greatly increased and the difficulties in the way of salvation are greatly multiplied by the false instructions that have been given to sinners. The consequence has been that instructions that used to be clear are now obscure. People have been taught so long that there is something so mysterious and unintelligible about conversion that they do not try to understand it.

It was once sufficient, as we learn from the Bible, to tell sinners to repent, or to believe on the Lord Jesus Christ. But now, faith has been talked about as a principle instead of an act, and repentance as something put into the mind, instead of an exercise of the mind. Sinners are perplexed. It is often a matter of the greatest difficulty to lead sinners out of the theological labyrinths and mazes into which they have been deluded, and to lead them along the straight and simple way of the gospel. It seems as if the greatest ingenuity had been used to mystify the minds of the people, and to weave a most subtle web of false philosophy, designed to involve a sinner in endless darkness. It is necessary to be as plain as A B C, and the most educated have to be talked to like children. Tell a sinner to believe, and he stares, saying, "Why, how you talk! Is not faith a principle? And how am I to believe until

---

[1] David Brainerd (1718-1747) was a man who worked as a missionary to the Native Americans. Though he had poor health, he showed remarkable dedication for the sake of the gospel. He died in the home of Jonathan Edwards, who subsequently published his diary. Known as the *Life and Diary of David Brainerd*, it is widely regarded as one of the most powerful autobiographical accounts ever written. It has inspired countless believers (including William Carey, David Livingstone, and Jim Elliot) in the service of Christ.

I get this principle?" So, if a minister tells a sinner, in the very words that the apostle used in the great revival on the Day of Pentecost, "Repent, every one of you" (Acts 2:38), he is answered, "Oh, I guess you are an Arminian[2]. I do not want any of your Arminian teaching. Do you not deny the Spirit's influences?" It is enough to make humanity weep, to see the fog and darkness that have been thrown around the plain instructions of the gospel.

2. These false instructions to sinners are infinitely worse than none. The Lord Jesus Christ found it more difficult to get the people to yield up their false notions of theology than anything else. This has been the great difficulty with the Jews to this day, that they have received false notions in theology, have distorted the truth on certain points, and you cannot make them understand the clearest points of the gospel. So it is with sinners: the most difficult thing is to get them away from these "refuges of lies," which they have found in false theology. They are so fond of holding on to these refuges (because they excuse the sinner, and condemn God), that it is found to be the most perplexing, difficult, and discouraging part of a minister's labor, to drive them out.

3. No wonder the gospel has taken so little effect, encumbered as it has been with these strange dogmas. The truth is, that very little of the gospel has come out upon the world, for these hundreds of years, without being obscured by false theology. People have been told that they must repent and, in the same breath, told that they could not repent, until the truth itself has been all mixed up with error, so as to produce the same practical effect with error. The gospel that was preached has been another gospel, or no gospel at all.

4. You can understand what is meant by "They have healed the wound of my people lightly" (Jeremiah 6:14, 8:11), and the danger of doing it. It is very easy, when sinners are under conviction, to say something that shall smooth over the case, and relieve their anxiety, so that they will either get a false hope, or will be converted with their views so obscure, that they will always be poor, feeble, wavering, doubting, inefficient Christians.

5. Much depends on the manner in which a person is dealt with, when under conviction. Much of his future comfort and usefulness depends on the clearness, strength, and firmness with which the instructions of the gospel are given when he is under conviction. If those who deal

---

[2] An Arminian is a person who holds a theology developed by Jacob Arminius (1560-1609). Arminius taught that an unregenerate person has a free will to accept or reject God.

with him are afraid to probe thoroughly, he will always be a poor, sickly, doubting Christian. The true mode is to deal thoroughly and plainly with the sinner, to tear away every excuse he can offer, and to show him plainly what he is and what he should be. Then he will bless God to all eternity that he encountered those who would be so faithful with his soul. For the lack of this thorough and searching management, many are converted who seem to be stillborn because they never were faithfully dealt with. We may charitably hope they are Christians, but still it is uncertain and doubtful: their conversion seems rather a change of opinion than a change of heart. But if, when sinners are under conviction, you pour in the truth, break up the old foundations, sweep away their "refuges of lies," and use the Word of God like fire and like a hammer, you will find that they will come out with clear views, strong faith, and firm principles — not doubting, halting, irresolute Christians, but as those who follow the Lord completely. That is the way to make strong Christians. This has been eminently the case in many revivals of modern days. I have heard old Christians say of the converts, "These converts have, at the very outset, all the clarity of view, and strength of faith, of old Christians. They seem to understand the doctrines of religion, and to know what to do, and how to promote revivals, better than one in a hundred of the old members in the church."

I once knew a young man who was converted away from home. The place where he lived had no minister, no preaching, and no Christianity. He went home three days after he was converted, and immediately determined to work for a revival. He set up meetings in his neighborhood, and prayed and labored, and a revival broke out — of which he had the principal management throughout a powerful work, in which most of the leading people of the place were converted. The truth was, he had been so dealt with that he knew what he was about. He understood the subject and knew where he stood himself. He was not all the while troubled with doubts, whether he was himself a Christian. He knew that he was serving God, and that God was with him, and so he went boldly and resolutely forward to his object. But if you undertake to make converts, without clearing up all their errors and tearing away their false hopes, you may make a host of hypocrites, or of puny, dwarfish Christians, always doubting and easily turned back from a revival spirit. The correct way is to bring them right out to the light. When a person is converted in this way, you can depend on him, and will know where to find him.

6. Protracted periods of conviction are generally due to defective instruction. Wherever clear and faithful instructions are given to sinners,

there you will generally find that convictions are deep and pungent but short.

7. Where clear and discriminating instructions are given to convicted sinners, if they do not soon submit, their convictions will generally leave them. Convictions in such cases are generally short. Where the truth is brought to bear upon the sinner's mind, and he directly resists the very truth that must convert him, there is nothing more to be done. The Spirit will soon leave him, for the very weapons he uses are resisted. Where instructions are not clear, but are mixed up with errors, the Spirit may strive, even for years, in great mercy, to get sinners through the fog of false instruction. But not so where their duty is clearly explained to them, and they are brought right up to the single point of immediate submission, all their false pretenses being exposed, and the path of duty made perfectly plain. Then, if they do not submit, the Spirit of God forsakes them, and their state is nearly hopeless.

If there are sinners in this house, and you see your duty clearly, be careful how you delay. If you do not submit, you may expect the Spirit of God will forsake you, and you are LOST.

8. Much of the instruction given to anxious sinners amounts to little less than the popish doctrine of indulgences. The Pope used to sell indulgences to sin, and this led to the Reformation under Luther. Sometimes people would purchase an indulgence to sin for a certain time, or to commit some particular sin, or a number of sins. Now, there is a vast deal in Protestant churches that is little less than the same thing. What does it differ from this, to tell a sinner to wait? It amounts to telling him to continue in sin for a while longer, while he is waiting for God to convert him. And what is that but an indulgence to commit sin? Any instruction given to sinners that does not require them immediately to obey God is an indulgence to sin. It is in effect giving them liberty to continue in sin against God. Such instructions are not only wicked, but also ruinous and cruel. If they do not destroy the soul, as no doubt they often do, they defer the sinner's enjoyment of God and of Christ, and he stands a great chance of being lost forever while listening to such instructions. Oh, how dangerous it is to give a sinner reason to think he may wait a moment before giving his heart to God!

9. So far as I have had opportunity to observe, those persons with whom conversion was most sudden have commonly turned out to be the best Christians. I know the opposite of this has often been held. But I am satisfied there is no reason for it, although many people even now regard it as suspicious if a person has been converted very suddenly. But the Bible gives no reason for this supposition. There is not a

se of protracted conviction recorded in the whole Bible. All the con-
ersions recorded there are sudden conversions. And I am persuaded
here never would be so many tedious convictions that often end in
othing, after all, if it were not for those theological perversions that
ave filled the world with Cannot-ism. In Bible days, sinners were told
o repent, and they did it then. Cannot-ism had not been introduced in
hat day. It is this speculation about the inability of sinners to obey God
hat lays the foundation for all the protracted anguish and distress, and
erhaps ruin, into which so many are led. Where a sinner is brought to
ee what he has to do, and he takes his stand at once, AND DOES IT,
ou generally find that such a person proves a decisive character. You
ill not find him one of those that you always have to warp up to duty,
ke a ship, against wind and tide. Look at those professing Christians
who always have to be dragged forward in duty, and you will gener-
lly find that they did not have clear and consistent instructions when
hey were converted. Most likely, too, they will be very much "afraid
f these sudden conversions."

fraid of sudden conversions! Some of the best Christians of my ac-
uaintance were convicted and converted in the space of a few min-
tes. In one quarter of the time that I have been speaking, many of
hem were awakened, and came right out on the Lord's side, and have
een shining lights in the church ever since. They have generally shown
he same decisive character in religion that they did when they first
ame out and took a stand on the Lord's side.

Part IV

SPIRITUAL GROWTH

Chapter 13

INSTRUCTIONS TO CONVERTS

"Feed my lambs." (John 21:15)

Those who read their Bibles will remember the situation in which these words occur, and by whom they were spoken. The Lord Jesus Christ spoke these words to Peter after he had denied his Lord and had subsequently professed repentance. By the terms "sheep" and "lambs" the Savior undoubtedly meant Christians, members of his church — the lambs probably represent young converts, those that have little experience and little knowledge of religion, and therefore need special attention to guard them from harm and to train them for future usefulness. And when our Savior told Peter to feed his sheep, he doubtless referred to the important role which Peter was to perform in watching over the newly formed churches in different parts of the world, and in training the young converts, and leading them along to usefulness and happiness.

My last lecture was on the subject of giving right instruction to anxious sinners. This naturally brings me to consider the manner in which young converts should be treated, and the instructions that should be given to them.

In speaking on this subject it is my intention to state:

I. Several things that should be considered, regarding the hopes of young converts.

II. Several things about their making a profession of Christianity, and joining the church.

III. The importance of having correct instruction given to young converts.

IV. What should not be taught to young converts.

V. What particular things are especially necessary to be taught to young converts.

I. THE HOPES OF YOUNG CONVERTS

1. Nothing should be said to create a hope. That is to say, nothing should ordinarily be suggested to persons under conviction to make them think they have experienced religion until they find it out themselves. I do not like this term, "experienced religion," and I use it only because it is a phrase in common use. It is an absurdity in itself. What is religion? Obedience to God. Suppose you should hear a good citizen say he had experienced obedience to the government of the country! You see that it is nonsense. Or suppose a child should talk about experiencing obedience to his father. If he knew what he was saying, he would say he had obeyed his father, just as the apostle Paul says to the Roman believers, "you who were once slaves of sin have become obedient from the heart to the standard of teaching to which you were committed" (Romans 6:17).

What I mean to say is that ordinarily it is best to let their hope or belief that they are converted spring up spontaneously in their own minds. Sometimes it will happen that persons may be really converted, but because of some notions that they have been taught about religion, they do not realize it. Their views of Christianity are so far from the truth that they do not think they are Christians. I will give you an illustration on this point.

Some years since, I labored in a place where a revival was in progress, and there was in the place a young lady from Boston. She had been brought up a Unitarian. She was a person of considerable education and was intelligent on many subjects. However, on the subject of religion she was very ignorant. Eventually she was convicted of sin. She became deeply convinced of her horrible enmity against God. She had been so educated as to have a sense of propriety, but her enmity against God became so great, and broke out so frightfully, that it was horrible to hear her talk. She used to come to the anxious meetings, where we conversed with each person separately. Her feelings of opposition to God were such that she used to create a disturbance. By the time I came within two or three seats of her, where she could hear what I said

a low voice to the others, she would begin to make remarks in rely, so that they could be heard. And she would say the most bitter
iings against God, against his providence, and his method of dealing
ith humankind, as if God were an infinite tyrant. I would try to hush
er, and make her keep still, because she distracted the attention of
thers. Sometimes she would stop and control her temper for a while,
nd sometimes she would rise and go out. I have seldom seen a case
here the enmity of the heart rose so high against God. One night at
ie anxious meeting, after she had been very restless, as I went towards
er, she began as usual to reply, but I hushed her, and told her I could
ot converse with her there. I invited her to see me the next morning,
hen I told her I would talk with her. She promised to come. But she
iid, "God is unjust — he is infinitely unjust. Is he not almighty? Why
ien has he never shown me my enmity before? Why has he let me
o on so long? Why does he let my friends at Boston remain in this
gnorance? They are the enemies of God as much as I am, and they are
oing to hell. Why does he not show them the truth in regard to their
ondition?" And in this temperament she left the room.

he next morning she came to see me as promised. I saw, as soon as she
ame in, that her countenance was changed, but I said nothing about it.
Oh," she said, "I have changed my mind about what I said last night
bout God. I do not think he has done me any wrong, and I think I
hall 'get religion' sometime, for now I love to think about God. I have
een all wrong. The reason why I had never known my enmity before
vas that I chose not to. I used to read the Bible, but I always passed
ver the passages that would make me feel as if I were a lost sinner.
'hose passages that spoke of Jesus Christ as God, I passed over without
onsideration. But now I see that it was my fault, not God's fault that I
lid not know any more about myself. I have changed my mind now."
he had no idea that this was religion, but she was encouraged now to
xpect religion at some future time, because she loved God so much. I
aid nothing to make her imagine that I thought her a Christian, but left
ter to find it out. And, for a time, her mind was so entirely occupied
vith thinking about God that she never seemed to ask whether she
'had religion" or not.

t is a great evil, ordinarily, to encourage persons to hope they are
Christians. It is very likely you will judge prematurely. Or if not, it
s better, in any case, that they should find it out for themselves — that
s, if they do not see it at once.

. When persons express a hope, and yet also express doubts, it is gen-
rally because the work is not thorough. If they are converted, they

need breaking up. They are still lingering around the world, or the have not broken off effectively from their sins, and they need to b pushed back rather than urged forward. If you see reason to doubt, o if you find that they have doubts, there is most probably some goo reason to doubt. Sometimes persons express a hope in Christ, and af terwards remember some sin that needs to be confessed to people, o some case where they have slandered, or defrauded, where it is neo essary to make things right, and where either their character, or thei purse, is so deeply implicated that they hesitate, and refuse to perforr their duty. This grieves the Spirit, brings darkness over their minds and appropriately leads them to doubt whether they are truly con verted. If a soul is truly converted, it will generally be found tha where there are doubts, there is on some point a neglect of duty. The should be searched as with a lighted candle, and brought up to do thei duty, and not tolerated to hope until they do it. Ordinarily, it is prope to throw in some plain and searching truth that will go through them something that will wither their false hopes. Do it while the Spirit o God is dealing with them, and do it in a right way, and there is no danger of its doing harm.

To illustrate this: I knew a person who was a member of the church but was an abominable hypocrite — proved to be so by her conduct and afterwards fully confessed to be so. In a revival of religion sh was awakened and deeply convicted, and after a while she became hopeful. She went to a minister to talk with him about her hope, and he poured the truth into her mind in such a manner as to annihilat all her hopes. She then remained under conviction many days, and a last she broke out in hope again. The minister knew her temperament and knew what she needed, and he tore away her hope again. Then she broke down. So deeply did the Spirit of God probe her heart that for a time, it took away all her bodily strength. Then she came ou subdued. Before, she had been one of the proudest of rebels agains God's government, but now she became humbled, and was one of the most modest, tender, and lovely of Christians. No doubt that was jus the way to deal with her. It was just the treatment that her situation required.

It is often useful to deal with individuals in this way. Some persons ar naturally unpleasant in their temperament. It is particularly importan that such persons should be dealt with most thoroughly whenever they first begin to express hope in Christ. Unless the work with them is, in the first place, uncommonly deep and thorough, they will be vastly less useful and happy than they would have been had the probe been thoroughly and skillfully applied to their hearts. If they are encour aged at first, without being thoroughly dealt with, if they are left to go on as though all were well, if they are not sufficiently probed and broken down, these unlovely traits of character will remain unsubdued and will be always emerging, to the great injury both of their personal peace and their general influence and usefulness as Christians.

It is important to act while they are just in these special circumstances, so that they can be molded into proper form. Do not hold back, even if it is a child, or a brother, or a husband, or a wife. Let it be a thorough work. If they express a hope, and you find they bear the image of Christ, they are Christians. But if it should appear doubtful — if they do not appear to be fully changed, just tear away their hope, by searching them with discriminating truth, and leave the Spirit to do the work more deeply. If still the image is not perfect, do it again — break them down into a childlike spirit, and then let them hope. They will then be clear and thorough Christians. By such a mode of treatment I have often known people of the most crooked and hateful natural character so transformed, in the course of a few days that they appeared like different beings. You would think the work of a whole life of Christian cultivation had been done at once. Doubtless this was the intent of our Savior's dealing with Peter. He had been converted, but became puffed up with spiritual pride and self-confidence, and then he fell. After that, Christ broke him down again by searching him three times with the question, "Simon, son of John, do you love me?"[1] After this, he seems to have been a stable and devoted saint the rest of his days.

3. There is no need of young converts having or expressing doubts about their conversion. There is no more need of a person doubting whether he is now in favor of God's government than there is for a person to doubt whether he is in favor of our Government or another. In fact, it is obviously absurd for a person to talk of doubting on such a point, if he is intelligent and understands what he is talking about. It has long been supposed to be a virtue, and a mark of humility, for a person to doubt whether he is a Christian. However this notion that there is virtue in doubting is a device of the devil. "I say, neighbor, are you in favor of our government, or do you prefer that of Russia?" "Why, I have some hopes that I love our own Government, but I have many doubts." Amazing! "Woman, do you love your children?" "Why, sir, I sometimes have a trembling hope that I love them, but you know that the best have their doubts." "Wife, do you love your husband?" "I do not know — I sometimes think I do, but you know the heart is deceitful, and we should be careful and not be too confident." Who would

---

[1] See John 21:15-19.

want such a wife? "Man, do you love your wife, do you love your family?" "Ah, you know we are poor creatures, we do not know our own hearts. I think I do love them, but perhaps I am deceived." Ridiculous!

Ordinarily, the very idea of a person expressing doubts renders his piety truly doubtful. A real Christian has no need to doubt. When one is full of doubts, ordinarily you should doubt for him and help him doubt. Affection to God is as much a matter of consciousness as any other affection. A woman knows she loves her child. How? By consciousness. She is conscious of the exercise of this affection. And she sees it carried into action every day. In the same way a Christian may know that he loves God: by his consciousness of this affection, and by seeing that it influences his daily conduct.

Especially in the case of young converts, these doubts generally arise from their having been wrongly dealt with, not sufficiently taught, or not thoroughly humbled. In any case they should never be left in such a state, but should be brought to such a thorough change that they will doubt no longer.

A Christian who always entertaining doubts cannot be useful. It not only makes him gloomy, but it makes his religion a stumbling block to sinners. What do sinners think of such a religion? They say, "These converts are afraid to think they have got anything real. They are always doubting whether it is a reality, and they should know whether there is anything in it or not. If it is anything, these people seem to have it, but I am inclined to think it rather doubtful. At any rate, I will let it pass for the present. I do not believe God will condemn me for not attending to that which appears so uncertain." No, a settled hope in Christ is necessary to usefulness. Therefore you should deal with young converts to lead them to a consistent, well-grounded, stable hope. Ordinarily, this can be done, if pursued wisely, at the proper time, which is the beginning of their Christian life. They should not be left until it is done.

I know there are exceptions. There are cases where the best instructions will be ineffective. Sometimes you find a person incapable of reasoning on a certain topic, and so his errors will not yield to instruction. But most commonly they mistake the state of their own hearts, because they are under the influence of a physical disease. Sometimes persons in depression will go almost into despair. People who are acquainted with physiology would easily explain the matter. The only way to deal with such cases is first to improve their health, and get their nervous system into a proper tone, and thus remove the physical cause of their gloom and depression. Then they will be able to receive and apply your instructions. But if you cannot remove their gloom and doubts and fears in this way, you can at least avoid doing the positive harm that is caused by giving wrong instructions.

I have known even experienced Christians to fix upon them the error of thinking it was necessary, virtuous, or a mark of humility, to be always in doubt. Satan would take advantage of it, and of the state of their health, and drive them almost to despair. You should guard against this by avoiding the error when teaching young converts. Teach them that instead of there being any virtue in doubting, it is a sin to have any reason to doubt, and a sin if they doubt without any reason, and a sin to be gloomy and to disgust sinners with their despondency. And if you teach them thoroughly what religion is, and make them see clearly what God wishes to have them do, and lead them to do it promptly and decidedly, ordinarily they will not be harassed with doubts and fears, but will be clear, openhearted, cheerful, and growing Christians — an honor to the religion they profess, and a blessing to the church and the world.

II. MAKING A PROFESSION OF CHRISTIANITY

I proceed to mention some things worthy of consideration in regard to young converts making a profession of Christianity, or joining the church.

1. Young converts should ordinarily offer themselves for admission to some church of Christ immediately. By "immediately," I mean that they should do it the first opportunity they have. They should not wait. If they start in Christian life by waiting, most likely they will always be waiting, and never do anything to much purpose. If they are taught to wait under conviction, before they give themselves to Christ, or if they are taught to wait after conversion, before they give themselves publicly to God by joining the church, they will probably go halting and stumbling through life. The first thing they should always be taught is: NEVER WAIT WHERE GOD HAS POINTED OUT YOUR DUTY.

2. While I say it is the duty of young converts to offer themselves to the church immediately, I do not say that in all cases they should be received immediately. The church has a definite right to assume the responsibility of receiving them immediately or not. If the church is not satisfied in the case, it has the power to bid candidates wait until inquiries can be made as to their character and their sincerity. This is more necessary in large cities than it is in the country, because so many applications are received from people who are entire strangers. But if the church thinks it necessary to postpone an applicant, the responsi-

bility is not his. He has not postponed obedience to the command of Christ, and so he has not grieved the Spirit, and so he may not be injured if he is faithful in other respects. In contrast, if he had neglected the duty voluntarily, he would soon have got into error, and would very likely have backslidden.

If there is no particular reason for delay, the church should ordinarily receive them when they apply. If they are sufficiently instructed on the subject of religion to know what they are doing, and if their general character is such that they can be trusted as to their sincerity and honesty in making a profession, I see no reason why they should be delayed. But if there are sufficient reasons, in the view of the church, for making them wait a reasonable time, let the church so decide, on its responsibility to Jesus Christ. However, the responsibility that the church thereby assumes should be remembered. If those are kept out of the church who should be in it, the Holy Spirit is grieved.

It is impossible to lay down particular rules on this subject, applicable to all cases. There is so great a variety of reasons which may warrant keeping persons back, that no general rules can cover them all. Our practice, in this church, is to put forward persons for a month after they make application, before they are received into full communion. The reason for this is that the Session may have opportunity to ask about individuals who offer themselves since so many of them are strangers. But in the country, where there are regular congregations, and all the people have been instructed from their youth in Christian doctrines, and where everybody is completely known, the case is different, and ordinarily I see no reason why people of good character should not be admitted immediately. If a person has not been a drunkard, or otherwise of bad character, let him be admitted at once, as soon as he can give a rational and satisfactory account of the hope that is in him.

That is evidently what the apostles did. There is not the least evidence in the New Testament that they ever put off a person who wanted to be baptized and to join the church. I know this does not satisfy some people, because they think the case is different. But I do not see it this way. They say the apostles were inspired. That is true, but it does not follow that they were so inspired to know the characters of people, to be prevented from making mistakes in this matter. In fact, we know they were not inspired in this way because they did make mistakes, just as ministers may do now. Therefore, it is not true that their being inspired changes the case on this point. Simon Magus was supposed to be a Christian, and was baptized and admitted into communion, remaining in good standing until he tried to purchase the Holy Spirit ith money.[2]

is important that the churches should act wisely on this point. Great
vil has been done by this practice of keeping people out of the church
long time in order to see if they were Christians. This is almost as
bsurd as it would be to throw a young child out into the street, to see
rhether it will live, and say, "If it lives, and promises to be a healthy
hild, we will take care of it," when that is the very time it needs nurs-
ng and care, the moment when the scale is turning whether it shall
ve or die. Is that the way to deal with young converts? Should the
hurch throw her newborn children out to the winds and say, "If they
ve there, let them be taken care of. But if they die there, then they
hould die"? I have not a doubt that thousands of converts, because of
iis treatment, have gone through life without joining any church, but
ave lingered along, full of doubts, fears, and darkness, and gone to
ie grave without the comforts and usefulness which they might have
njoyed. This is simply because the church, in folly, has made them
vait outside, to see whether they would grow and thrive without those
rdinances which Jesus Christ established particularly for their benefit.

esus Christ says to his church, "Here, take these lambs, and feed them,
nd shelter them, and watch over them, and protect them." What does
he church do? Why, turn them out alone upon the cold mountains,
mong the wild beasts, to starve or perish, to see whether they are
live or not! The whole system is as illogical as it is unscriptural. Did
esus Christ tell his churches to do so? Did the God of Abraham teach
ny such doctrine like this about the children of Abraham? Never. He
iever taught us to treat young converts in such a barbaric manner. The
ery way to lead them into doubts and darkness is to keep them away
rom the church, from its fellowship, and its ordinances.

have understood there is a church which has passed a resolution that
io young converts shall be admitted until they have "had a hope" for
t least six months. Where did they get any such rule? Not from the
3ible, nor from the example of the early churches.

. In examining young converts for admission, their consciences should
iot be ensnared by examining them too extensively or minutely on
loctrinal points. From the manner in which examinations are con-
lucted in some churches, it would seem as if they expected that young
onverts would be all at once acquainted with the whole system of di-
rinity, and able to answer every puzzling question in theology. The
ffect of it is that young converts are perplexed and confused, and give

---

See Acts 8:9-24.

their assent to things they do not understand, and thus their conscienc
is ensnared, and consequently weakened. Why, one great goal of re
ceiving young converts into the church is to teach them doctrines. Bu
if they are to be kept out of the church until they understand the whol
system of doctrines, this end is defeated. It is absurd. There are certai
cardinal doctrines of Christianity, which are embraced in the exper:
ence of every true convert. These young converts will testify to them :
questioned in such a way as to draw out knowledge, and not in such
way as to puzzle and confound. The questions should draw out from
them what they have learned by experience, and not what they ma
have got in theory before or since their conversion. The goal is not t
find out how much they know, or how good scholars they are in di
vinity, as you would test in school. It is to find out whether they hav
a change of heart, to learn whether they have experienced the grea
truths of religion by the power in their own souls. You see therefor
how absurd and harmful it must be to examine, as is sometimes done
like a lawyer cross-examining a suspicious witness. It should rather b
like a faithful physician eager to find out his patient's true condition
and therefore leading him, by questions and hints, to disclose the rea
symptoms of the case.

You will always find, if you ask your questions correctly, that real con
verts will see clearly those great fundamental points — the divine au
thority of the Scriptures, the necessity of the influences of the Hol
Spirit, the deity of Christ, the doctrines of total depravity and regen
eration, the necessity of the atonement, justification by faith, and th
justice of the eternal punishment of the wicked. By a proper cours
of inquiries you will find all these points come out, if you put you
questions in such a way that they are understood.

A church committee in this city has, as we are informed, passed a vot
that no person shall join that church until he will agree to the whol
Presbyterian Confession of Faith, and adopt it as his "rule of faith and
practice and Christian obedience." That is, they must read the bool
through, which is about three times as large as this hymn-book which
I hold, must understand it, and agree to it all, before they can be ad
mitted to the church. By what authority does a church say that ne
one shall join their communion until he understands all the points and
technicalities of this long Confession of Faith? Is that their charity, t
cram this whole Confession of Faith down the throat of a young con
vert, before they let him so much as come to the Communion? He says
"I love the Lord Jesus Christ, and wish to obey his command." "Very
well, but do you understand and adopt the Confession of Faith?" He
says, "I do not know, for I never read that, but I have read the Bible

and I love that, and wish to follow the instructions in it, and to come to the table of the Lord." "Do you love the Confession of Faith? If not, you shall not come," is the reply of this charitable committee. "You shall not sit down at the Lord's table until you have adopted all this Confession of Faith." Did Jesus Christ ever authorize a church committee to say this — to tell that child of God, who stands there with tears, and asks permission to obey his Lord, and who understands the grounds of his faith, and can give a satisfactory reason of his hope — to tell him he cannot join the church until he understands the Confession of Faith? Shut the door against young converts until they swallow the Confession of Faith! Will such a church prosper? Never!

4. Sometimes people who are known to entertain a hope dare not make a profession of religion for fear they should be deceived. I would always deal decidedly with such cases. A hope that will not lead to a profession of religion is clearly worse than no hope, and the sooner it is torn away the better. Shall a person hope he loves God, and yet not obey Jesus Christ? Preposterous! Such a hope had better be given up at once.

5. Sometimes people professing to be converts will make the excuse for not joining the church that they can enjoy religion just as well without it. This is always suspicious. I should look out for such characters. It is almost certain they have no religion. Ordinarily, if a person does not desire to be associated with the people of God, he is rotten at the foundation. It is because he wants to keep out of the responsibilities of a public profession. He has a feeling within him that he had rather be free, so that he can eventually go back to the world again, if he likes, without the charge of instability or hypocrisy. Enjoy religion just as well without obeying Jesus Christ! It is false on the face of it. He overlooks the fact that religion consists in obeying Jesus Christ.

III. THE IMPORTANCE OF GIVING RIGHT INSTRUCTION

Ordinarily, the Christian character of converts throughout life is molded according to the manner in which they are dealt with when first converted. There are many who have been poorly taught at first, but have been afterwards re-converted, and if they are then properly dealt with, they may be made something of. But the proper time to do this is when they are first brought in, when their minds are soft and tender, and easily yield to the truth. Then they may be led with a hair, if they believe it is the truth of God. And whatever notions of Christianity they get then, they are likely to forever cling to afterwards. It is almost impossible to get a person away from the notions he acquires when he is a young convert. You may reason him down, but he clings to them. It is often the case where people have been taught certain things when first converted, that if they afterwards get a new minister who teaches somewhat differently, they will rise up against him as if he were going to subvert the faith, carry away the church into error, and throw everything into confusion. Thus you see that young converts are thrown into the hands of the church, and it passes to the church to mold them and form them into Christians of the right stamp. To a large extent their future comfort and usefulness depend on the manner in which they are instructed at the outset. The future character of the church, the progress of revivals, and the coming of the millennium depend on right instruction being given to those who are young converts.

IV. THINGS THAT SHOULD NOT BE TAUGHT

1. "You will not always feel as you do now." When the young convert is rejoicing in his Savior, and aiming to live for the glory of God and the good of mankind, how often is he met with this reply. Thus, his mind is prepared to expect that he shall backslide, and not to be much surprised when he does. This is just the way the devil wants young converts dealt with, to have old Christians tell them, "Your feelings will not last, but, you will eventually be as cold as we are." It has made my heart bleed to see it. When the young convert has been pouring out his warm heart to some older professing Christian, and expecting the warm burstings of a kindred spirit responding to his own, what does he meet with? This cold answer, coming like a northern blast over his soul, "You will not always feel this way." SHAME! Preparing the young convert to expect that he shall backslide as a natural matter! When he begins to decline, as it is most likely he will under the influences of this instruction, it produces no surprise or alarm in his mind, but he looks at it just as the natural thing, doing as everybody else does.

I have heard it preached as well as expressed in prayer, that seasons of backsliding are "necessary to test the church." They say, "When it rains, you can find water anywhere. It is only in seasons of drought that you can tell where the deep springs are." Wonderful logic! And so you would teach that Christians must get cold and dull, and backslide from God — and for what reason? Why, indeed, to show that they are not hypocrites. Amazing! You would prove that they are hypocrites in order to show that they are not.

Such doctrine as this is the very last that should be taught to young converts. They should be told that they have only begun the Christian life, and that their religion is to consist in going on in it. They should be taught to go forward all the time, and "grow in grace" continually. Do not teach them to taper off their religion — to let it grow smaller and smaller until it comes to a point. God says, "The path of the righteous is like the light of dawn, which shines brighter and brighter until full day" (Proverbs 4:18). Now, whose path is that which grows dimmer and dimmer into the full night? They should be brought to such a state of mind that the first indications of decay in spirituality or zeal will alarm them and spur them up to duty. There is no need that young converts should backslide as they do. Paul did not backslide. And I do not doubt that this very doctrine, "You will not always feel this way," is one of the grand devices of Satan to bring about the result that it predicts.

2. "Learn to walk by faith and not by sight." This is sometimes said to young converts about their continuing to show the power of religion, and is a manifest perversion of Scripture. If they begin to lose their faith and zeal, and get into darkness, some older professing Christian will tell them, "Ah, you cannot expect to have the Savior always with you, you have been walking by sight. You must learn to walk by faith and not by sight." That is, you must learn to get as cold as death, and then hang on to the doctrine of the Perseverance of the Saints as your only ground of hope that you shall be saved. And that is walking by faith! Cease to persevere, and then hold on to the doctrine of Perseverance! "One of guilt's blunders, and the loudest laugh of hell." Living in the enjoyment of God's favor and the comforts of the Holy Spirit is what they call "walking by sight"! Do you suppose young converts see the Savior at the time they believe on him? When they are so full of the enjoyments of heaven, do you suppose they see heaven, and so walk by sight? It is obviously absurd. It is not faith — it is presumption that makes the backslider hold on to the doctrine of Perseverance, as if that would save him, without any perceptible exercises of godliness in his soul. Those who attempt to walk by faith in this way had better be careful, or they will walk into hell with their "faith." Faith indeed! "Faith apart from works is useless" (James 2:20). Can dead faith make the soul live?

3. "Wait until you see whether you can hold out." When a young convert feels zealous and warm-hearted, and wants to give himself completely for God, some prudent, old, professing Christian will warn him not to go too fast. "You had better not be too forward in religion, until you see whether you can hold out. For if you take this high ground and then fall, you will disgrace religion." That is, in plain English, "Do not do anything that is religion, until you see whether you have religion." Religion consists in obeying God. Now, these wise teachers tell a young convert, "Do not obey God until you see" — what? — until

you see whether you have obeyed him — or, until you see whether you have obtained that substance, that mysterious thing which they imagine is created and put into a person, like a lump of new flesh, and called "religion." This waiting system is all wrong. There is no Scriptural basis for telling a person to wait, when the command of God is upon him, and the path of duty is before him. Let him go ahead.

Young converts should be fully taught that this is the only consistent way to find out whether they have any religion, to find that they are heartily engaged in doing the will of God. To tell the convert to wait, therefore, before he does these things, until he first has his evidence, is reversing the matter, and is absurd.

4. "Wait until you get strength, before you take up the cross." This is applied to various religious duties. Sometimes it is applied to prayer, just as if prayer were a cross. I have known young converts advised not to attempt to pray in their families, or "not to attempt quite yet" to pray in meetings and social circles. "Wait until you get strength." As if they could gain strength without exercise. Strength comes by exercise. You cannot get strength by lying still. Let a child lie in a cradle continually, and he would never have any strength. He might grow in size, but he never could be anything more than a great baby. This is a law of nature. There is no substitute for exercise in producing strength. It is so in the body, and it is just so with the mind. It is this way with the affections, with judgment, and with the conscience. All the powers of the soul are strengthened by exercise. I need not now discuss the logic of this. Everybody knows it is so. If the mind is not exercised, the brain will not grow, and the person will become a fool. If the affections are not exercised, he will become a stoic. To talk to a convert about neglecting Christian action until he gets strength, is absurd. If he wants to gain strength, let him go to work.

5. Young converts should not be made sectarian in their feelings. They should not be taught to dwell upon sectarian distinctions, or to be sticklish about sectarian points. They should examine these points, according to their importance, at a proper time, and in a proper way, and make up their minds for themselves. But they should not be taught to dwell upon them, or to make much of them at the beginning of their religious life. Otherwise there is great danger that their whole religion will run into sectarianism. I have seen most sad exhibitions of the effects of this upon young converts. And whenever I see professed converts taking a strong hold of sectarian peculiarities, no matter of what denomination of Christians, I always feel in doubt about them. When I hear them asking, "Do you believe in the doctrine of Election?" Or,

Do you believe in sprinkling?" Or, "Do you believe in immersing?" I el sad. I never knew such converts to be worth much. Their sectarian al soon sours their feelings, eats out all the heart of their religion, and olds their whole character into sinful, sectarian bigotry. They gener-lly become very zealous for the traditions of the elders, and very little oncerned for the salvation of souls.

THINGS THAT ARE IMPORTANT TO BE TAUGHT

One of the first things young converts should be taught is to dis-nguish between emotion and principle in religion. I want you to get old of the words, and have them fixed in your mind in order to have ou distinguish between emotion and principle.

y emotion, I mean that state of mind of which we are conscious, and hich we call feeling — an involuntary state of mind that arises when e are in certain circumstances or under certain influences. There may e powerful feelings, or they may subside into tranquility, or disappear ntirely. But these emotions should be carefully distinguished from eligious principle. By principle, I do not mean any substance or root or eed or sprout implanted in the soul. But I mean the voluntary decision f the mind, the firm determination to fulfill duty and to obey the will f God, by which a Christian should always be governed.

When a person is fully determined to obey God because it is RIGHT nat he should obey God, I call that principle. Whether he feels any vely religious emotion at the time or not, he will do his duty cheer-ully, readily, and sincerely, whatever may be the state of his feelings. his is acting upon principle, and not from emotion. Many young con-erts hold mistaken views upon this subject, and depend almost en-irely on the state of their feelings to go forward in duty. Some will not ead a prayer meeting, unless they feel as if they could make an elo-uent prayer. Many are influenced almost entirely by their emotions, nd they give way to this, as if they thought themselves under no obli-ation to duty, unless urged on by some strong emotion. They will e very zealous in religion when they feel like it, when their emotions re warm and lively, but they will not act out religion consistently, and arry it into all the concerns of life. They are religious only as they are notivated by a gush of feeling. But this is not true Christianity.

Young converts should be carefully taught that when duty is before hem they are to do it. However dull their feelings may be, if duty alls, DO IT. Do not wait for feeling, but DO IT. Most likely the very motions for which you would wait will be called up when you begin o do your duty. If the duty is prayer, for example, and you do not have

the feelings you would like, do not wait for emotions before you pra
In doing it, you are most likely to have the emotions for which yo
were inclined to wait, and which constitute the conscious happiness c
religion.

2. Young converts should be taught that they have renounced the owr
ership of all their possessions, and of themselves, and that if they hav
not done this they are not Christians. They should not be left to thin
that anything is their own: their time, property, influence, facultie:
body or soul. "You are not your own" (1 Corinthians 6:19). Convert
belong to God, and when they submitted to God they made a free su
render of all to him, to be ruled and used at his pleasure. They hav
no right to spend one hour as if their time were their own, no righ
to go anywhere, or do anything for themselves, but should hold all a
the disposal of God, and use all for the glory of God. If they do no
they should not call themselves Christians, for the very idea of being
Christian is to renounce self and become entirely consecrated to Goc
A person has no more right to withhold anything from God than h
has to rob or steal. It is robbery in the highest sense of the term. I
is an infinitely higher crime than it would be for a clerk in a store t
go and take the money of his employer, and spend it on his own lust
and pleasures. If God calls on them to use anything they have, thei
money, their time, or to give their children, or to dedicate themselve
in advancing his kingdom, and they refuse, because they want to us
them in their own way, or prefer to do something else, it is vastly mor
guilty than for a clerk or an agent to go and embezzle the money tha
is entrusted him by his employer.

God is, in an infinitely higher sense, the Owner of all, than any em
ployer can be said to be the owner of what he has. The Church of Chris
never will be disentangled from the world, never will be able to go for
ward without these continual declines and backslidings, until Chris
tians, and churches generally, hold the ground that it is just as much
matter of discipline for a church member to deny his stewardship b
his practice as to deny the deity of Christ, and that covetousness, fairl
proved, shall just as soon exclude a person from the Communion a
adultery.

The Church is strongly orthodox in notions, but very heretical in prac
tice. The time must come when the church will be just as vigilant ir
guarding orthodoxy in practice as orthodoxy in doctrine, and just a
prompt to turn out heretics in practice, as heretics that corrupt the doc
trines of the gospel. In fact, it is vastly more important. The only
design of doctrine is to produce practice, and it does not seem to be

understood by the church that true faith "works by love and purifies the heart," that heresy in practice is conclusive proof of heresy in sentiment. The church is very sticklish for correct doctrine, but very apthetic about correct living. This is preposterous. Has it come to this, that the Church of Jesus Christ is to be satisfied with correct notions on some abstract points, and never move her orthodoxy to practice? Let it be so no longer.

It is urgent these matters are set right. And the only way to set them right is to begin with those who are just entering upon religion. Young converts must be told that they are just as worthy of condemnation (and that the church can hold no fellowship with them), if they show a covetous spirit, and turn a deaf ear when the whole world is calling for help, as if they were living in adultery, or in the daily worship of idols.

3. Teach them how to cultivate a tender conscience. I am often amazed to find how little conscience there is even among those whom we hope are Christians. And here we see the reason of it. Their consciences were never cultivated. They never were taught how to cultivate a tender conscience. They have dealt so rudely with their conscience, and resisted it so often, that it has got blunted, and does not act. The usefulness of a Christian greatly depends on his knowing how to cultivate his conscience. Young converts should be taught to keep their conscience just as tender as the apple of the eye. They should watch their conduct and their motives, and let their motives be so pure and their conduct so selfless as not to offend, or injure, or stifle conscience. They should maintain such a habit of listening to conscience, that it will always be ready to give forth a stern verdict on all occasions.

It is astonishing to see how much the conscience may be cultivated by a proper course. If rightly attended to, it may be made so pure, and so powerful, that it will always respond exactly to the Word of God. Present any duty to such a Christian, or any self-denial, or suffering, and only show him the Word of God, and he will do it without a word of objection. In a few months, if properly taught, young converts may have a conscience so delicately poised that the weight of a feather will turn them. Only bring a "Thus says the Lord," and they will be always ready to do that, be it what it may.

4. Young converts should be taught to pray without ceasing. That is, they should always keep a watch over their minds, and be all the time in a prayerful spirit. They should be taught to pray always, whatever may take place. For the lack of right instruction on this point many young converts suffer loss and get far away from God. For instance, sometimes it happens that a young convert will fall into some sin, and

then he feels as if he could not pray, and instead of overcoming thi
he feels so distressed that he waits for the keen edge of his distress to
pass away. Instead of going right to Jesus Christ in the midst of hi
agony, confessing his sin out of the fullness of his heart, and getting
a renewed pardon and restored peace, he waits until all the sharpnes
of his feelings has subsided. Then his repentance, if he does repent, i
cold and half-hearted. Let me tell you, beloved, never to do this. When
your conscience presses you, go then to Christ, confess your sin fully
and pour out your heart to God.

Sometimes people will neglect to pray because they are in the dark
and feel no desire to pray. But that is the very time when they need
prayer. That is the very reason why they should pray. You should go
right to God and confess your coldness and darkness of mind. Tell him
just how you feel. Tell him, "O Lord, I have no desire to pray, but
know I should pray." And immediately the Spirit may come and lead
your heart out in prayer, and all the dark clouds will pass away.

5. Young converts should be faithfully warned against adopting a false
standard in religion. They should not be left to fall in behind older
professing Christians, or keep these people before their minds as a
standard of holy living. They should always look at Christ as their
model. They should not aim at being as good as the old church members are, and they should not think they are doing well because they
are as awake as the old members of the church. They should aim at being holy. The church has been greatly injured for the lack of attention to
this matter. Young converts have come forward, and their hearts were
warm, and their zeal ardent enough to aim at a high standard, but they
were not directed properly, and so they soon settled down into the notion that what was good enough for others was good enough for them
and therefore they stopped to aim higher than those who were before
them. And in this way the church, instead of rising, with every revival,
higher and higher in holiness, is kept nearly stationary.

6. Young converts should be taught to do all their duty. They should
never make a compromise with duty, nor think of saying, "I will do this
to make up for neglecting that." They should never rest satisfied until
they have done their duties of every kind, in relation to their families,
the church, Sunday Schools, the impenitent around them, the disposal
of their property, and the conversion of the world. Let them do their
duty, as they feel it when their hearts are warm, and never attempt to
pick and choose among the commandments of God.

7. They should be made to feel that they have no separate interest. It
is time Christians were made actually to feel that they have no interest

whatever, separate from the interests of Jesus Christ and his kingdom. They should understand that they are incorporated into the family of Jesus Christ, as members in full, so that their whole interest is identified with his. They are embarked with him, they have gone on board, and taken their all. Henceforth they have nothing to do, nor anything to say, except as it is connected with this interest and bearing on the cause and kingdom of Christ.

8. They should be taught to maintain singleness of motive. Young converts should not begin to have a double mind on any subject, nor let selfish motives mingle with good motives in anything they do. But this can never be so long as Christians are allowed to hold a separate interest of their own, distinct from the interest of Jesus Christ. If they feel that they have a separate interest, it is impossible to keep them from paying attention to it, and having an eye to it as well as to Christ's interest, in many things that they do. It is only by becoming entirely consecrated to God, and giving up all to his service, that they can ever keep their eye single and their motives pure.

9. They should set out with a determination to aim at being useful in the highest degree possible. They should not rest satisfied merely with being useful, or remaining in a situation where they can do some good. But if they see an opportunity where they can do more good, they must embrace it, whatever may be the sacrifice to themselves. No matter what it may cost them, no matter what danger or what suffering may be involved, no matter what change in their outward circumstances, or habits, or employments, it may lead to. If they are satisfied that they will on the whole do more good, they should not even hesitate. How else can they be like God? How can they think to bear the image of Jesus Christ, if they are not prepared to do all the good that is in their power? When a person is converted he comes into a new world, and should consider himself as a new person. If he finds he can do most good by remaining in his old employment, let it be so. But if he can do more good in some other way, he is obligated to change. It is for the lack of attention to this subject, at the outset, that Christians have got such low ideas on the subject of duty. That is the reason why there are so many useless members in our churches.

10. They must be taught not to aim at comfort but usefulness in religion. There are a great many spiritual epicureans in the churches, who are all the while seeking to be happy, while they are taking very little trouble to be useful. They would much rather spend their time in singing joyful hymns, and pouring out their happy feelings in a gushing tide of exultation and triumph, than in an agonizing prayer for sin-

ners, or in going about pulling dying people out of the fire. They seem to feel as if they were born to enjoy themselves. But I do not think such Christians show fruits as to make their example one to be imitated. Such was not the temperament of the apostles. They travailed for souls, they labored in weariness and painfulness, and were "often near death," to save sinners (2 Corinthians 11:23). Ordinarily, Christians are not qualified to drink deep at the fountain of joy. In ordinary cases, a deep agony of prayer for souls is more profitable than high flights of joy. Let young converts be taught plainly not to plan on a life of joy and triumph. They may be called to go through fiery trials. Satan may sift them like wheat. But they must go forward, not intending so much to be happy as to be useful, not talking about comfort but duty, not desiring flights of joy and triumph, but hungering and thirsting after righteousness, not studying how to create new flights of rapture, but how to know the will of God and do it. They will be happy enough in heaven. There they may sing the song of Moses and the Lamb. And they will in fact enjoy a more solid and rational happiness here, by thinking nothing about it, but patiently devoting themselves to do the will of God.

11. They should be taught to have moral courage, and not to be afraid of going forward in duty. The Bible insists fully on Christian boldness and courage in action as a duty. I do not mean that they should indulge in bravado, like Peter, saying what they will do, and boasting of their courage. The boaster is generally a coward at heart. But I mean moral courage — a humble and fixed decision of purpose, that will go forward in any duty, unangered and unawed, with the meekness and firmness of the Son of God.

12. They should be so instructed as to be sound in the faith. They should be made, as early and as far as possible, complete and correct in regard to their doctrinal belief. As soon as may be, without turning their minds off from their practical duties in promoting the glory of God and the salvation of people, they should be taught fully and plainly all the leading doctrines of the Bible. Doctrinal knowledge is necessary to growth in grace. Knowledge is the food of the mind. "Desire without knowledge is not good" (Proverbs 19:2). The mind cannot grow without knowledge any more than the body without food. And therefore it is important that young converts should be thoroughly indoctrinated, and made to understand the Bible. By "indoctrinating," I do not mean teaching them the catechism, but teaching them to draw knowledge from the fountainhead. Create in their minds such an appetite for knowledge that they will eat the Bible up — will devour it — will love it, and love it all. "All Scripture is breathed out by God

id profitable... that the man of God may be competent, equipped for ery good work" (2 Timothy 3:16-17).

i. Great trouble should be taken to guard young converts against critizing. Young converts, when they first come out on the Lord's side, id are all warm and zealous, sometimes find older professing Chrisans so cold and dead, that they are strongly tempted to criticize. This iould be corrected immediately — otherwise the habit will poison .eir minds and destroy their religion.

l. They must learn to say "NO." This is a very difficult lesson to many. :e that young woman. Formerly she loved the merry circle, and took elight in its pleasures. She joined the church, and then found herself istant from all her old associates. They do not ask her now to their ills and parties, because they know she will not join them. Perhaps iey keep entirely away for a time, for fear she should talk with them >out their souls. But they eventually grow a little bold, and some f them venture to ask her just to take a ride with a few friends. She oes not like to say "No." They are her old friends, only a few of them re going, and surely a ride is so innocent a recreation that she may :cept the invitation. But, now she has begun to agree, the ice is broken, nd they have her again as one of them. It goes on, and she begins to ttend their social visits — "only a few friends, you know" — until ventually the carpet is taken up for a dance. Next, perhaps, she has one for a sleigh ride on Saturday night, coming home after midnight, nd then sleeping all morning on Sunday to make up for it — perhaps 'ommunion Sunday, too. All for the lack of learning to say "No."

ee that young man. For a while he was always in his place in Sunday chool and in the prayer meeting. But eventually his old friends begin > treat him with attention again, and they draw him along, step by tep. He reasons that if he refuses to go along with them in innocent iings, he will lose his influence with them. And so he goes on, until rayer meeting, Bible class, and even private Bible reading and prayer re neglected. Ah, young man, stop there! If you do not wish to expose ie cause of Christ to scorn and contempt, learn to resist the beginnings f temptation.

5. Teach them not to count anything a sacrifice that they do for God. ome people are always telling about the sacrifices they make in reliion. I have no confidence in such piety. Why keep talking about their acrifices, as if everything they do for God is a sacrifice? If they loved ;od they would not talk like this. If they considered their own intersts and the interest of Christ identical, they would not talk of making acrifices for Christ — it would be like talking of making sacrifices for

themselves.

16. It is of great importance that young converts should be taught t be strictly honest. I mean more by this than perhaps you would thinl It is a great thing to be strictly honest. It is being very different fror the world at large, and different even from the great body of professin Christians. The holiest man I ever knew, and one who had been man years a Christian and a minister, once made the remark to me, "Brothe it is a great thing to be strictly honest and straight in everything, so tha God's pure eye can see that the mind is perfectly upright."

It is of great importance that young converts should understand wha it is to be strictly honest in everything, so that they can maintain " clear conscience toward both God and man" (Acts 24:16). Alas, alas how little conscience there is! How little of that real honesty, that pure simple uprightness, which should mark the life of a child of God. How little do many honor even a clear promise. I heard the other day that o the individuals who subscribed to the Anti-Slavery Society, less thar half will pay their subscriptions. Their excuse is that they signed wher they were excited and do not choose to pay now. As if their being excited released them from the obligation to keep their promise. The promised, signed their names, and now will not pay? And they cal that honesty!

I have heard that a number of people pledged hundreds of dollar to the Oneida Institute, promising to pay the money when called or When they were called on, they refused to pay the money. And the reason is that all in the Institute have turned Abolitionists! Very well Suppose they have. Does that change your promise? Did you sign or the condition that if abolitionism were introduced, you would be ex empt? If you did, then you are exempt. But if you gave your promis without any condition, it is dishonest to refuse. And yet some of yo might be almost angry if anybody were to accuse you of refusing t pay money that you had promised.

Look at this seriously. Who does God say will go to heaven? Read the fifteenth psalm, and see. "He who swears to his own hurt and doe not change." What do you think of that? If a person has promised anything, except to commit sin, let him keep his promise, if he mean to be honest and to go to heaven. But these people will make promises and because they cannot be prosecuted, will break them as if they were nothing. They would not let a check of theirs be returned from the bank. Why? Because they would lose credit, and would be sued. Bu the Oneida Institute, and the Anti-Slavery Society, and other societies will not sue for the money, and therefore these people take offense a omething, and refuse to pay. Is this honest? Will such honesty as this get them admitted to heaven? What? Break your promises, and go up and carry a lie in your hand before God? If you refuse or neglect o fulfill your promise you are a liar. If you persist in this, you shall have your part in the lake that burns with fire and brimstone. I would not for ten thousand worlds die with money in my hands that I had unrighteously withheld from any object to which I had promised it.

f you are not able to pay the money, that is a good excuse. But then, ay so. But if you refuse to pay what you have promised, because you have changed your mind, be sure that you are guilty. You cannot pray until you pay that money. Will you pray, "O Lord, I promised to give hat money, but I changed my mind, and broke my promise. But still, O Lord, I pray you to bless me, and forgive my sin, although I keep my money. Make me happy in your love"? Will such prayers be heard? Never.

Chapter 14

ADDITIONAL INSTRUCTIONS TO CONVERTS

"Feed my lambs." (John 21:15)

I propose to continue the subject by:

I. Noticing several other points on which young converts should be instructed.

II. Showing the manner that the church should treat young converts.

III. Mentioning some of the evils that naturally result from defective instructions given in that stage of Christian experience.

I. FURTHER INSTRUCTIONS TO YOUNG CONVERTS.

1. It is of great importance that young converts should be made early to understand what religion consists of. Perhaps you will be surprised at my mentioning this. "What! Are they converts, and do not know what religion consists of?" I answer, "They would know, if they had received no instruction except that drawn from the Bible." But many people have absorbed such notions about religion, that not only young converts, but also a great part of the church members do not know what religion consists of. There are many ministers who do not. I do not mean to say that they have no religion, for it may be charitably believed they have. But what I mean is that they cannot give a correct statement of what does, and what does not, constitute real religion.

It is important that young converts should be taught what religion does not consist in.

(a) Not in doctrinal knowledge. Knowledge is essential to religion, but it is not religion. The devil has doctrinal knowledge, but he has no religion. A person may have any amount of doctrinal knowledge, without a particle of religion. Yet some people have very strange ideas on this subject, as though an increase of doctrinal knowledge indicated an increase of piety. In a certain instance, where some young converts had made rapid progress in doctrinal knowledge, a person who saw it remarked, "How these young converts grow in grace!" Here he confused improvement in knowledge with improvement in piety. The truth was that he had no means to judge their growth in grace, and their progress in doctrinal knowledge was not evidence of it.

(b) They should be taught that religion is not a substance. It is not any root, or sprout, or seed, or anything else as part of the mind itself. People often speak of religion as if it were something that is covered up in the mind, just as a spark of fire may be covered up in the ashes, which produces no effects, but yet lives, and is ready to act as soon as it is uncovered. And similarly they think they may have religion, as something remaining in them, although they do not show it by obeying God. But they should be taught that this is not of the nature of religion. It is not part of the mind itself, nor of the body. Nor is it a root, or seed, or spark that can exist, and yet be hid and produce no effects.

(c) Teach them that religion does not consist in raptures, ecstasies, or high flights of feeling. There may be a great deal of these where there is religion. But it should be understood that they are all involuntary emotions, and may exist in full power where there is no religion. They may be the mere workings of the imagination, without any truly religious affection at all. People may have them to such a degree as actually to swoon away with ecstasy, even on the subject of religion, without having any religion. I have known a person almost carried away with rapture, by a mere view of the natural attributes of God, his power and wisdom, as displayed in the starry heavens, and yet the person had no religion. Religion is obedience to God, the voluntary submission of the soul to his will.

(d) Neither does religion consist in going to services, or reading the Bible, or praying, or any other of what are commonly called religious duties. The very phrase, "religious duties," should be struck out of the vocabulary of young converts. They should be made to know that these acts are not religion. Many become very strict in performing certain things, which they call "religious duties," and think that is beg religious, while they are apathetic about the ordinary duties of life, hich actually constitute a life of piety. Prayer may be an expression id an act of piety, or it may not be. Going to church or to a prayer leeting, may be considered either as a means, an act, or an expresion of pious sentiment. But the performance of these does not make person a Christian. There may be great strictness and zeal in these, ithout a particle of religion. If young converts are not taught to unerstand the difference, they may be led to think there is something eculiar in what are called religious duties, and to imagine they have great deal of religion because they abound in certain actions that are ommonly called "religious duties," although they may at the same me be deficient in honesty, faithfulness, punctuality, temperance, or iy other of what they choose to call their common duties. They may e very precise in some things, may "tithe mint and dill and cumin" Matthew 23:23), and yet neglect "the weightier matters of the law," istice and the love of God.

) Religion does not consist in desires to do good actions. Desires that o not result in choice and action are not virtuous. Nor are such desires ecessarily vicious. They may arise involuntarily in the mind, in view f certain objects. While they produce no voluntary act, they are no iore virtuous or vicious than the beating of the pulse, except in cases here we have indirectly willed them into existence, by voluntarily utting ourselves under circumstances designed to excite them. The rickedest person on earth may have strong desires after holiness. Did ou ever think of that? He may see clearly that holiness is the only way f happiness. And the moment he understands holiness as a means of appiness, he naturally desires it. It is to be feared that many are deeiving themselves with the idea that a desire for holiness, as a means f happiness, is religion. Many, doubtless, give themselves great credit or desires that never result in choosing right. They feel desires to do ieir duty, but do not choose to do it, because they on the whole have ven stronger desires not to do it. In such desires there is no virtue. An ction or desire, to be virtuous in the sight of God, must be an act of ie will. People often talk absurdly on this subject, as though their deires could be anything good, while they remain mere desires. "I think desire to do so-and-so." But do you do it? "Oh, no, but I often feel desire to do it." Whatever desires a person may have, if they are not arried out into actual choice and action, they are not virtuous. And no egree of desire is itself virtuous. If this idea could be made prominent, nd fully riveted in the minds of people, it would probably annihilate ie hopes of half the members of the churches, who are living on their ood desires, while doing nothing for God.

(f) They should be made to understand that nothing that is selfish i religion. Whatever desires they may have, and whatever choices an actions they may put forth, if the reason is selfish, there is no religion i them. A person may just as much commit sin in praying, or reading th Bible, or going to a religious service, as in anything else, if his motiv is selfish. Suppose a person prays simply with a view to promote h own happiness. Is that religion? What is it but attempting to mak God his Almighty Servant? It is nothing else but to attempt to have th universe, God and all, contribute to make him happy. It is the sublim degree of wickedness. It is so far from being piety that it is in fac superlative wickedness.

(g) Nothing is acceptable to God, as religion, unless it is performe heartily to please God. No outward action has anything good, or any thing that God approves, unless it is performed from right motives an from the heart. Young converts should be fully taught that all religio consists in obeying God from the heart. All religion consists in volun tary action. All that is holy, all that is lovely, in the sight of God, all tha is properly called religion, consists in voluntary action, in voluntaril obeying the will of God from the heart.

2. Young converts should be taught that the duty of self-denial is one c the leading features of the gospel. They should understand that the are not pious any further than they are willing to take up their cros daily, and deny themselves for Christ. There is little self-denial in th church, and the reason is that the duty is so much lost sight of in giv ing instruction to young converts. How seldom are they told that self denial is the leading feature in Christianity! In pleading for benevolen objects, how often will you find that ministers and agents do not ever ask Christians to deny themselves for the sake of promoting the object They only ask them to give what they can spare. In other words, t give to the Lord that which costs them nothing.[1] What an abomina tion! They only ask for the surplus, for what is not wanted, for wha can just as easily be given as not.

There is no religion in this kind of giving. A person might give a ver large sum to a benevolent goal, and there would be no religion in hi doing so, if he could give the money as easily as not, nor would there b any self-denial in it. Jesus Christ exercised self-denial to save sinners God the Father exercised self-denial in giving his Son to die for us, anc in bearing with our wickedness. The Holy Spirit exercises self-denia in condescending to strive with such unholy beings to bring them tc God. The angels exercise self-denial, in watching over this world. The

---

[1] A reference to David's statement in 2 Samuel 24:24.

apostles planted the Christian religion among the nations by the exercise of self-denial. And are we to think of being religious without any self-denial? Are we to call ourselves Christians, the followers of Christ, the "temples of the Holy Spirit" (1 Corinthians 6:19), and to claim fellowship with the apostles, when we have never deprived ourselves of anything toward our personal enjoyment for the sake of promoting Christ's kingdom? Young converts should be made to see that unless they are willing to give themselves completely for God, and are ready to sacrifice life and everything else for Christ, they "do not have the Spirit of Christ, and are not his" (Romans 8:9*).

3. They must be taught what sanctification is. "What!" you will say, "do not all who are Christians know what sanctification is?" No, many do not. Many would be as much at a loss to clearly say what sanctification is, as they would be to say what religion is. If the question were asked of every professing Christian in this city, "What is sanctification?" I doubt if one in ten would give a right answer. They would blunder just as they do when they try to say what religion is, and speak of it as something dormant in the soul, something that is put in, and lies there, something that may be practiced or not, and still be in them. So they speak of sanctification as if it were a sort of washing off of some defilement, or a purging from some physical impurity. Or they will speak of it as if the faculties were steeped in sin, and sanctification is taking out the stains. This is the reason why some people will pray for sanctification, and practice sin, evidently supposing the sanctification is something that precedes obedience. They should be taught that sanctification is not something that precedes obedience, some change in the nature or the constitution of the soul. But sanctification is obedience. It is progressive and consists in obeying God more and more perfectly.

4. Young converts should be taught to understand what perseverance is. It is astonishing how people talk about perseverance. As if the doctrine of perseverance is, "Once in grace, always in grace" or, "Once converted, sure to go to heaven."[2] This is not the idea of perseverance. The true idea is, that if a person is truly converted, he will CONTINUE to obey God. As a consequence, he will surely go to heaven. But if a person gets the idea that because he is "converted," therefore he will assuredly go to heaven, that person will almost assuredly go to hell.

---

[2] Today the doctrine of the Perseverance of the Saints is often wrongly stated as "once saved, always saved." This phrase does not capture the key idea that the Christian is saved because of continued faith that produces obedience. It wrongly makes it seems as if a profession of faith saves you, even if that faith does not continue. The key word is *perseverance*.

5. Young converts should be taught to be religious in everything. They should aim to be religious in every aspect of life, and in all that they do. If they do not aim at this, they should understand that they have no religion at all. If they do not intend and aim to keep all the commandments of God, what pretense can they make to piety? "For whoever keeps the whole law but fails in one point has become accountable for all of it" (James 2:10). He is justly subject to the whole penalty. If he disobeys God habitually in one particular way, he does not actually obey him in any particular way. Obedience to God consists in the state of the heart. It is being willing to obey God, willing that God should rule in all things. But if a person habitually disobeys God, in any one particular way, he is in a state of mind that renders obedience in anything else impossible. To say that in some things a person obeys God, out of respect to his authority, and that in some other things he refuses obedience, is absurd. The fact is that obedience to God consists in an obedient state of heart, a preference of God's authority and commandments to everything else. If, therefore, an individual appears to obey in some things, and yet continually and knowingly disobeys in any one thing, he is deceived. He offends in one point, and this proves that he is guilty of all. In other words, he does not, from the heart, obey at all. A person may pray half of his time and have no religion. If he does not keep the commandments of God, his very prayer will be hateful to God. "If one turns away his ear from hearing the law, even his prayer is an abomination." (Proverbs 28:9). Do you hear that? If a person refuses to obey God's law, if he refuses to comply with any one duty, he cannot pray, he has no religion, and his very devotions are hateful.

6. Young converts, by proper instructions, are easily brought to have "self-control in all things" (1 Corinthians 9:25). Yet this is a subject greatly neglected in regard to young converts, and almost lost sight of in the churches. There is a great deal of indulgence in the churches. I do not just mean intemperate drinking, but indulgent eating and living in general. There is actually little conscience about it in the churches, and therefore the progress of reform in the matter is so slow. Nothing but an enlightened conscience can carry forward a permanent reform. Ten years ago, most ministers used strong drink, and kept it in their houses to treat their friends and their ministering brethren with. And the great body of the members in the churches did the same. Now, there are but few of either, who are not actual drunkards, that will do so. But still there are many that indulge without hesitation in the use of wine. Chewing and smoking tobacco are also acts of indulgence. If they use these mere stimulants when there is no necessity for them, what is that but indulgence? That is not having "self-control in all things." Until

Christians shall have a conscience on this subject, and be made to feel that they have no right to be indulgent in anything, they will only make little progress in religion. It is well known, or should be, that tea and coffee have no nutrients in them. They are mere stimulants. They go through the system without being digested. The milk and sugar you put in them are nourishing. They would be just as nourishing if you mixed them with rum, and made milk punch. But the tea and coffee afford no nourishment. Yet I dare say, that a majority of the families in this city give more in a year for their tea and coffee than they do to save the world from hell. Probably this is true about entire churches. Even agents of benevolent societies will dare to go through the churches soliciting funds, for the support of missionary and other institutions, and yet use tea, coffee, and, in some cases, tobacco. Strange! No doubt many are giving five times as much for mere indulgence as they give for every effort to save the world.

If professing Christians could be made to realize how much they spend for what are mere poisons, and nothing else, they would be amazed. Many people will strenuously maintain that they cannot survive without these stimulants, these poisons, and they cannot give them up.[3] No, not even to redeem the world from eternal damnation. And very often they will absolutely show anger, if argued with, just as soon as the argument begins to pinch their consciences. Oh, how long shall the church show her hypocritical face at the missionary meeting, and pray to God to save the world, while she is actually throwing away five times as much for sheer intemperance, as she will give to save the world! Some of you may think these are little things, and that it is quite beneath the dignity of the pulpit to lecture against tea and coffee. But I tell you it is a great mistake of yours if you think these are little things, when they make the church odious in the sight of God, by exposing her hypocrisy and lust. Here is an individual who pretends he has given himself up to serve Jesus Christ, and yet he refuses to deny himself any darling lust, and then he will go and pray, "O Lord, save the world. O Lord, your kingdom come!" I tell you it is hypocrisy. Shall such prayers be heard? Unless people are willing to deny themselves, I would not give a penny for the prayers of enough such professing Christians to cover the whole of the United States.

These things must be taught to young converts. It must come to this point in the church, that people shall not be called Christians, unless

---

[3] Today soft drinks would be another example of the indulgences that are commonly consumed. Professing Christians spend countless millions of dollars on these unhealthy drinks, far more than is spent on missions.

they will cut off the right hand, and pluck out the right eye, and deny themselves for Christ's sake. A little thing? See it poison the spirit of prayer! See it debase and sensualize the soul! Is that a trifle beneath the dignity of the pulpit, when these intemperate indulgences, of one kind and another, cost the church five times, if not fifty times, more than all she gives for the salvation of the world?

The time to teach these things with effect is when the converts are young. If converts are not properly taught then, if they get a wrong habit, and begin with an easy, self-indulgent mode of living, it rarely happens that they become thoroughly reformed. I have conversed with older professing Christians on these subjects, and have been astonished at their stubbornness in indulging their lusts. And I am convinced that the church never can rise out of this sloth until young converts are faithfully taught, at the outset of their religious course, to have self-control in all things.

7. They should be taught to have just as much religion in all their business as they have in prayer, or in going to a religious service. They should be just as holy, just as watchful, aim just as singly at the glory of God, be just as sincere and solemn in all their daily employments, as when they come to the throne of grace. If they are not, their Sabbath performances will be an abomination.

8. They should be taught that it is necessary for them to be just as holy as they think ministers should be. There has for a long time been an idea that ministers are obligated to be holy and practice self-denial. And so they are. But it is strange they should suppose that ministers are obligated to be any more holy than other people. They would be shocked to see a minister showing levity, or chasing after the latest fashions, or losing his temper, or living in a fine house, or riding in a coach. Oh, that is dreadful! It does not look well in a minister. Indeed! For a minister's wife to wear such a fine bonnet, or such a silk shawl — oh no, it will never do! But they think nothing of these things in a layman, or a layman's wife! That is no offense at all! I am not saying that these things do look well in a minister. I know they do not. But they look, in God's eyes, the same in a minister as they do in a layman. You have no more right to indulge in vanity, and folly, and pride, than a minister. Can you go to heaven without being sanctified? Can you be holy without living for God, and doing all that you can to his glory? I have heard supposedly good men speak against ministers having large salaries, and living in an expensive style, when they themselves were actually spending a great deal more money for the support of their families than any minister. What would be thought of

minister living in the style in which many professing Christians and ders of churches are living in this city? Why, everybody would say ey were hypocrites. But it is just as much evidence of hypocrisy in layman to spend God's money to gratify his lusts, or to please the orld, or his family, as it is for a minister to do so.

is distressing to hear some of our foremost laymen talk of its being ishonorable to religion, to give ministers a large salary, and let them ve in an expensive style, when it is a fact that their own expenses are ir above those of almost any minister. All this arises out of fundamen-lly wrong notions absorbed while they were young converts. Young inverts have been taught to expect that ministers will have all the re-gion — especially all the self-denial. So long as this continues there in be no hope that the church will ever do much for the glory of God, r for the conversion of the world. There is nothing of this in the Bible. Vhere has God said, "You ministers, love God with all your heart, and iul, and mind, and strength"? Or, "You ministers, do everything for ie glory of God"? No, these things are said to everyone alike. The one /ho attempts to excuse himself from any duty or self-denial, from any /atchfulness or sobriety, by putting it off upon ministers, or who ven-ires to adopt a lower scale of holy living for himself than he thinks is roper for a minister, is in great danger of proving himself a hypocrite, nd paying in hell the cost of his foolishness.

fuch depends on the instructions given to young converts. Once they et into the habit of supposing that they may indulge in things that iey would condemn in a minister, it is extremely unlikely that they /ill ever get out of it.

. They should aim at being perfect. Every young convert should be iught that if it is not his purpose to live without sin, he has not yet egun to be religious. What is religion but a supreme love to God and supreme purpose of heart or disposition to obey God? Without this, iere is no religion at all. It is the duty of all to be perfect, and to itend entire, perpetual, and universal obedience to God. It should e their constant purpose to live completely for God, and obey all his ommandments. They should live so that if they should sin it would e an inconsistency, an exception, an individual case, in which they act ontrary to the fixed and general purpose and quality of their lives. hey should not sin at all — they are obligated to be as holy as God is. 'oung converts should be taught to set out in the right course, or they vill never be right.

0. They should be taught to show their light. If the young convert loes not show his light, and hold it up to the world, it will go out. If

he does not stir himself, and go forth and try to enlighten those aroun
him, his light will go out, and his own soul will soon be in darknes.
Sometimes young converts seem inclined to sit still and not do any
thing in public until they have a great deal of light. But this is not th
way. Let the convert use what he has. Let him hold up his little twir
kling candle, boldly and honestly, and then God will make it like
blazing torch. But God will not take the trouble to keep a light burnin
that is hid. Why should he? What is the use?

This is the reason why so many people have so little enjoyment in re
ligion. They do not exert themselves to honor God. They keep wha
little they do enjoy so entirely to themselves, that there is no good rea
son why God should give blessings and benefits on them.

11. They should be taught how to win souls to Christ. Young convert
should be taught particularly what to do to accomplish this, and hov
to do it. They should be then taught to live for this end as the grea
leading goal of life. How strange has been the course sometimes pu
sued! These persons have been converted, and — there they are. The
get into the church, and then they are left to go along just as they di
before. They do nothing, and are taught to do nothing, for Christ. Th
only change is that they go more regularly to church on Sunday, an
let the minister feed them, as it is called. But suppose he does fee
them, they do not grow strong, for they cannot digest it, because the
do not exercise. They have spiritual indigestion. Now, the great goa
for which Christians are converted and left in this world is, to pull sin
ners out of the fire. If they do not do this, they had better be dead. An
young converts should be taught this as soon as they are born into th
kingdom. The first thing they do should be to go to work for this end
— to save sinners.

II. HOW THE CHURCH SHOULD TREAT YOUNG CONVERTS

1. Older professing Christians should be able to give young converts
great deal of instruction, and they should give it. The truth is, howeve
that most professing believers in the churches do not know how to giv
good instruction to young converts. If they attempt to do so, they giv
only that which is false. The church should be able to teach her chil
dren. When she receives them she should be as busy in training then
to act, as mothers are in teaching their little children the things the
will need to know and do. But this is far enough from being the cas
in general. And we can never expect to see young converts habitually
taking right hold of duty, and going straight forward without declin
and backsliding, until the time comes when all young converts are in
telligently trained by the church.

2. Young converts should not be kept back behind the rest of the church. How often is it found that the old professing Christians will keep the young converts back behind the rest of the church, and prevent them from taking any active part in religion, for fear they should become spiritually proud. Young converts in such churches are rarely or never called on to take a part in meetings, or set to any active duty, or the like, for fear they should become lifted up with spiritual pride. Thus the church becomes the modest keeper of their humility, and teaches them to file in behind the old, stiff, dry, cold members and elders, for fear that if they should be allowed to do anything for Christ, it will make them proud. The correct way to make young converts humble and keep them so, is to put them to their work and keep them there. That is the way to keep God with them, and as long as God is with them, he will take care of their humility. Keep them constantly engaged in religion, and then the Spirit of God will dwell in them, and so they will be kept humble by the most effective process. But if young converts are left to fall in behind the old professing Christians where they can never do anything, they will never know what spirit they are of, and this is the very way to run them into the danger of falling into the worst type of spiritual pride.

3. They should be watched over by the church, and warned of their dangers, just as a tender mother watches over her young children. Young converts do not know at all the dangers by which they are surrounded. They do not know the devices of the devil, the temptations of the world, the power of their own passions and habits, and the thousand forms of danger. If not properly watched and warned, they will run right into such dangers. The church should watch over and care for her young children — just as mothers watch their little children in this great city, for fear the carts run over them, or they stray away. Or as mothers watch over them while growing up, for fear they may be drawn into the whirlpools of iniquity. The church should watch over all the interests of her young members, know where they are, and what are their habits, temptations, dangers, privileges — the state of religion in their hearts, and their spirit of prayer. Look at that anxious mother, when she sees paleness on the forehead of her little child. "What is the matter with you, my child? Have you eaten something bad? Have you gotten cold? What is wrong?" Oh, how different it is with the children of the church, the lambs that the Savior has committed to the care of his church! Alas! Instead of restraining her children, and taking care of them, the church lets them go anywhere, and look out for themselves. What should we say of a mother who should knowingly let her children totter along to the edge of a cliff? Would we not say

she was horribly guilty for doing so, and that if the child should fall and be killed, its blood would rest on the mother's head? What, then, is the guilt of the church, in knowingly neglecting her young converts? I have known churches where young converts were totally neglected, and viewed with suspicion and jealousy. Nobody went near them to strengthen or encourage or counsel them. Nothing was done to lead them to usefulness, to teach them what to do or how to do it, or to open to them a field of labor. And then — what then? Why, when they find that young converts cannot stand everything, when they find them growing cold and backward under such treatment, they just turn around and abuse them, for not standing firm!

4. Be tender in reproving them. When Christians find it necessary to reprove young converts, they should be exceedingly careful in their manner of doing it. Young converts should be faithfully watched over by the elder members of the church, and when they begin to lose ground, or to turn aside, they should be promptly admonished, and, if necessary, reproved. But to do it in a wrong manner is worse than not to do it at all. It is sometimes done in a manner that is abrupt, harsh, and apparently critical, more like scolding than like brotherly admonition. Such a manner, instead of inspiring confidence, or leading to reformation, will harden the heart of the young convert, and confirm him in his wrong ways. At the same time, it closes his mind to the influence of such critical guardians. The heart of a young convert is tender, and easily grieved, and sometimes a single unkind look will set him into such a state of mind as will fasten his errors upon him, and make him grow worse and worse.

You who are parents know how important it is when you reprove your children, that they should see that you do it from the best of motives, for their benefit, because you wish them to be good, and not because you are angry. Otherwise they will soon come to regard you as a tyrant, rather than a friend. Just so with young converts. Kindness and tenderness, even in reproof, will win their confidence, and attach them to you, and give an influence to your brotherly instructions and counsels, so that you can mold them into finished Christians. Instead of this, if you are severe and critical in your manner, that is the way to make them think you wish to rule over them. Many people, under pretense of being faithful, as they call it, often hurt young converts by such a severe and overbearing manner, as to drive them away, or perhaps crush them into gloom and apathy. Young converts have only little experience, and are easily thrown down. They are just like a little child when it first begins to walk. You see it tottering along, and it stumbles over a straw. You see the mother take everything out of the way, when her lit-

:le one is going to try to walk. Just so with young converts. The church should take up every stumbling block, and treat converts in such a way as to make them see that if they are reproved, Christ is in it. Then they will receive it as it is meant, and it will do them good.

5. Kindly point out things that are at fault in the young convert, which he does not see. He is but a child, and knows so little about religion, so that there will be many things that he needs to learn, and a great many that he should fix. Whatever there is that is wrong in spirit or unlovely in his manner that will impede his usefulness or impair his influence as a Christian, should be kindly pointed out and corrected. To do this in the right way, however, requires great wisdom. Christians should make it a subject of much prayer and reflection, that they may do it in such a way to not do more harm than good. If you rebuke him merely for the things that he did not see, or did not know to be improper, it will grieve and disgust him. Such instruction should be carefully timed. Often, it is well to take the opportunity after you have been praying together, or after a kind conversation on religious subjects which has made him feel that you love him, seek his good, and earnestly desire to promote his sanctification, his usefulness, and his happiness. Then, a mere hint will often do the work. Just suggest that "Such a thing in your prayer," or "Your conduct in so-and-so did not strike me pleasantly. Would you think about it, and perhaps you will consider it better to avoid it happening again?" Do it right, and you will help him and do him good. Do it in the wrong way, and you will do ten times more harm than good. Often, young converts will err through ignorance. Their judgment is not ripe, and they need time to think and make an enlightened judgment on some point that at first appears to them doubtful. In such cases the older members should treat them with great kindness and patience, should kindly instruct them, and not immediately denounce them for not seeing at first what perhaps they themselves did not understand until years after they were converted.

6. Do not speak of the faults of young converts behind their backs. This is too common among old professing Christians. Eventually the converts hear of it. What an influence it must have to destroy the confidence of young converts in their elder brethren, to grieve their hearts and discourage them, and perhaps to drive them away from the good influence of the church.

III. SOME OF THE EVILS OF DEFECTIVE INSTRUCTION

1. If the instruction given to young converts is not correct and full, they will not grow in grace, but their religion will dwindle away and

decay. Their course, instead of being like the path of the righteous, growing brighter and brighter into the full day (Proverbs 4:18), will grow dimmer and dimmer, and finally, perhaps, go out in darkness. Wherever you see young converts let their religion taper off until it comes to nothing, you may understand that it is the natural result of defective instruction. The logical result of teaching young converts the truth, and the whole truth, is that they grow stronger and stronger. Truth is the food of the mind — it is what gives the mind strength. And where religious character grows feeble, in nine cases out of ten it is because of their being neglected, or falsely instructed, when they were young converts.

2. They will be left in doubt as to whether they are Christians. If their early instruction is false, or defective, there will be so much inconsistency in their lives, and so little evidence of real piety, that they themselves will finally doubt whether they have any. Probably they will live and die in doubt. You cannot make a little evidence go a great way. If they do not see clearly, they will not live consistently. If they do not live consistently, they can have only little evidence. If they do not have evidence, they must doubt, or live in presumption.

3. If young converts are not well instructed, they will inevitably backslide. If their instruction is defective, they will probably live in such a way as to disgrace Christianity. The truth, kept steadily before the mind of a young convert, in proper proportions, has a natural tendency to make him grow "to mature manhood, to the measure of the stature of the fullness of Christ" (Ephesians 4:13). If any one point is made too prominent in the instruction given, there will probably be just that disproportion in his character. If he is fully instructed on some points and not on others, you will find a corresponding defect in his life and character.

If the instruction of young converts is greatly defective, they will press on in religion no farther than they are strongly propelled by the first emotions of their conversion. As soon as that is spent they will come to a standstill, and then they will decline and backslide. And after you will always find that they will go forward only when stirred by some powerful excitement. These are your "periodical" Christians, who are so likely to wake up in a time of revival, and bluster about as if they had the zeal of angels for a few days, and then die away as dead and cold as a northern winter. Oh, how desirable, how infinitely important it is, that young converts should be so taught that their religion will not depend on impulses and excitements, but that they will go steadily onward in the Christian course, advancing from strength to strength, d giving forth a clear and safe and steady light all around.

EMARKS

The church is truly guilty for her past neglect of the instruction of ung converts. Instead of bringing up their young converts to be orking Christians, churches have generally acted as if they did not ow how to employ young converts. They have acted like a mother ho has a large family of daughters, but knows not how to put them work, and so lets them to grow up idle and untaught, useless and spised, and to be the easy prey of every scheming villain.

the Church had only done her duty in training up young converts to ork and labor for Christ, the world would have been converted long o. But instead of this, how many churches actually oppose young nverts who attempt to put themselves to work for Christ. Many d professing Christians look with suspicion upon every movement f young converts, and talk against them, saying, "They are too for- ard, they should not to put themselves forward, but wait for those ho are older." Instead of bidding young converts "Godspeed," and eering them on, very often they hinder them, and perhaps put them own. How often have young converts been stopped from going for- ard, and turned into rank behind a formal, lazy, inefficient church, ntil their spirit has been crushed, and their zeal extinguished. After few ineffective struggles to throw off the cords, they have decided sit down with the rest, and wait. In many places young converts nnot even attempt to hold a prayer meeting by themselves, without eing rebuked by the pastor or some deacon, for being so forward, and arged with spiritual pride. "Oh," it is said, "you are young converts, e you? And so you want to get together, and call all the neighbors to- ether to look at you, because you are young converts. You had better rn preachers at once!" A celebrated Doctor of Divinity in New Eng- nd boasted, at a public table, of his success in keeping all his converts till. He had great difficulty, he said, for they were in a terrible fever do something, to talk, or pray, or start meetings, but by the greatest igilance he had kept it all down, and now his church was just as quiet it was before the revival. Wonderful achievement for a minister of sus Christ! Was that what the blessed Savior meant when he told eter, "Feed My lambs"?

. Young converts should be trained to work just as carefully as young ecruits in an army are trained for war. Suppose a captain in the army ould get his company enlisted, and then take no more pains to teach nd train, and discipline them, than are taken by many pastors to train nd lead forward their young converts. Why, the enemy would laugh at such an army. Call them soldiers! Such an army would resemb the church that does not train her young converts. Instead of beir trained to stand shoulder to shoulder from the onset, they feel no pra tical confidence in their leaders, no confidence in their neighbors, ar no confidence in themselves. Hence they scatter at the first shock battle. Look at the church now. Ministers are not agreed as to wh shall be done, and many of them will fight against their brethren, qua reling about "new measures," or something. As to the members, the cannot feel confidence when they see the leaders so divided. And the if they attempt to do anything — what ignorance, what awkwardnes what discord, what weakness we see, and what miserable work the make of it! And so it must continue, until the church shall train u young converts to be intelligent, single-hearted, self-denying, workir Christians.

3. The Church has entirely mistaken the way in which she is to b sanctified. The experiment has been carried on long enough, of tryir to sanctify the church, without finding anything for the members do. But holiness consists in obeying God. Sanctification, as a proces means obeying him more and more perfectly. And the way to promo it in the Church is to give everyone something to do. Look at these larg churches, where they have five hundred or seven hundred member and have a minister to feed them from Sabbath to Sabbath, while ther are so many of them together that the majority have nothing at all do, and are never trained to make any direct efforts for the salvation souls. And in that way they are expecting to be sanctified and prepare for heaven! They never will be sanctified this way. That is not the wa God has appointed. Jesus Christ has made his people coworkers wit him in saving sinners, for this very reason, because sanctification cor sists in doing those things that are required to promote this work. Th is one reason why he has not employed angels in the work, or carrie it on by direct revelation of truth to the minds of men. It is because is necessary as a means of sanctification that the church should syn pathize with Christ in his feelings and his labors for the conversio of sinners. And in this way the entire church must move, before th world will be converted. When the day comes that the whole body professing Christians will realize that they are here on earth as a bod of missionaries, and when they live and work accordingly, then the da of humanity's redemption will draw near.

Christian, if you cannot go abroad to labor, why are you not a mis sionary in your own family? If you are too feeble even to leave you room, be a missionary there in your room. How many unconverte servants have you in your house? Call in your unconverted servants and your unconverted children, and be a missionary to them. Think of your physician, who, perhaps, is pouring himself out to save your body. Think that you receive his kindness and never make him the greatest return in your power.

It is necessary that the church should take hold of her young converts at the outset, and set them to work in the right way. The hope of the church is in the young converts.

4. We see what a responsibility rests on ministers and elders, and on all who have opportunity to assist in training young converts. How distressing is the picture that often forces itself upon the mind, where many are converted, and yet so little trouble is taken with young converts that in a single year you cannot tell the young converts from the rest of the church. And then we see the old church members turn around and complain of these young converts, and perhaps slander them, when in truth these old professors themselves are mostly to blame — oh, it is too bad! This reaction that people talk so much about after a revival would never come, and young converts never would backslide as they do, if the church would be prompt and faithful in attending to their instruction. If they are truly converted, they can be made thorough and energetic Christians. And if they are not made such Christians, Jesus Christ will require it at the hands of the church.

Chapter 15

THE BACKSLIDER IN HEART

"The backslider in heart will be filled with the fruit of his ways." *(Proverbs 14:14)*

cannot conclude this series of lectures, without warning converts against backsliding. In discussing this subject, I will show:

. What backsliding in heart is not.

I. What backsliding in heart is.

II. What are evidences of backsliding in heart.

V. What are consequences of backsliding in heart.

V. How to recover from this state.

I. WHAT A BACKSLIDING HEART IS NOT

It does not consist in the decrease of highly excited religious emotions. The decrease of religious feeling may be evidence of a backslidden heart, but it does not consist in the cooling off of religious feeling.

II. WHAT BACKSLIDING IN HEART IS

1. It consists in taking back that consecration to God and his service, that constitutes true conversion.

2. It is the leaving by a Christian of his first love.

3. It consists in the Christian withdrawing himself from that state of entire devotion to God, which constitutes true religion, and coming

again under the control of a self-pleasing spirit.

4. The text implies that there may be a backslidden heart even when the forms of religion and obedience to God are maintained. As we know that people can perform the same or similar acts from widely different, and often from opposite, motives, we are certain that people may keep up all the outward appearances of religion, when in fact they are backslidden in heart. No doubt the most intense selfishness often takes on a religious type, and there are many considerations that might lead a backslider in heart to keep up the forms, while he had lost the power of godliness in his soul.

III. WHAT ARE EVIDENCES OF A BACKSLIDDEN HEART

1. Obvious formality in religious exercises. There may be a stereotyped, formal way of saying and doing things from habit rather than the outpouring of the religious life. This formality will be emotionless and cold as an iceberg, and will demonstrate a total lack of sincerity in the performance of religious duty. In prayer and in Christian exercises the backslider in heart will pray, praise, confess, or give thanks with his lips, so that all can hear him, but in such a way that no one can feel him. Such a formality would be impossible where there existed a present, living faith and love, and religious zeal.

2. A lack of religious enjoyment is evidence of a backslidden heart. We always enjoy the words and actions that please those whom we most love. Furthermore, when the heart is not backslidden, communion with God is maintained, and therefore all religious duties are not only performed with pleasure, but the communion with God is a source of rich and continual enjoyment. If we do not enjoy the service of God, it is because we do not truly serve him. If we love him supremely, it is impossible that we should not enjoy his service at every step. Always remember then: whenever you lose the enjoyment of serving God, you can know that you are not serving him correctly.

3. Religious bondage is another evidence of a backslidden heart. God has no slaves. He does not accept the service of those who serve him because they must. He accepts nothing but a service of love. A backslider in heart finds his religious duties a burden to him. He has promised to serve the Lord. He dare not wholly break off from the form of service, and he tries to be dutiful, while he has no heart in prayer, in praise, in worship, or in any of those exercises which are so spontaneous and delightful, where there is true love to God. The backslider in heart is often like a dutiful, but unloving wife. She tries to do her duty to her husband, but utterly fails because she does not love him.

er effort to please her husband is forced, not the spontaneous out-
urst of a loving heart. Her relationship and her duties become the
urden of her life. She goes around complaining about the burden of
ire on her, and will not be likely to advise young ladies to marry. She
committed for life, and must therefore perform the duties of married
fe, but it is such a bondage! Just so with religious bondage. The pro-
·ssing Christian must perform his duty. He drags painfully about it,
ıd you will hear him naturally sing backslider's hymns:

> Reason I hear, her counsels weigh,
> And all her words approve;
> And yet I find it hard to obey,
> And harder still, to love.

. A reckless temperament. While the heart is full of love, the temper-
ment will naturally be controlled and sweet. The will keeps it con-
·olled, and does not tolerate it to explode in outrageous abuse, or if at
ıy time it should break loose in hateful words, it will soon be brought
own, and by no means allowed to gain control and show itself to the
nnoyance of others. A loving heart will especially confess and break
own, if at any time bad temperament gains control. Whenever, there-
ɔre, there is an irritable, uncontrolled temperament allowed to show
self to those around, you can know there is a backslidden heart.

. A spirit of uncharitableness is evidence of a backslidden heart. By
ıis, I mean a lack of that disposition that puts the best light upon ev-
ryone's conduct that can be reasonable — a lack of confidence in the
ood intentions and professions of others. We naturally believe the
ood professions of those whom we love. We naturally attribute to
ıem right motives, and put the best allowable construction upon their
vords and deeds. Where there is a lack of this, there is conclusive evi-
ence of a backslidden or unloving heart.

. A critical spirit is conclusive evidence of a backslidden heart. This
; a spirit of fault finding, of maligning the motives of others, when
heir conduct allows a charitable construction. It is a disposition to
asten blame on others, and judge them harshly. It is a spirit of dis-
rust of Christian character and profession. It is a state of mind that
eveals itself in harsh judgments, harsh sayings, and the manifestation
·f uncomfortable feelings toward individuals. This state of mind is en-
irely incompatible with a loving heart. Whenever a professing believer
hows a critical spirit, you can know there is a backslidden heart.

. A lack of interest in God's Word is also evidence of a backslidden heart. Perhaps nothing more conclusively proves that a professing Christian has a backslidden heart, than his losing his interest in the Bible. While the heart is full of love, no book in the world is so precious as the Bible. But when the love is gone, the Bible becomes not only uninteresting but often repulsive. There is no faith to accept its promises, only enough conviction left to dread its threatening. But in general the backslider in heart is apathetic about the Bible. He does not read it much, and when he does read it, he does not have enough interest to understand it. Its pages become dark and uninteresting, and therefore it is neglected.

8. A lack of interest in secret prayer is also evidence of a backslidden heart. Young Christian, if you find yourself losing your interest in the Bible and in secret prayer, stop immediately, return to God, and give yourself no rest, until you enjoy the light of his countenance. If you feel disinclined to pray, or to read your Bible, if when you pray and read your Bible, you have no heart, if you are inclined to make your secret devotions short, or are easily induced to neglect them, or if your thoughts, affections, and emotions wander, you can know that you are a backslider in heart, and your first business is to be broken down before God, and to see that your love and zeal are renewed.

9. A lack of interest in the conversion of souls and in efforts to promote revivals of religion. This of course reveals a backslidden heart. There is nothing that a loving heart takes more interest in than in the conversion of souls — in revivals of religion, and in efforts to promote them.

10. A lack of interest in published accounts or narratives of revivals of religion is also evidence of a backslidden heart. While one retains his interest in the conversion of souls and in revivals of religion he will, of course, be interested in all accounts of revivals of religion anywhere. If you find yourself, therefore, not interested in these accounts, take it for granted that you are backslidden in heart.

11. The same is true of missions, and missionary work and operations. If you lose your interest in the work and in the conversion of the lost and do not delight to read and hear of the success of missions, you can know that you are backslidden in heart.

12. The loss of interest in benevolent enterprises generally is evidence of a backslidden heart. I say, "the loss of interest," for surely, if you were ever converted to Christ, you have had an interest in all benevolent enterprises that came within your knowledge. Religion consists in selfless benevolence. Of course, a converted soul takes the deepest interest in all benevolent efforts to reform and save humankind, in good

government, in Christian education, in the cause of temperance, in the abolition of slavery, in provision for the needs of the poor, and in short, in every good word and work. In proportion as you have lost your interest in these, you have evidence that you are backslidden in heart.

3. The loss of interest in truly spiritual conversation is another evidence of a backslidden heart. "Out of the abundance of the heart the mouth speaks" (Matthew 12:34). This our Lord Jesus Christ announced as a law of our nature. No conversation is so sweet to a truly loving heart, as that which relates to Christ, and to our living Christian experience. If you find yourself losing interest in conversation on heart religion, and of the various and wonderful experiences of Christians, if you have known what the true love of God is, you have fallen from it, and are a backslider in heart.

4. A loss of interest in the conversation and company of highly spiritual people is evidence of a backslidden heart. We take the greatest delight in the company of those who are most interested in the things that are most dear to us. Hence, a loving Christian heart will always seek the company of those who are most spiritually minded, and whose conversation is most evangelical and spiritual. If you find yourself lacking in this respect, then know for certain that you are backslidden in heart.

5. The loss of interest in the question of sanctification is evidence of a backslidden heart. I say again, the loss of interest, for, if you ever truly knew the love of God, you must have had a great interest in the question of entire consecration to God, or of entire sanctification. If you are a Christian, you have felt that sin was an abomination to your soul. You have had inexpressible longings to be rid of it forever, and everything that could throw light upon that question of agonizing importance was most intensely interesting to you. If this question has been dismissed, and you no longer take an interest in it, it is because you are backslidden in heart.

6. The loss of interest in those newly converted, is also evidence of a backslidden heart. The Psalmist says, "Those who fear you shall see me and rejoice, because I have hoped in your word" (Psalm 119:74). This he puts into the mouth of a convert, and who does not know that this is true? There is joy in the presence of the angels of God, over one sinner that repents. Is there not joy among the saints on earth, over those that come to Christ, and are as babes newly born into the kingdom? Show me a professing Christian who does not show an absorbing interest in converts to Christ, and I will show you a backslider in heart and a hypocrite. He professes religion, but has none.

17. An uncharitable state of mind in regard to professed converts, is also evidence of a backslidden heart. Love "believes all things, hopes all things" (1 Corinthians 13:7), is very ready to judge kindly and favorably of those who profess to be converted to Christ, and will naturally watch over them with interest, pray for them, instruct them, and have as much confidence in them as it is reasonable to have. A disposition, therefore, to pick at, criticize, and criticize them, is evidence of a backslidden heart.

18. The lack of the spirit of prayer is evidence of a backslidden heart. While the love of Christ remains fresh in the soul, the indwelling Spirit of God will reveal himself as the Spirit of grace and supplication. He will create strong desires in the soul for the salvation of sinners and the sanctification of saints. He will often make intercessions in them, with great longings, strong crying and tears, and with groanings too deep for words, for those things that are according to the will of God. To express it in Scriptural language, according to Paul, "Likewise the Spirit helps us in our weakness. For we do not know what to pray for as we ought, but the Spirit himself intercedes for us with groanings too deep for words. And he who searches hearts knows what is the mind of the Spirit, because the Spirit intercedes for the saints according to the will of God" (Romans 8:26-27). If the spirit of prayer departs, it is a sure indication of a backslidden heart, for while the first love of a Christian continues he is sure to be drawn by the Holy Spirit to wrestle much in prayer.

19. A backslidden heart often reveals itself by the manner in which people pray. For example, praying as if in a state of self-condemnation, or very much like a convicted sinner, is evidence of a backslidden heart. Such a person will reveal the fact that he is not at peace with God. His confessions and self-accusations will show to others what perhaps he does not well understand himself. His manner of praying will reveal the fact that he has not communion with God. Instead of being filled with faith and love, he is convicted of sin and conscious that he is not in a state of acceptance with God. He will naturally pray more like a convicted sinner than like a Christian. It will be seen by his prayer that he is not in a state of Christian liberty — that he is having a Seventh of Romans experience, instead of that which is described in the Eighth.

20. A backslidden heart will further reveal itself in praying almost exclusively for self, and for those friends that are regarded almost as parts of self. It is often very striking and even shocking to attend a backsliders' prayer meeting, and I am very sorry to say that many prayer meetings of the church are little else. Their prayers are timid and hes-

tating, and reveal the fact that they have little or no faith. Instead of surrounding the throne of grace and pouring their hearts out for a blessing on those around them, they have to be urged up to duty, to "take up their cross." Their hearts do not and will not spontaneously pour out to God in prayer. They have very little concern for others, and when they pretend to lead in prayer, it will be observed that they pray just like a company of convicted sinners, almost altogether for themselves. They will pray for that which, should they obtain it, would be religion, just as a convicted sinner would pray for a new heart. The fact that they pray for religion as they do, shows that they have none, in their present state of mind. Ask them to pray for the conversion of sinners, and they will either completely forget to do so, or just mention sinners in such a way as will show that they have no heart to pray for them.

I have known professing Christian parents to get into such a state that they had no heart to pray for the conversion of their own children, even when those children were under conviction. They would keep up family prayer, and attend a weekly prayer meeting, but would never get out of the rut of praying round and round for themselves. A few years ago I was laboring in a revival in a Presbyterian Church. At the close of the evening sermon I found that the daughter of one of the elders of the church was in great distress of mind. I observed that her convictions were very deep. We had been holding a meeting with inquirers in the vestry, and I had just dismissed the inquirers, when this young lady came to me in great agitation and begged me to pray for her. The people had mostly gone, except a few who were waiting in the body of the church for those friends who had attended the meeting of inquiry. I called the father of this young lady into the vestry that he might see the very anxious state of his daughter's mind.

After a short personal conversation with her in the presence of her father, I called on him to pray for her, and said that I would follow him, and I urged her to give her heart to Christ. We all knelt, and he went through with his prayer, kneeling by the side of his sobbing daughter, without ever mentioning her case. His prayer revealed that he had no more religion than she had, and that he was very much in her state of mind — under an awful sense of condemnation. He had kept up the appearance of religion. As an elder of the church, he was obliged to keep up appearances. He had gone around and around upon the treadmill of his duties, while his heart was utterly backslidden. It is often almost nauseating to attend a prayer meeting of the backslidden in heart. They will go around, one after the other, in reality praying for their own conversion. They do not so express it, but that is the real significance of their prayer. They could not make it more evident that they are backsliders in heart.

21. Absence from stated prayer meetings for petty reasons is a sure indication of a backslidden heart. No meeting is more interesting to Christians than the prayer meeting, and while they have any heart to pray, they will not be absent from prayer meeting unless prevented from attending by the providence of God. If a call from a friend at the hour of meeting can prevent their attendance, unless the call is made under very unusual circumstances, it is strong evidence that they do not wish to attend, and hence, that they are backsliders in heart. A call at such a time would not prevent their attending a wedding, a party, a picnic, or an amusing lecture. It is hypocrisy for them to pretend that they really want to go, when they can be kept away for petty reasons.

22. The same is true of the neglect of family prayer for petty reasons. While the heart is engaged in religion, Christians will not readily omit family devotions, and whenever they are ready to find an excuse for the omission, it is certain evidence that they are backslidden in heart.

23. When secret prayer is regarded more as a duty than as a privilege, it is because the heart is backslidden. It has always appeared to me almost ridiculous, to hear Christians speak of prayer as a "duty." It is one of the greatest of earthly privileges. What should we think of a child coming to its parent for its dinner, not because it is hungry, but as a duty? How would it strike us to hear a beggar speak of the "duty" of asking alms of us? It is an infinite privilege to be allowed to come to God, and ask for the supply of all our wants. But to pray because we must, rather than because we may, seems unnatural. To ask for what we want, and because we want it, and because God has encouraged us to ask, and has promised to answer our request, is natural and reasonable. But to pray as a duty and as if we were obliging God by our prayer, is quite ridiculous, and is a certain indication of a backslidden heart.

24. Pleading for worldly amusements is also an indication of a backslidden heart. The most grateful amusements possible, to a truly spiritual mind, are those engagements that bring the soul into the most direct communion with God. While the heart is full of love and faith, an hour, or an evening, spent alone in communion with God, is more delightful than all the amusements that the world can offer. A loving heart is jealous of everything that will interfere with its communion with God. It has not relish for mere worldly amusements. When the soul does not find more delight in God than in all worldly things, the heart is sadly backslidden.

. Religious apathy, with worldly wakefulness, is a sure indication a backslidden heart. We sometimes see people who feel deeply and uickly on worldly subjects, but who cannot be made to feel deeply on ligious subjects. This clearly indicates a backslidden state of mind.

. A self-indulgent spirit is a sure indication of a backslidden heart. By lf-indulgence, I mean a disposition to gratify the appetites, passions, nd propensities, to "carry out the desires of the body and the mind" phesians 2:3).

nis, in the Bible, is represented as a state of spiritual death. I am nvinced that the most common occasion of backsliding in heart is be found in the clamor for indulgence of the various appetites and ropensities. The appetite for food is frequently, and perhaps more equently than any other, the occasion of backsliding. Few Christians, fear, understand any danger in this direction. God's command is, Whether you eat or drink, or whatever you do, do all to the glory of od" (1 Corinthians 10:31). Christians forget this, and eat and drink to lease themselves, consulting their appetites instead of the laws of life nd health. More people are ensnared by their tables than the church aware of. The table is a snare of death to so many that no person can ount. A great many people who avoid alcoholic drinks altogether, will dulge in tea and coffee, and even tobacco, and in food that, both in uantity and quality, violates every law of health. They seem to have o other law than that of appetite. This appetite they so deprave by use that, by indulging it, ruins body and soul together. Show me a luttonous professing Christian, and I will show you a backslider.

7. A seared conscience is also evidence of a backslidden heart. While ne soul is wakeful and loving, the conscience is as tender as the apple f the eye. But when the heart is backslidden, the conscience is silent nd seared on many subjects. Such a person will tell you that he is not iolating his conscience, in eating or drinking, or in self-indulgence of ny kind. You will find a backslider has but little conscience. The same ill very generally be true in regard to sins of omission. Many duties ay be neglected and a seared conscience will remain silent. Where onscience is not awake, the heart is surely backslidden.

8. Loose moral principles are a sure indication of a backslidden heart. backslider in heart will write letters on the Sabbath, engage in secular eading, and in much worldly conversation. In business, such a person ill take little advantages, play business tricks, and conform to the abits of worldly business people in the transaction of business. He ill be guilty of deception and misrepresentation in making bargains, ill demand exorbitant interest, and take advantage of the necessities

of his fellow people.

29. Being influenced by the fear of man is evidence of a backslidde heart. While the heart is full of the love of God, God is feared, and n man. A desire for the applause of people is kept down, and it is enoug to please God, whether people are pleased or displeased. But when th love of God is abated, "the fear of man," that "lays a snare" (Proverb 29:25), gets hold of the backslider. To please man rather than God, then his aim. In such a state he will sooner offend God than man.

30. A sticklishness about forms, ceremonies, and nonessentials, give evidence of a backslidden heart. A loving heart is particular only abou the substance and power of religion, and will not stickle about its form

31. Criticizing measures in promoting revivals of religion, is a sure ev dence of a backslidden heart. Where the heart is fully set upon the cor version of sinners and the sanctification of believers, it will naturall approach the subject in the most direct manner, and by most effectiv means designed to accomplish the end. It will not object to, nor stum ble at, measures that are evidently blessed of God, but will exert th utmost wisdom in devising the most suitable means to accomplish th great end on which the heart is set.

IV. THE CONSEQUENCES OF BACKSLIDING IN HEART

The text says, "The backslider in heart will be filled with the fruit of hi ways."

1. He shall be filled with his own works. But these are dead works, the are not works of faith and love, which are acceptable to God, but are th filthy rags of his own righteousness. If they are performed as religiou services, they are but loathsome hypocrisy, and an abomination to God There is no heart in them. "You are those who justify yourselves befor men, but God knows your hearts. For what is exalted among men i an abomination in the sight of God" (Luke 16:15). "I know that you d not have the love of God within you" (John 5:42).

2. He shall be filled with his own feelings. Instead of that sweet peac and rest, and joy in the Holy Spirit, that he once experienced, he wi find himself in a state of unrest, dissatisfied with himself and every body else, his feelings often painful, humiliating, and as unpleasar and unlovely as can be conceived. It is often very difficult to live wit backsliders. They are often ill tempered, critical, and irritating, in a their ways. They have forsaken God, and in their feelings there is mor of hell than of heaven.

3. They will be filled with their own prejudices. Their willingness t

know and do the truth has gone. They will very naturally commit themselves against any truth that bears upon a self-indulgent spirit. They will endeavor to justify themselves, will neither read nor hear that which will rebuke their backslidden state, and they will become deeply prejudiced against everyone that would reprove them, counting him as an enemy. They hedge themselves in, shut their eyes against the light, stand on the defensive, and criticize everything that would search them out.

4. A backslider in heart will be filled with his own enmities. He will irritate almost every relationship, will allow himself to be annoyed, and to get into such relations with some people, and perhaps with many, that he cannot pray for them honestly, and can hardly treat them with common civility. This is an almost certain result of a backslidden heart.

5. The backslider in heart will be full of his own mistakes. He is not walking with God. He has fallen out of the divine order. He is not led by the Spirit, but is walking in spiritual darkness. In this state he is sure to fall into many and grievous mistakes, and may get entangled in such a way as to damage his happiness, and perhaps destroy his usefulness for life. Mistakes in business, mistakes in forming new relations in life, mistakes in using his time, his words, his money, his influence. Indeed, all will go wrong with him as long as he remains in a backslidden state.

6. The backslider in heart will be filled with his own lustings. His appetites and passions, which had been kept down, have now resumed their control, and having been so long suppressed, they will seem to avenge themselves by becoming more clamorous and despotic than ever. The animal appetites and passions will burst forth, to the astonishment of the backslider, and he will probably find himself more under their influence and more enslaved by them than ever before.

7. The backslider in heart will be filled with his own words. While in that state, he will not, and cannot, control his tongue. It will prove itself to be unruly, full of deadly poison. By his words he will involve himself in many difficulties and perplexities, from which he can never extricate himself until he comes back to God.

8. He will be full of his own trials. Instead of keeping out of temptation, he will run right into it. He will bring upon himself many trials that he never would have had, had he not departed from God. He will complain of his trials, but yet he will constantly multiply them. A backslider feels his trials keenly, but, while he complains of being so tried by everything around him, he is constantly aggravating them. Being the author of them, he seems industrious to bring them upon himself

like an avalanche.

9. The backslider in heart shall be full of his own folly. Having rejected divine guidance, he will evidently fall into the depths of his own foolishness. He will inevitably say and do many foolish and ridiculous things. Being a professing Christian, these things will be all the more noticed, and of course bring him all the more into ridicule and contempt. A backslider is indeed the most foolish person in the world. Having personal knowledge of the true way of life, he has the infinite folly to abandon it. Knowing the fountain of living waters, he has forsaken it, and made "cisterns, broken cisterns, that can hold no water" (Jeremiah 2:13*). Having been guilty of this infinite folly, the whole course of his backslidden life must be that of a fool, in the biblical sense of the term.

10. The backslider in heart will be full of his own troubles. God is against him, and he is against himself. He is not at peace with God, with himself, with the church, or with the world. He has no inward rest. Conscience condemns him. God condemns him. All that know his state condemn him. "'There is no peace,' says my God, 'to the wicked'" (Isaiah 57:21).

11. The backslider in heart will be full of his own cares. He has turned back to selfishness. He counts himself and his possessions as his own. He has everything to care for. He will not hold himself and his possessions as belonging to God, and put aside the responsibility of taking care of himself and all that he possesses. He does not cast his cares upon the Lord, but undertakes to manage everything for himself, in his own wisdom, and for his own ends. Consequently, his cares will be multiplied and come upon him like a flood.

12. The backslider in heart will be full of his own questions. Having forsaken God, having fallen into the darkness of his own folly, he will be filled with questions and doubts about what course he shall pursue to accomplish his selfish ends. He is not walking with, but contrary to God. Hence, the providence of God will constantly cross his path, and baffle all his schemes. God will frown darkness upon his path, and take trouble to confound his projects, and blow his schemes to the winds.

13. The backslider in heart will be filled with his own anxieties. He will be anxious about himself, about his business, about his reputation, about everything. He has taken all these things out of the hands of God, and claims them and treats them as his own. Hence, having faith in God no longer, and being unable to control events, he must of necessity be filled with anxieties with regard to the future. These

anxieties are the inevitable result of his madness and folly in forsaking God.

14. The backslider in heart will be filled with his own disappointments. Having forsaken God, and taken the attitude of self-will, God will inevitably disappoint him as he pursues his selfish ends. He will frame his ways to please himself, without consulting God. Determined to have his own way, he will be greatly disappointed if his plans are frustrated. Yet the course of events under the government of God must bring him a series of disappointments.

15. The backslider in heart must be full of his own losses. He regards his possessions as his own, his time as his own, his influence as his own, his reputation as his own. The loss of any of these, he accounts as his own loss. Having forsaken God, and being unable to control the events upon which the continuance of those things is conditioned, he will find himself suffering losses on every side. He loses his peace. He loses his property. He loses much of his time. He loses his Christian reputation. He loses his Christian influence, and if he persists he loses his soul.

16. The backslider in heart will be full of his own crosses. All religious duty will be irksome, and, therefore, a cross to him. His state of mind will make many things crosses that in a Christian state of mind would have been very pleasant. Having lost all heart in religion, the performance of all religious duty is a cross to his feelings. There is no help for him, unless he returns to God. His whole life will be a series of crosses and trials.

17. The backslider in heart will be full of his own disgraces. He is a professing believer. The eyes of the world are upon him, and all his inconsistencies, worldly mindedness, follies, bad tempers, and hateful words and deeds, disgrace him in the estimation of all people who know him.

18. The backslider in heart will be full of his own delusions. Having an evil eye, his whole body will be full of darkness. He will almost certainly fall into delusions in regard to doctrines and in regard to practices. Wandering on in darkness, as he does, he will very likely swallow the most glaring delusions. Spiritism, Mormonism, Universalism, and every other "ism" that is apart from the truth, will be very likely to gain possession of him. Who has not observed this of backsliders in heart?

19. The backslider in heart will be filled with his own bondage. His profession of religion brings him into bondage to the church. He must do something to sustain religious institutions, but to do so is a bondage.

If he does it, it is because he must, and not because he may. Again, he is in bondage to God. If he performs any duty that he calls religious, it is rather as a slave than as one who is free. He serves from fear or hope, just like a slave, and not from love. Again, he is in bondage to his own conscience. To avoid conviction and remorse, he will do or omit many things, but it is all with reluctance, and not at all of his own cordial goodwill.

20. The backslider in heart is full of his own self-condemnation. Having enjoyed the love of God, and forsaken him, he feels condemned for everything. If he attempts religious duty, he knows there is no heart in it, and hence condemns himself. If he neglects religious duty, he of course condemns himself. If he reads his Bible, it condemns him. If he does not read it, he feels condemned. If he goes to religious meetings, they condemn him. If he stays away, he is condemned also. If he prays in secret, in his family, or in public, he knows he is not sincere, and feels condemned. If he neglects or refuses to pray, he feels condemned. Everything condemns him. His conscience is up in arms against him, and the thunder and lightning of condemnation follow him wherever he goes.

V. HOW TO RECOVER FROM A STATE OF BACKSLIDING

1. Remember from where you are fallen. Take up the question at once, and deliberately contrast your present state with that when you walked with God.

2. Take to heart the conviction of your true position. No longer delay to understand the exact situation between God and your soul.

3. Repent at once, and "do the works you did at first"[1] over again.

4. Do not attempt to get back, by reforming your mere outward conduct. Begin with your heart, and at once set yourself right with God.

5. Do not act like a more convicted sinner, and attempt to recommend yourself to God by any impenitent works or prayers. Do not think that you must "reform, and make yourself better" before you can come to Christ, but understand distinctly, that coming to Christ, alone, can make you better. However distressed you may feel, know for certain that until you repent and unconditionally accept his will, you are no better, but are constantly growing worse. Until you throw yourself upon his sovereign mercy, and thus return to God, he will accept nothing at your hands.

---

[1] See Revelation 2:4-5.

Do not imagine yourself to be in a justified state, for you know you are not. Your conscience condemns you, and you know that God would condemn you. Come, then, immediately to Christ, like a guilty, condemned sinner, as you are. Own up, and take all the shame and blame to yourself, and believe that despite all your wanderings from God, he loves you still — that he has loved you with an everlasting love, and therefore with lovingkindness is drawing you.

Chapter 16

GROWTH IN GRACE

"But grow in the grace and knowledge of our Lord and Savior Jesus Christ."
(2 Peter 3:18)

I must conclude this series of lectures by giving converts instructions on the subject of Growth in Grace. I shall pursue the following method, showing:

I. What grace is, as the term is used here.

II. What the command to "grow in grace" does not mean.

III. What it does mean.

IV. The conditions of growth in grace.

V. What is not proof of growth in grace.

VI. What is proof of growth in grace.

VII. How to grow in grace.

I. WHAT GRACE IS

Grace is favor. The word is often used in the Bible to signify a free gift. The grace of God is the favor of God.

II. WHAT TO "GROW IN GRACE" DOES NOT MEAN

It does not command the gradual giving up of sin. It would seem that some have understood it this way. But we are nowhere in the Bible commanded to give up sin gradually — we are everywhere commanded to give it up instantly and completely.

III. WHAT IT DOES MEAN

The text commands us the duty of growing in the favor of God, of growing in his esteem — in a worthiness of his favor.

IV. CONDITIONS OF GROWTH IN GRACE

1. Growth or increase in anything implies a beginning. Growth in the favor of God implies that we have already found favor in his sight, that we are already indebted for receiving grace, and that we are already in grace, in the sense of having a place among his favored ones.

2. Consequently, growth in grace implies that we have already repented of our sin, have actually and practically abandoned all known sin. It cannot be that we are in favor with God if we are still indulging in known sin against him. Being in favor with God implies, of course, that we are pardoned and favored by him, for the sake of our Lord and Savior Jesus Christ. Pardon is favor, and implies the renunciation of rebellion against God. The conditions of the divine favor, as revealed in the Bible, are repentance and abandonment of all known sin, and faith in our Lord Jesus Christ. As a condition of growth in grace, we must have the beginning of grace. In other words, we must be already Christians, must be in a state of acceptance with God, must have accepted Christ, must be in a state of obedience to all the recognized will of God. Without this, we cannot be in a state of grace, or in the favor of God. But being in this state, there is room for everlasting growth. As we know more of God, we shall be capable of loving him more, of having a more universal and implicit confidence in him. And there can be no end to this while we have any being, either in this or any other world. Our love and confidence in him may be complete, so far as we know him. This love and confidence will secure his favor, but there will be no end to our growth in knowledge of him, and, consequently, there is room for eternal growth in grace. The more we love God, the more we believe, the more we know of him, if we conform to this knowledge, the more God must be pleased with us, the higher shall we stand in his favor, and more and greater gifts he will continue to give us.

3. Of course, growth in the knowledge of God is a condition of growth in his favor. We might grow in knowledge, without growing in his favor, because we might not love and trust him in accordance with this increased knowledge. But we cannot love and trust him more perfectly, unless we become more perfectly acquainted with him. If our love and faith keep pace with our growing knowledge, we must grow in his favor. But growth in knowledge must be a condition of growth in love and faith.

4. Growth in the knowledge of God, as revealed in Christ Jesus, must

be a condition of growth in his favor. It is in and through Christ Jesus that God reveals himself to man. It is in Christ Jesus that we get the true idea of the personality of the infinite God. Hence, the text says, "Grow in the grace and knowledge of our Lord and Savior Jesus Christ."

5. Growth in grace is conditioned on increased knowledge of what is involved in entire consecration to God.

True conversion to God involves the consecration of ourselves and of all that we have to him, as far as we understand what is implied in this. But, at first, converts are by no means aware of all that is involved in the highest forms of consecration. They will soon learn that there are certain things that they did not think of, and that they did not give up to God. At first, perhaps, all that was in their thought was, to lay their naked soul upon the altar, and give up their whole heart to God. But soon they may learn that they did not think of all their possessions, of everything that was dear to them. They did not surrender all, leaving "not a hoof behind" (Exodus 10:26). They surrendered all of which they thought, but they were not fully enlightened, they did not think, nor could they think, at the time, of every appetite, passion, propensity, of every desire and affection, and of everything dear to them, in the whole creation, to make a thorough surrender and delivery of these to God.

To gain such knowledge is a work of time. Growth in the favor of God is conditioned on making a full surrender and consecration to God of everything we are, and have, and desire, and love, as fast as these objects are presented to thought. As long as we exist, and knowledge increases, there is no doubt that we shall be called upon to grow in grace, by consecrating to God every new object of knowledge, of desire, and of affection, that we may come to know, and desire, and love, to all eternity.

As you get new light, you must enlarge your consecration from day to day, and from hour to hour, or you will cease to grow in grace. Whenever you stop short, and do not leave everything that you are, that you possess, or that you love, upon the altar of consecration, that moment you cease to grow in grace. I pray that you will let this saying sink deep into your hearts.

6. Another condition of growth in grace is intense sincerity and steadiness in seeking increased religious light, by the illumination of the Holy Spirit. You will gain no effective religious light except by the inward showing and teaching of the Holy Spirit. This you will not obtain unless you continue in the true attitude of a disciple of Christ. Remem-

ber, he says, "Any one of you who does not renounce all that he has cannot be my disciple" (Luke 14:33). He will not, by his Holy Spirit, be your Divine Teacher unless you renounce self, and live in a state of continual consecration to him. To obtain and preserve the teachings of Christ, by the Holy Spirit, you must continually and sincerely pray for this divine teaching of the Spirit, and watch against resisting and grieving him.

7. Another condition of growth in grace is a constant conformity to all the teachings of the Holy Spirit, keeping up with our convictions of duty and with our growing knowledge of the will of God.

8. A more and more implicit faith in God is a condition of growth in grace. By implicit, I mean a confidence in God's character so profound that we trust him in the dark as well as in the light, as well when we do not understand the reasons of his dealings with us, or of his requirements, as when we do. Abraham had faith that did not "waver concerning the promise of God" (Romans 4:20), though what was promised seemed irrational and impossible. An implicit faith is an unwavering, unquestioning faith, a state of mind that will rest in God, in his promises, in his faithfulness, in his love, whatever appearances may be and however difficult and apparently unreasonable his commands or providential dealings may be. Abraham's faith is often commended in the Bible. God had promised him a son, but did not give him the promised seed until he was a hundred years old, and Sarah was ninety. But in spite of Sarah being past age, and he as good as dead, he believed that God was able to fulfill his promise. Then, when he had received his beloved son, with the assurance that this was to be his heir, and that through him the promise was to be fulfilled through all generations, God tested his faith severely, by commanding him to offer his Isaac as a burnt sacrifice. Yet he obeyed, without the least hesitation, believing "that God was able even to raise him from the dead" (Hebrews 11:19). He made all the arrangements to obey this difficult command with such calmness that neither Sarah nor Isaac suspected that any such thing was in mind. This was an example of implicit faith. Growth in grace, or in the favor of God, is conditioned upon growth in implicit confidence in him.

9. A more thoroughly sanctified sensibility is a condition of growth in the favor of God. By the sensibility, I mean the part of our nature that feels and desires, to which belongs all that we call desire, affection, emotion, feeling, appetite, passion, propensity, and lust. The sensibility is an involuntary power, and moral actions and qualities cannot strictly come from it. The states of the sensibility have moral charac-

er only as they come from the action of the will. The nature of man
n his depraved condition is very ugly, and although the will may be
iven up to God, the sensibility may be very ugly in the sight of One
hat looks directly upon it, and knows perfectly every excited desire,
assion, propensity, and lust. It is mainly through the sensibility that
re are assailed with temptations. It is through this that the Christian
rarfare is kept up. The Christian warfare consists in the battle of the
rill with these various appetites, passions, propensities, and lusts, to
eep them in subjection to the will of God. If the will maintains its in-
egrity, and clings to the will of God, the soul does not sin in its battle
rith the excited states of the sensibility. But these rebellious propensi-
es embarrass the will in the service it renders to God. To keep them in
ontrol occupies much time, thought, and strength. Hence the soul can-
ot give to God as complete a service, while exerting the full strength
f the will to control these propensities, as it otherwise might give.

hese appetites, passions, and propensities, although not sinful in them-
elves, have been regarded and spoken of as indwelling sin. Strictly,
hey cannot be sin, because they are involuntary. But they are often a
reat hindrance to our growth in the favor of God. "For the desires of
he flesh are against the Spirit, and the desires of the Spirit are against
he flesh, for these are opposed to each other, to keep you from doing
he things you want to do" (Galatians 5:17). This means that we can-
ot do for God what we otherwise would, because we have to battle
o much with the states of the sensibility, to keep them in control. As
he sensibility becomes more and more subdued and in harmony with
he will's devotion to God, we are left free to render to God a more un-
mbarrassed service. Therefore, the more thorough the sanctification
f the sensibility, the more thoroughly we are in favor with God.

0. A growing thoroughness of consecration, of spirit, soul, and body,
s the condition of more growth in the favor of God. It is common, at
irst, for the steadfastness of the will's devotion to God to be overcome
y the clamor of the excited appetites, passions, and propensities, or by
he various states of the sensibility. Whenever the will yields to these
xcited states, you sin. But, in such cases, the sin is not willful, in the
ense of being deliberate and intentional. It is rather a slip, a momen-
ary yielding under the pressure of highly excited feeling. Neverthe-
ess, this yielding is sin. However excited the states of the sensibility
nay be, if the will does not yield, there is strictly no sin. However,
vhile the will is steadfast, maintaining its consecration and obedience
o God, the appetites originating in the body and the various propensi-
ies of the soul may be in such confusion and in such a state of morbid
levelopment, that the soul may be unfit for the employments and en-

joyments of heaven.

Hence, the taking on of a greater fullness of the divine nature is a con dition of growth in the favor of God. Both the will and the sensibilit of God are in a state of utmost perfection and harmony. All of his de sires and feelings are in perfect harmony with his intelligence and hi will. Not so with us, in our state of physical depravity. The depravit of sensibility must be physical, because it is involuntary. Still, it is de pravity. It is a lapsed or fallen state of the sensibility. This fallen aspec of our nature must be recovered, sanctified, and completely restored t harmony with a consecrated will, and an enlightened intelligence, o we are never prepared for heaven. As we become more and more th partakers of the divine nature, and of the divine holiness, we are mor fully sanctified in spirit, soul, and body, and of course grow more an more in the favor of God.

11. A greater and more all-pervading fullness of the Holy Spirit's res idence is another condition of growth in the favor of God. You can not have it too thoroughly impressed upon you that every step in th Christian life is to be taken under the influence of the Holy Spirit. Th goal is the universal guidance of the Holy Spirit, so that in all thing you shall be led by the Spirit of God. "Walk by the Spirit, and you wil not gratify the desires of the flesh" (Galatians 5:16). "If by the Spiri you put to death the deeds of the body, you will live" (Romans 8:13) "To set the mind on the flesh is death, but to set the mind on the Spiri is life and peace" (Romans 8:6). Always remember, therefore, that t grow in grace, you must grow in the possession of the fullness of th Holy Spirit in your heart.

12. A deeper personal acquaintance with the Lord Jesus Christ, in al his official work and relations, is a condition of growth in grace. His na ture, work, and relations are the theme of the Bible. The Bible present him to us in a great variety of relations. In my *Systematic Theology* I hav considered some sixty or more of these official relations of Christ to th human race, and these are presented rather as illustrations rather tha covering the whole ground of his relations to us. Now, it is one thing to know Christ simply on paper, as spoken of in the Bible, by readin or hearing of him. It is quite another thing to know him personally, ir these relations. The Bible is the medium of introduction to him per sonally. What is there said of him is designed to lead us to seek afte a personal acquaintance with him. It is by this personal acquaintanc with him that we are made like him. It is by direct, personal interactior with his divine mind that we take on his image. "We all, with unveilec face, beholding the glory of the Lord, are being transformed into th

same image from one degree of glory to another" (2 Corinthians 3:18). "Faith comes from hearing," (Romans 10:17) and faith secures for us a personal acquaintance with Christ. Christ has promised to manifest himself personally to those who love and obey him. Do not stop short of securing this personal manifestation of Christ to your souls.

Your growth in grace will depend upon this. Do not think of stopping short of personally knowing Christ, not only in all these relations, but in the fullness of these relations. Do not overlook the fact that the appropriation of Christ, in each of these relations, is a personal act of faith. It is putting on the Lord Jesus Christ, taking him as yours, in each of these relations: as your wisdom, righteousness, sanctification, and redemption — as your Prophet, to teach you, your King, to govern you, your High Priest, to atone for you, your Mediator, your Advocate, your Strength, your Savior, your Hiding place, your High Tower, your Captain and Leader, your Shield, your Defense, your Exceeding Great Reward. In each of these relations, and in all other of his official relations, you need to take him by faith for personal interaction with him in these relations. Growing in a personal acquaintance with him, in these relations, is an indispensable condition of growth in his favor.

V. SOME SIGNS THAT ARE NOT PROOF OF GROWTH

1. Growth in knowledge is not conclusive evidence of growth in grace. Some degree of knowledge is necessary to our being in favor with God. Growth in knowledge, as I have shown, is a condition of growth in grace. But knowledge is not grace, and growth in knowledge does not constitute growth in grace. A person may grow ever so much in knowledge, and have no grace at all. In hell, they cannot but grow in knowledge, as they grow in experience, and in the knowledge of God's justice. But there, their growth in knowledge only aggravates the guilt and misery of hell. They know more and more of God and his law, and their own guilt. And the more they know, the more wretched they are. From their increased knowledge they never learn piety.

2. It is not certain evidence that an individual grows in grace because he grows in gifts. A professing Christian may increase in gifts, that is, he may become more fluent in prayer, and more eloquent in preaching, or more passionate in exhortation, without being any more holy. We naturally increase in that in which we exercise ourselves. And if any person often exercises himself in exhortation, he will naturally, if he makes effort, increase in fluency and pungency. But he may do all this, and yet have no grace at all. He may pray ever so sincerely, and increase in fluency and apparent passion, and yet have no grace. People who have no grace often do so. It is true, if he has grace, and exer-

cises himself in these things, as he grows in grace, he will grow in gifts. No person can exercise himself in obeying God, without improving in those exercises. If he does not improve in gifts, it is a true sign he does not grow in grace. But, on the other hand, it is not sure evidence that he grows in grace because he improves in certain exercises, for he will naturally improve with practice, whether he is a Christian or a hypocrite.

3. It is not proof that a person grows in grace because he thinks he is doing so. Someone may be very favorably impressed with his own progress in religion, when it is evident to others that he is not only making no progress, but is actually declining. An individual who is growing worse and worse is not usually well aware of the fact. It is not uncommon for both impenitent sinners and Christians to think they are growing better, when they are growing no better.

This results from the very nature of the case. If any person is growing worse, his conscience will, for the time being, become more and more seared, and his mind more and more dark, as he stifles conscience and resists the light. Then he may imagine he is growing better, just because he has less sense of sin. While his conscience continues to sleep, he may continue under the fatal delusion. A person will judge his own spiritual state as he compares himself with a high or low standard. If he keeps Christ before him, in his fullness, as his standard, he will doubtless always, at least in this state of existence, have only a low estimate of his own attainments. While at the same time, if he sets before himself the church, or any member of the church, as a standard, he will be very likely to form a high estimate of his progress in religion, and be very well satisfied with himself. This is the reason why there is such a difference between various people's views of their own condition and the condition of the church. They compare themselves and the state of the church with different standards. Hence, one takes a very humbling view of his own condition, and complains of that of the church. Another thinks such complaints of the church hostile, for to him the church appears to be doing very well. The reason why he does not think the church cold, and in a low state, is that Christ is not his standard of comparison. If a person shuts his eyes, he will not see the defilement on him, and may think he is clean, while to all around he appears loathsome.

VI. WHAT IS PROOF OF GROWTH

1. The manifestation of more implicit and complete trust in God is evidence of growth in grace. The exercise of greater implicit confidence, as I have said, is the condition of growing in the favor of God. The

manifestation of this confidence is proof that this growing confidence exists. Therefore it is satisfactory evidence of growth in the favor of God. If you are conscious in your own soul that you do exercise more implicit and universal confidence in God, this is conclusive proof to you that you are growing in grace. As you show in your life, temperament, and spirit, this growing confidence, you prove to yourself and to others that you are growing in the favor of God. As you grow in implicit confidence in him, you must grow in his favor.

2. Another evidence of growth in grace is becoming more weaned from the world. The will may be in an attitude of devotion to God, while the world's seductive charms very much embarrass the healthy action of the Christian life. As the soul becomes crucified and dead to the world, it grows in the favor of God.

3. Feeling less reluctant when called to the exercise of self-denial, is evidence of growth in grace. It shows that the feelings are becoming less and less despotic, that the will is getting more the mastery of them, that the sensibility is getting more into harmony with the devotion of the will and the dictates of the intelligence.

4. Less temptation to sins of omission is another evidence of growth in grace. This means less temptation to shun the cross, to neglect unpleasant duties, less temptation to laziness, to neglect responsibility, to neglect of prayer, to reading the Scriptures, and to private and family devotions. In short, less and less temptation to shun the performance of any duty is evidence of growth in grace. These temptations consist in the excited states of the sensibility. As these become less in strength and frequency, we learn that our sensibility is becoming more completely subjugated to the rule of the intellect and the decisions of the will, and consequently, that the work of sanctification of the spirit, soul, and body is progressing, and that therefore we are growing in the favor of God.

5. A growing intensity and steadiness of zeal in promoting the cause of God is evidence of growth in the favor of God. Sometimes Christian zeal is comparatively cool, at other times deep and intense. Sometimes it will be steady, at other times irregular and fleeting. As Christians grow in piety, their zeal becomes deep, intense, and steady, and as you are conscious of this, and in your life and spirit give evidence of it to others, you have and give proof that you are growing in the favor of God.

6. Losing more and more the consciousness of self, in every action of life, is evidence of growth in the favor of God. Some have so much con-

sciousness of self in everything, and so much consideration for self in everything they say and do, as to be embarrassed in all their Christian life, whenever they attempt to act or speak in the presence of others. As they lose this self-consciousness, and have less consideration for self, their service of God becomes more free and unembarrassed, and they are therefore better servants. Sometimes young converts cannot speak or pray, or perform any public duty, without being either proud or ashamed according to how they believe they were perceived by those around them. While this is so, their piety is in a feeble state. They must lose sight of their own glory, and have a single eye to the glory of God, to find acceptance with him. But as they lose sight of self, and set God always before them, having an eye only to his glory, they grow more and more in his favor.

7. Consequently, a growing deadness to the flattery or criticism of others is evidence of growth in grace. Paul had grown in grace so much that he counted it a small thing to be judged by man since he sought only to commend himself to God (1 Corinthians 4:3-4). As you find yourself growing in this state of deadness to the flatteries or criticisms of people, you have evidence that you grow in grace.

8. Growing calmness and quietness under great afflictions give evidence of growth in the favor of God. There is shown a more explicit faith, a fuller and more cordial acceptance of the will of God, as revealed in these afflictions. The soul is shown to be more firmly at anchor upon its rock, Christ.

9. A growing tranquility under sudden and crushing disasters and losses is evidence of growth in grace. The more tranquil the soul can remain, when sudden storms of providence come upon it, sweeping away loved ones, and ruining earthly hopes, the greater is its evidence of being under the particular favor of God. The tranquility is both a result and evidence of the favor of God.

10. "Patience with joy" (Colossians 1:11) is evidence of growing in favor with God. When you cannot only tolerate, but accept, the will of God, as revealed in calling you to suffer, especially when you can accept these sufferings and endure them patiently and with joyfulness, you have evidence that you are growing in the favor of God.

11. An increasing deadness to all that the world has to offer, or to threaten, is evidence of growth in the favor of God.

12. A growing rest in, and contentment with, all the allotments of Providence, is evidence of growth in grace.

3. Less temptation to murmur or complain at any allotment of Providence is evidence of growth in grace.

4. Less and less temptation to resentment, and the spirit of retaliation, when we are in any way insulted or abused, is evidence that the sensibility is becoming more and more thoroughly subdued, and consequently, that we are growing in favor with God.

5. Less temptation to dwell upon, to magnify our trials and troubles, to think of them, and speak of them to others, is evidence that we think less and less of self, and accept our trials and troubles with more and more contentment in God. It is sad to hear some professedly good people, always dwelling on their own troubles and trials. But, if they grow in grace, they will think less and less of these, and be more inclined to think of them as "light afflictions." The more we grow in grace, the less stress we lay upon the evils we meet with in the way. A good man said to me once, who was really passing through what the world would call very severe trials and afflictions (he had lost a beloved wife, and his children had died one after another), "I have many mercies, and few afflictions." When, under such circumstances, a person can say, "The lines have fallen for me in pleasant places; indeed, I have a beautiful inheritance," (Psalm 16:6) he has the most satisfactory evidence that he is growing in the favor of God. For this state of mind is both a result and evidence of the favor of God.

6. Being less and less disturbed and troubled by the events of life, especially those that go counter to our own plans, hopes, expectations, and desires, and that thwart our most cherished aims, is evidence of growth in grace.

7. A growing confidence in the wisdom, benevolence, and universality of the providence of God, a state of mind that sees God in everything, is evidence of growth in grace. Some minds become so spiritual that they hardly seem to reside in the body, but appear continually to perceive the presence of God in every event, almost as if they were disembodied, and beheld God face to face. They seem to dwell, live, move, and have their being, in the spiritual rather than in the natural world. They are continually under such a sense of the divine presence, agency, and protection, as hardly to appear like inhabitants of earth. They are a living, walking mystery to those in the midst of whom they dwell. The springs of their activity are so divine, their life is so much hidden in God, they act under influences so far above the world, that they cannot be judged by the same standards as other people. Worldly minds cannot understand them. Their hidden life is so unknowable to those who are far below them in their spiritual life, that they are

necessarily regarded as quite eccentric, as being mystics or obsessec as having very peculiar religious views, as being enthusiasts, and pei haps fanatics. These people are in the world, but they live above th world. They have so greatly escaped from the pollutions that are in th world that they can truly say with Paul, "But far be it from me to boa: except in the cross of our Lord Jesus Christ, by which the world ha been crucified to me, and I to the world" (Galatians 6:14). Such peopl are growing in the grace of God.

18. Being less and less disposed to dwell upon the faults and weak nesses of others is evidence of growth in grace.

19. Being less and less disposed to speak severely, or to judge unchai itably of others is evidence of growth in grace. A growing delicacy, o tenderness, in speaking of their real or supposed faults, is evidence c growth in grace.

20. An increasing reluctance to regard or treat any one as an enem and an increasing ease in treating them kindly, in sincerely praying fo them, and in efforts to do them good, is evidence of growth in grace.

21. Less and less temptation to remember an injury, and the decreas of all desire to retaliate when injured is evidence of growth in grace.

22. A growing readiness and cordiality in forgiving and putting ai injury out of sight, and a kind of moral inability to do anything bu seek the highest good of those who have injured us most deeply, i evidence of growth in grace.

23. When we find in our own experience, and show to others, that it i more and more natural to regard all people as our brothers, especiall to drop out of view all sectarian discriminations, all ideas and preju dices of caste, and of color, of poverty, and of riches, of blood relatior and of natural, rather than of spiritual ties, and to make common caus with God, in aiming to do good to all people, to enemies and friend alike, we have then the highest evidence of our growing in the favor o God.

24. Especially is it true, when we find ourselves very warm and sincer in making great sacrifices for those that hate us, and having a willing ness to lay down our lives for the promotion of their eternal salvation that we have evidence of growth in grace.

25. Still more especially, when we find ourselves less and less inclinec to account anything a sacrifice that we can do for God, or for the soul of people. When we can count our lives not dear to us, if called to la them down to save the souls of enemies, when, for the joy of saving

them, we can "endure the cross, and despise the shame," or make any sacrifice that we are called to, we have evidence that we are growing in favor with God.

26. When we find less and less reluctance to making full confession to those whom we have injured, when with increasing readiness we lay our hearts open to be searched, when we find conviction of wrongdoing, when, in such cases, we cannot rest until we have made the fullest confession and reparation within our power, and when to "own up," and confess, and make the fullest satisfaction, is a luxury to us, rather than a trial and a cross, we have evidence that we are growing in the favor of God.

27. When we are more and more impressed and affected by the mercies of God, and by the kindnesses of our fellow people, when we more deeply and thoroughly appreciate manifestations of kindness in God, or in any one else, when we are more and more humbled and affected by these kindnesses, and find it more and more natural "to do justice, and to love kindness, and to walk humbly" (Micah 6:8), and live gratefully, we have evidence that we are growing in favor with God.

28. When we find ourselves drawn, with increasing sincerity, to continue to know more of the Lord, we have evidence of growth in grace.

29. When we find ourselves more and more readily affected, vitalized, and stimulated by religious truth, we have evidence that we are growing in grace.

30. A growing jealousy for the honor of God, for the purity and honor of his church, for the rights of God, and for the rights of all people, is evidence of growing in conformity to God and growing in his favor.

VII. HOW TO GROW IN GRACE

1. Fulfill the conditions noticed under the fourth head of this lecture.

2. Remember that every step of progress must be made by faith, and not by works. The mistakes that some good people have made on this subject are truly amazing. Growth in grace is nearly always represented as consisting in the formation of habits of obedience to God. The fact is, that every step of progress in the Christian life is taken by a fresh and fuller appropriation of Christ by faith, a fuller baptism of the Holy Spirit. As our weaknesses and besetting sins are revealed to us by the circumstances of temptation through which we pass, our only efficient help is found in Christ, and we grow only as we step by step more fully appropriate him, in one relation or another, and more fully "put him on" (see Romans 13:14). As we are more emptied of self-dependence,

as we more and more renounce all expectation of forming holy habits by any obedience of ours, and as by faith we secure deeper and deeper baptisms of the Holy Spirit, and put on the Lord Jesus Christ, more and more thoroughly, and in more of his official relations, the faster we grow in the favor of God. Nothing can be more erroneous and dangerous than the commonly accepted idea of growing in grace by the formation of holy habits. By acts of faith alone, we appropriate Christ, and we are as truly sanctified by faith as we are justified by faith. In my *Systematic Theology*, in pointing out the conditions of entire or permanent sanctification, I have noticed some sixty of the official relations of Christ. As I have there insisted and as I here insist, growth in holiness, and consequently, in the favor of God, is secured only by fresh, fuller, and more thorough appropriations of Christ, in all these official relations. If you would grow in grace you must do it through faith. You must pray in faith for the Holy Spirit. You must appropriate and put on Christ through the Holy Spirit. At every forward step in your progress, you must have a fresh anointing of the Holy Spirit through faith.

APPENDIX

Below are the sources for each of the chapters in the book. The abbreviation LPC stands for *Lectures to Professing Christians* (1836), WOS for the *Way of Salvation* (1852), and LRR stands for the *Lectures on Revivals of Religion* (1835, revised 1868). The third column contains the lecture number as it is found in the source. Charles Finney's original works are in the public domain.

Chapter	Source	Lecture #	Original title
1	LPC	2	False Professors
2	WOS	8	Salvation of Sinners Impossible
3	LPC	9	True and False Repentance
4	LRR	3	How to Promote a Revival
5	LRR	4	Prevailing Prayer
6	LRR	5	The Prayer of Faith
7	LRR	6 and 7	The Spirit of Prayer / On Being Filled with the Spirit
8	LRR	8	Meetings for Prayer
9	LRR	9	Means to be Used with Sinners
10	LRR	10	To Win Souls Requires Wisdom
11	LRR	17	False Comforts for Sinners
12	LRR	18	Directions to Sinners
13	LRR	19	Instructions to Converts
14	LRR	20	Instructions to Converts (continued)
15	LRR	21	The Backslider in Heart
16	LRR	22	Growth in Grace

The Fleming H. Revell Company published an edition of *Lectures on Revivals of Religion* that was used as the reference standard for that portion of this work (there have been several variant editions published over the years). In addition, where annotated, some material from their footnotes was incorporated into this edition.

CPSIA information can be obtained
at www.ICGtesting.com
Printed in the USA
LVHW031407111221
705932LV00017B/177